AF334567

Stealing
from the
World's Best Schools

What One U.S. Teacher Learned
by Visiting Countries that are Doing Education Right

KEITH BALLARD

With Brooke Staggs

Contents

To my family,

my mother and deceased father,

Tom Teagle,

and Brooke Staggs.

Foreword

Teach me something worthwhile. Teach me something that will pay the rent. Teach me something that will improve my quality of life. Anything else is a waste of my time.

This is a mantra many American educators hear from students all the time.

I suppose we can also say this about the books we read. Give me something to read that tells me a better way to do things or makes me grow as a person, or my time is wasted.

I know it's been worth my time reading this remarkable book. I suspect it will be for you, too, if you're someone at all troubled by the current state of American schools or simply interested in helping to make the United States more globally competitive once again.

We need an honest account of the true status of our American school system and how we measure up to the other guys around the world. As a 20-year veteran teacher and retired Naval officer myself, I'm jaded by all of the lies and fake stories fed to me by school administrators. I need someone to speak to me frankly and to give me easy-to-understand goals to work towards. Don't make it difficult. I don't want to cast stones at people. I just want to know what I'm up against and what I need to do to make things better. And there's nothing like first-hand information, backed by solid research, to drive those lessons home.

That's precisely what award-winning teacher, world traveler, and adventurer Keith Ballard offers in this book. Using results from the worldwide PISA test, or Program for International Student Assessment, as a metric, he paints a stark picture of our American K-12 educational system in terms of its potential preparatory value. And he highlights some of the best practices employed by schools he's personally visited during this global journey of classrooms, from vocational education to teaching methodologies that high-testing countries use in order to prepare their kids for life and service in their nation.

In the introduction of this book, you'll meet a man who likes to run into life head-on. Whether scaling Mt. Aconcagua, the highest peak in

South America, challenging the frigid waters while swimming from San Francisco to Alcatraz Island, or perhaps barreling out of an airplane in a parachute at 10, 000 feet, Keith is the kind of man that likes to experience things close up and then bring those real-life experiences into the classroom.

So it came as no surprise to those of us who knew Keith that, when he decided to conduct a study of classrooms around the world, he did something that's never been done before, to my knowledge, in the field of American education. On his own dime, Keith became the first documented K-12 teacher in the world who has visited eight schools in each of the 17 highest performing PISA educational countries in the world, with a few more countries thrown in for good measure. (I'll never forget when Keith called me for advice before he visited North Korea. My words of wisdom were simple: "Don't do anything stupid.") Instead of reading a book or looking at a video, he set out for himself in search of an answer to a simple question: "What are the other top-performing nations doing in their schools that make them test better than us in the U.S.?" He didn't know his path clearly in the beginning, but he knew where his journey would take him. And he captured his quest to answer that question in this book and gifted it to us, so we can travel with him to experience firsthand what it's like in schools and classrooms around the world.

I understand Keith's passion. The reason he asked me to write this foreword, I suspect. We've had many long talks about educational topics such as the treatment that vocational education has been given in our local and regional schools. I saw as a teacher myself how students increasingly feel they have no choice in their education and are stuck learning information that won't help them. Remembering back to my own high school days, we had several vocational options we could select from such as metal shop, wood shop, auto shop or an agricultural option. Today, these vocational areas and more are largely underfunded in many school districts or don't exist at all. Watching vocational education being defunded and given more and more low priority is a scourge to our country, and a dangerous mistake.

Before my 20-year teaching career, I retired as a naval officer. I've flown high performance airplanes, parachuted out of all sorts of rotary and fixed-wing aircraft, and road motorcycles since my youth. I've traveled the globe and have been a bit of an adrenaline-junkie, too. I've observed and experienced other cultures close-up. I've finished five university programs and am an award-winning teacher myself. I've also had some firsts in education, teaching at both rich and poor schools. But nothing like what Keith has accomplished with this book, which has given us a real standard to shoot for.

If you want to see what the best public schools are doing around the world, read this book. If you want to see what our young students are competing against on a global scale, read this book. Listen to Keith's arguments. Look at how he crafts his case. Read with a pencil in hand, so you can write notes as you study. Write down your own ideas. You can think more about them when you revisit them later. This is how Keith organized *Stealing from the World's Best Schools*, with this intent in mind. This is the beginning of involvement.

This book will be a gut check for many. We need a good gut check. We better have the resolve to face up to some very serious problems in our American educational system, such as how our U.S. students measure-up globally to other countries. Our U.S. students are competing on a global scale, whether this competition is in terms of providing goods or services. We, as an American public, need to know what our competition is doing—and how we fare in comparison. Keith makes the point that it's our students, in our schools today, who will work in our industries of tomorrow. Who will participate on our nation's behalf, and on our behalf, when we're older citizens rocking in our rocking chairs. It's crucial that we get a clear picture of our educational status now, using the world's schools as a measuring stick, and use strategies laid out in this book as a blueprint for rebuilding our own education system. Otherwise, we, as a nation, will suffer the future economic consequences.

—Dr. John Norman Simmons, EdD, retired educator and Naval officer

Inspiration on a Mountaintop

What no one ever tells you about climbing the world's tallest mountains is just how boring long stretches of the journey can be. Looking back, I'm grateful for that boredom. Because without it, this book wouldn't exist.

It was December 2010, and I was nearly two weeks into scaling Mt. Aconcagua, the highest peak in South America and one of the so-called "seven summits" of the world. We were a couple days off course because the weather had been so bad. But we'd finally made it 19,357 feet up to Camp Berlin, the highest camp on our route. The next day, we'd go for Aconcagua's summit.

This was my second attempt at reaching the top of Mt. Aconcagua. We made it halfway up the year before when a giant snowstorm forced us to turn back. Of course, the mountain didn't care.

On this attempt, I'd developed a condition called hypoxia, where I'd bolt awake feeling like I was choking. It's particularly scary because you aren't sure if you have pulmonary edema, which can be deadly. I also was experiencing acute mountain sickness, which left me feeling like I had a bad hangover. I forced myself to eat some freeze-dried lasagna that night at Camp Berlin, trying to keep my energy up. To make things worse, it was so windy outside that our little camp stove kept blowing out. My climbing partner and I decided to cook inside our small tent, but the cooker fell over and caught my sleeping bag on fire. I threw the bag outside the tent, rubbing it on the ice below to put out the flames. Part of my $600 sleeping bag was scorched, but I just felt fortunate that our whole tent hadn't burned to the ground, leaving us with only our down parkas to shield us from temperatures that were dipping to minus 40 degrees Fahrenheit.

With freezing winds and snow showers whipping around us, I remember looking up at the clouds covering Mt. Aconcagua's snowy peak. The task of climbing another 3,500 feet to the summit and back down looked daunting. We were set to leave at 3:30 a.m. the next morning, with no sun to warm things up until about 8 a.m. and a 12-hour trek ahead.

You need a reason to climb a mountain like Aconcagua because there's a lot of pain and discomfort and cost involved. I thought I had one, imagining some great sense of accomplishment I would feel when I achieved this massive goal I'd set for myself, something few people ever accomplish. But looking up at that jagged peak, I was miserable. All I could think was: Why am I here?

When I was honest with myself, I had to admit I was searching for answers to questions I'd started to ask some six years earlier, in a middle school music class in Southern California.

In 2004, I was 12 years into my teaching career and proud of what I'd accomplished. To reach middle schoolers at Sweetwater Union High School District, which educates some 40,000 students in the southern tip of San Diego County, a couple miles from the Mexican border, I had introduced mariachi and steel drum programs that drew national attention, sparking student performances on *The Today Show* and in front of former Presidents Bill Clinton and George W. Bush. My efforts to infuse lessons about scales and chords with messages about self-esteem, cultural sensitivity and the importance of academics helped me earn more than 25 teaching awards. That included the 2003 Milken National Educator Award, which is known as the "Oscars of Teaching."

While I felt I was doing well as a teacher, I also felt like my hands were tied in the classroom by systemic philosophies and policies that weren't helping American students get what they needed to succeed in a global economy. I watched so many of our middle school students regularly fail to prepare for class, neglecting to even charge up the iPads they needed to use for the day's work, let alone complete their homework. I saw them reading on average at a third-grade level, with math scores not much better. I watched students who'd come alive in my music classes struggle with academics and drop out before graduating high school, with teachers also fleeing the profession at astounding rates.

As I looked at the academic shortcomings, the lack of motivation, and the discipline issues around me, I felt like I was working in a broken system. Not just the school where I was teaching, or the district or even the state. Our entire country was failing students in so many ways.

It's a problem that has plagued American schools for half a century. Fifty years ago, by common consensus among economists all over the world, the United States had the best educational system and our workforce was the best prepared of any workforce in the world. This propelled the United States' global leadership in one arena after another, from manufacturing to technology, through the mid-1970s. Sadly, our nation has lost that status in recent decades, even though government spending per student has more than doubled after figuring in the cost of inflation. We're not at the bottom, by any stretch. But while other countries have capitalized on their underdog status, working harder and transforming their education systems to make up for their smaller size or higher rates of poverty, we've become complacent. Now we're sitting comfortably in the middle, with no progress on improving our international standing in recent decades. As journalist Fareed Zakaria put it: "The biggest force behind falling American rankings is not that the United States is doing things much worse, but that other countries have caught up and are doing far better."

Unfortunately, most Americans don't seem to recognize that reality. "The first step in solving any problem is recognizing there is one. America is not the greatest country in the world anymore." Character Will McAvoy said those lines in 2012, during the first minutes of the HBO series *The Newsroom*, before spouting off figures about the United States' declining educational, healthcare and economic status.

Consider these facts:

- In 10 other countries with top-performing education systems, the average high school student graduates 2.5 years ahead academically of the average American student.

- In the most recent Program for International Student Assessment or PISA test, 22 other countries outperformed American students in science, 35 countries outperformed American students in math and 20 countries did better than the U.S. in reading.

- When the majority of U.S. high school graduates are admitted to college, they are actually studying what many other countries' students were studying in high school. Simply said, our students are studying a high school curriculum and paying college prices.

- Most countries with high-performing education systems spend much more on support of families with young children than the U.S. does, including state-of-the-art early childhood educational programs that start for kids as young as one year old.

- Millennials in the United States are now among the most poorly educated workforce in the industrialized world when it comes to measuring basic skills. That's why, in order for many U.S. companies to compete globally, they have to import "brains" from places such as China and India because many human resources directors claim they cannot find such world-class talent in America.

- States in the U.S. continue to lower teaching standards due to epidemic shortages in the classroom—an approach top educational countries would never consider.

Attempts to reform education in the United States over the past 40 years have been riddled with quick-fix and "silver bullet" solutions. Many of these reforms have focused on punishing the teacher or school for the students' failures, helping to drive massive teacher burnout and shortages across the country. I knew from my own experiences in the classroom that the problem is not with the teachers or the teachers' unions but with a system that was designed a century ago for a smokestack economy. That system has been a catalyst in creating both a first-world economy and a large third-world economy, where many students have been poorly prepared and are doomed to live a life of poverty. This gap will only grow as globalization and artificial intelligence expand, replacing by some estimates 50 percent of American jobs in coming decades.

Frustrated and discouraged by a system I felt powerless to change, I took to filling my weekends and summer breaks with daring exploits I thought I could control. I navigated the icy waters of San Francisco Bay in the Alcatraz swim. I climbed Yosemite's famed El Capitan. But even at the literal highest point, when I was at Camp Berlin near the summit of Mt. Aconcagua in 2010, I felt weighed down by the problems I knew were waiting back in my classroom.

The only thing you can really do to kill the boredom when you're camped out on the side of a mountain, waiting for your body to acclimate to the altitude or for the weather to change or for daylight to break, is to make sure you have a few good books to keep you distracted. On my brother's recommendation, I'd climbed Mt. Aconcagua carrying *The Dragon and the Elephant: Understanding the Development of Innovation Capacity in China and India,* which discusses how the two nations had remade their economies so they could become manufacturing superpowers. One of the best ways you can understand another country is to go inside its schools and see how the education system is structured. That will tell you a lot about what the future may hold for that nation's people. So as I read *The Dragon and the Elephant*, I swore to myself that if I reached Aconcagua's summit, I would start a new chapter in my own life.

Most Americans—from parents to teachers to school administrators to policymakers—have no idea what the rest of the world is doing in terms of highly successful countries that have significantly raised their education standards. And that problem is getting worse, not better, as a push for isolationism grows in some American circles. By contrast, most of the countries with successful education systems regularly visit other high-performing nations. Of the nine principals that I would later interview in Finland, for example, all had visited schools in at least five other countries. And I never met a Finnish teacher who had not visited schools in at least two different countries. So while I was huddled in my tent, 19,356 feet up a mountain in Argentina, I started hatching a plan to spend my free time and the $25,000 prize money that comes with winning the Milken Educator Award to visit schools in other countries to see what they were doing differently, and to diagnose where the American school system had gone wrong in preparing students for the modern world.

I focused my mission on countries that have performed best in recent years on the Program for International Student Assessment or PISA tests, which is an international program that measures the reading, mathematics and science literacy of 15-year-old students around the world every three years. During summer vacations from 2011 to 2018, I visited more than 170 public schools around the world to observe, document and report on what the top performing education systems in the world do differently than the United States. To my knowledge, I'm the first K-12 teacher in the world who has visited eight schools in each of the 17 highest performing PISA educational countries in the world: Singapore, Japan, China, Taiwan, South Korea, Canada, Ireland, Finland, Estonia, Germany, Belgium, Netherlands, Switzerland, Liechtenstein, Slovenia, Poland and New Zealand. I also studied schools in several other countries that have made substantial educational gains in recent years, including Vietnam. I even managed to visit five schools in North Korea.

I funded and arranged these trips myself, sometimes sleeping in my car and talking my way into meetings with top education officers. Along the way, I documented my school visits through some 200 videos on my YouTube channel so I could share first-hand footage of what the world's best schools looked like from the inside.

When I got back home, I was bursting to share all that I'd seen and to discuss ideas for implementing some of these best practices in American schools. I felt certain many people would be as excited as I was about what

I'd seen. After all, everyone in the United States has an interest in the success of our public school system, from the tens of millions of parents with kids in school, to the millions of educators on the job, to the businesses who depend on a qualified workforce. Meanwhile, numerous surveys show that a majority of people in each of these groups is dissatisfied with the current education system.

I landed more than 40 live TV interviews after returning from my first international education tour, with segments on NBC, ABC, CBS, CW, FOX and PBS. I also published four articles in professional education journals and was an invited speaker at more than a half dozen education conferences. But when I approached the superintendent in my own Sweetwater Union High School District about the potential benefits of learning from top schools around the world, she said to me, "Why would we need to visit those other countries when we have great schools here?" Even my own principal at Southwest Middle School would not allow me to make a presentation to my colleagues for fear that they might learn something contrary to the party line. Clearly, not everyone had accepted the reality of the American educational system or embraced the idea of taking cues from other countries who are outperforming the United States by most measures.

That's where this book comes into play.

In the pages ahead, I'll offer research and first-hand accounts of how countries with top-performing education systems do things differently than the United States in eight key areas, from supporting families to standardized testing to charter schools. I will tell the story of how these countries improved their systems to world class status and why the United States continues to perform so poorly, even with the amount of money it spends. I also will share ideas you can steal from the world's best schools right now, whether you're a parent hoping to ensure a better education for your child, a teacher desperate for quick solutions that actually make a difference in the classroom, or a policymaker with the power to create needed, sweeping changes.

The intent is not to bash the U.S. education system, which I've been a part of for nearly three decades. In fact, there are many things I hope never change about American schools. Our schools are generally diverse and inclusive, for example, with solid funding for special education. Most students have access to technology. We also have an abundance of extracurricular activities and organized sports programs for both male and female students, which isn't a given in all nations I visited. But as Will McAvoy said, until we identify the problems, we can't start to discuss real solutions.

With no major federal reforms in sight, some U.S. school districts and even entire states have started trying to implement international best practices on their own. On paper, Maryland has designed a system that's probably as close to a top-tier education system as any seen in the United States. Now the question is whether they can get the funding and have the political will to actually put such reforms in place. Massachusetts, which has a slightly larger population than the entire country of Finland, otherwise is generally considered to have the best overall education system in the U.S. today. Students from Massachusetts have even outperformed students from top performing nations such as Singapore on recent PISA exams. But that model just hasn't been replicated in other states, many of which are larger and have higher poverty rates than Massachusetts. That's why nationally mandated reforms, with federal support and financial pressure to make them happen, are key to lifting performance at all U.S. schools.

It's tough to reengineer a plane as it's flying. Unlike places such as China, which had a decisive opportunity to reinvent its education system when the country first opened to the outside world four decades ago, the United States hasn't had a natural reset button for its education system. Perhaps the COVID-19 pandemic, which has rattled America's education systems, can help shake us awake. Maybe it'll take us falling further behind in the global economy. But we also could decide not to wait for some circumstance to force such changes, and instead to all take an active role in advocating for sweeping reforms today.

I know what you're thinking, and I've heard all of the excuses. There's this one: "Our students will never be disciplined like Chinese students because we aren't a communist country." Then there's this: "We have too many immigrants (or too much poverty, or a thousand other distinctions) to make the Finnish system work here." It's true that we have historical, cultural and political issues at play in the United States that would require systemic changes beyond the education system for practices that work in some of the top-performing countries to work here. Even then, some policies likely will never fit in the United States. But if I've learned anything on this journey, it's that there's also no one-size-fits-all method for fixing education. Even the top-performing countries contradict each other when it comes to many issues, such as how many hours of homework are assigned or how many days of school students attend each year. That's why looking at two or three countries isn't enough.

By examining the best practices of nearly two dozen countries with widely different cultures and policies, then selectively implementing aspects of successful programs here, the U.S. could significantly improve the quality of our educational system. This could help our students prosper in a hypercompetitive world, which would elevate businesses, the economy, and our entire nation, while improving life for every kid who sets foot in an American classroom.

I envisioned that future in 2010, when I was crouched in my wind-whipped tent, looking up at the peak of Mt. Aconcagua.

I reached the summit the next morning. Looking out at the world from 22,841 feet up, I almost felt like if I squinted I could see some 5,000 miles, all the way back to the middle school classroom packed with instruments and dreams, sheet music and frustrations that had sent me in search of this mountain peak. After taking in the view for a short time, we headed back down the mountain and back toward the reality I'd been trying to escape for six years.

That's when this journey began.

"The greatest work we will ever do will be within the walls of our home."

David O. McKay

Spencer Peng with his mother, Elizabeth Ding, who taught English at Qingdao #51 Middle School in China.

Chapter One

Family Support: It's a Two-Way Street

How does a public school teacher from a low-income school in Southern California land interviews with top education officials and tours of top school systems around the world? For me, it started with a Craigslist ad.

Ten years ago, my personal travels had largely been limited to Mexico and South America. I knew nothing about visiting China, let alone how to get a foot in the door of this global superpower's impressive school systems. I didn't know then to contact the country's ministry of education, for example, or how to go through other proper channels. But I was a man on a mission. I was so certain that the answers to fixing America's struggling educational system could be readily found if only we were willing to steal ideas from the world's best schools. And I knew that my mission to witness those best educational practices in action—and to bring them back home to share with the world—had to start in China, which took the No. 1 spot on the latest Program for International Student Assessment or PISA exams, broadly used as the key benchmark for comparing student achievement the world over.

So I did what I'd always done, whether I was trying to reach middle school music students or to reach the top of a mountain: I got creative.

There was a Craigslist ad near my home in San Diego, California, promoting a Chinese immigrant who was offering to teach Mandarin. When I told the tutor my reason for contacting him, he said he was on board to help. But after taking my $200 retainer and making some calls, he told me he was unable to get me into any Chinese schools, which can be notoriously difficult given the strict Communist government. I decided to try my Craigslist scheme one more time. That's when I met Spencer.

It was a match made in heaven. Spencer was a student at the increasingly competitive University of California San Diego. He'd attended top-tier public schools in China before coming to the United States for college. And Spencer's mom was a middle school teacher in China who happened to be visiting when I contacted Spencer online about helping with my mission. The three of us met at a Starbucks in June 2011. Three months later, I was visiting Spencer's elementary, middle and high schools in China, witnessing classroom by classroom how the rigorous, sometimes ruthless education he'd received had prepared him to compete in a global economy in ways that classrooms back in my district simply weren't doing.

The first school I visited outside the United States was Qingdao #58, a highly selective high school in China's eastern Shandong Province. I had barely gotten out of my taxi to enter the school's guard gate when I saw hundreds of students in white and red uniforms running to the school track. A selection of patriotic music was blaring from the speaker system, luring me over. I made a quick introduction to my host teacher and followed the students, running while trying to make sure I didn't drop my briefcase and camera bag.

I arrived at the track, winded and sweating, to find approximately 2,500 students lining up in strict platoon-like formations with little supervision from their teachers. I had read about the high level of student discipline in Chinese schools, but seeing it in person for the first time gave me chills. The only similar thing I had seen in my life to this was watching U.S. Marines forming up at the MCRD Training Center in San Diego. The Qingdao #58 students ran side by side, chanting loudly, with no one lagging or sitting on the sidelines. My host teacher told me the students had to run four laps around the track three times per day. This was considered a "break" from their other courses, with students still required to attend regularly scheduled PE classes.

After the run was complete, many of the students began walking briskly to their next class. When the bell rang, most of them were in their classrooms, with anyone running late sprinting that way. I remember shaking my head in disbelief at the comparison to a typical day at my middle school, where students casually stroll to their classes and sit indolently on the ground during PE. When the final bell rings and they're supposed to be in class, my students continue to drift in late, aware that there are no significant consequences for tardiness. Even when students are finally sitting in their seats, most teachers—myself included—find it a challenge just to get the students to stop talking as we take attendance. In terms of motivation and discipline, our school systems couldn't be farther apart. And I took all of that in before I'd even set foot inside a Chinese classroom.

One of the first people I met at Qingdao #58 was the petite and spectacled Meng. She took time between teaching classes to tell me about how she'd once left her familiar world in China behind to teach for one year at a public high school in Boston.

During the teacher exchange program, Meng's colleagues at her Massachusetts school made her feel welcome, and she said she largely saw in them the same passion and dedication to helping students that her colleagues back home put into their work. But one area where Meng experienced extreme culture shock was with the lack of discipline from her American students. And she attributed that problem to a lack of parental involvement in their kids' education.

"The parents, they don't care. So the students, the kids, they don't care," Meng said.

Of course, I knew it wasn't fair to flatly say that American parents don't care about their kids' schooling. In my nearly three decades as a public-school teacher in Arizona and California, I've encountered thousands of parents who were deeply invested in giving their children the best education possible. And I'm an American parent myself, with a teenager attending public schools in San Diego County.

Still, I couldn't deny the reality of one experience that Meng said perfectly illustrated this problem for her. Heck, I'd experienced the same thing myself year after year—and it only seemed to be getting worse.

Meng told me about getting ready for Open House night at her Boston school. She was eager to connect with her students' families, expecting dozens of people to come flooding into her classroom as soon as she opened the doors. Instead, Meng said, exactly three parents showed up.

In China, she said, "All the parents, they come. Even sometimes both the mom and dad come here. If the parents are not here, out of town on business, the grandparents come."

That one night left a lasting impression on Meng, convincing her that American families don't support their children's education with the same vigor as parents in countries with top-performing education systems, such as China.

This was a message I heard over and over as I set out on my self-funded trip around the world to speak with teachers, administrators and students at schools in the 17 countries that perform best on the PISA test.

So what is PISA? It is the largest international comparative study of education in the world. The program was launched in 2000 by the Organisation for Economic Cooperation and Development, an inter-governmental organization of industrialized countries, as a way to measure how countries around the world are preparing students for the global economy. Tests are given every three years to 15-year-olds regardless of grade level, achievement or socioeconomic status. The program tests reading, mathematics, and science literacy, with a test on financial literacy as an optional addition for the most recent test. The focus is not on memorization of facts, but on assessing skills such as collaborative problem solving. PISA also includes a questionnaire that gathers information on students' attitudes and motivations. Seventy-nine countries participated in the 2018 PISA test, which is the last exam with results available at the time this book was published. PISA publishes results that rank participating countries and economies according to their performance in reading, math and science.

Why did I choose to base my research around countries that performed well on PISA exams? As you'll recall from the introduction, my motivation for this project was to figure out why the United States was falling behind globally and how school systems fit into that picture. Several longitudinal studies show that, even after accounting for factors such as socioeconomic and educational status of parents, students who perform better on PISA at age 15 have stronger education and employment outcomes at the age of 25. That brighter future is what I want for our students and for the health of our nation at large. So it only made sense to try to figure out what countries that perform well on PISA are doing differently than the United States, which consistently earns decent scores on the reading exam but particularly struggles with math, and so sits near the middle of PISA rankings when looking at an average of reading, math and science scores. Perhaps even more concerning, the United States has a much smaller percentage of students who score at the highest levels on PISA's math exams, which means even our best and brightest are generally lagging behind top students in other countries. And those dynamics really haven't changed since the first PISA exams were administered, with U.S. scores essentially remaining flat.

That's why I visited eight or more schools in each of the 17 countries that now regularly earn top scores across all PISA subjects, including Singapore, Japan, China, Taiwan, South Korea, Canada, Ireland, Finland, Estonia, Germany, Belgium, Netherlands, Switzerland, Liechtenstein, Slovenia, Poland and New Zealand.

In a majority of these countries, there is clear evidence of parents overall remaining highly involved in their children's education, from setting high expectations to attending school functions to making sure kids take time to do their homework each night. In the United States, that support from the home simply tends to be less consistent and thorough. The consensus is that the value of education and a drive to produce educated workers who can compete in a global economy just isn't built into American culture the same way it is in most countries that consistently perform the best on international student testing.

This contrast showed up when results from the first PISA exams were published in 2001.

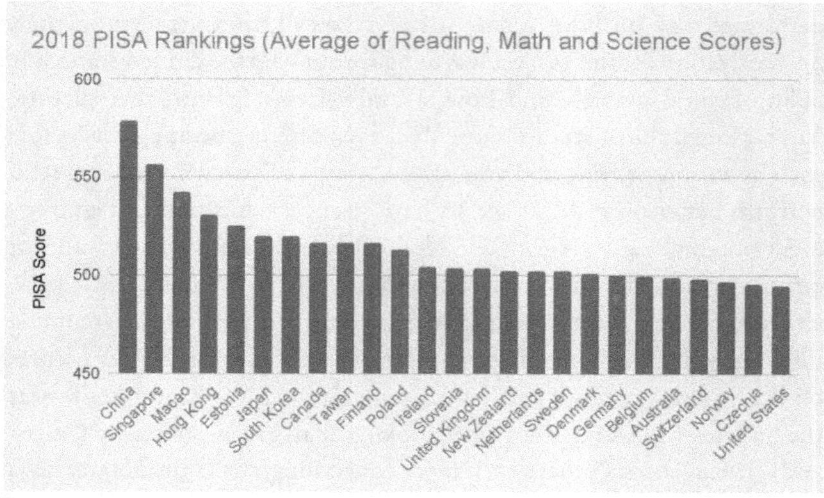

In Germany, when residents learned their country had scored in the bottom half among the 32 participating countries in reading, math and science, it sent shockwaves through the nation, triggering headlines in every newspaper and a demand from parents to know what went wrong. "The whole of Germany said, 'Oh my god,'" recalls Frank Eberth, who lives in the state of Bavaria and talked with me about raising two children in German public schools. "I always thought we had a good school system." Worried it was an early indicator of falling behind in the global economy, German officials immediately launched a major overhaul of the nation's education system. That effort has led to steady gains in PISA results, with Germany ranking No. 19 out of 77 countries tested in 2018.

By comparison, when Americans learned they'd scored dead middle in reading and science and in the bottom half of countries (just one slot above Germany) in math in the 2001 PISA results, the reaction was minimal. It generated sporadic headlines and some education officials called for changes, but minimal news coverage and little reaction from parents. Even nearly a decade later, when two more rounds of PISA results had been released showing Germany making gains while the United States' performance hardly changed, a 2009 survey showed German families very concerned about PISA scores while most American families paid little attention to the test if they even knew what it was. The idea of "American exceptionalism" persisted even when, at least by this quantifiable measure, it was simply no longer accurate.

It would be easy for me as an educator to become frustrated with this reality, point the finger at the home and blame a lack of parental involvement for all of the woes in the American school system. I can't begin to estimate the number of times I've tried to reach the parents of a struggling student only to find that the only phone number they've left us is disconnected or to never get a call back. When I do reach parents, many times they'll promise to start checking their child's homework or work on discipline issues or get needed supplies, but they won't follow through. Too often it feels like we're working at it alone instead of in partnership with parents and guardians, who are with these kids far more than we are. American teachers spend an average of 18,720 hours with students over their 13 years in the public education system, while parents theoretically are with their kids for much of the other 138,960 hours packed into a kid's first 18 years of life.

We also know from countless studies that no matter how great the classroom experience is, if a student isn't getting solid support at home to encourage them, give them the opportunity to read and do homework, and put a priority on education, the odds are stacked against that child succeeding. A 2015 report from Johns Hopkins University sums it up like this: "Research has established consistent and reliable connections between families' involvement in student learning—through practices such as shared reading, homework monitoring, and volunteering at school—with attendance and academic achievement. Studies also show that family engagement matters to the success of the school as an enterprise."

We absolutely need families to be more focused on their kids' learning. This chapter serves as a challenge to all parents, that we look at how families in nations with top-tier education systems support their children's education and strive to do better ourselves.

Still, I've been a teacher for too long to place this blame solely on parents.

From outside my classroom door at Southwest Middle School, I can see the dense housing built on the hill in Tijuana, Mexico, and can hear the helicopters that constantly patrol the border. Some 97 percent of the student population at my middle school is Latino. Many of my students' parents work two or three jobs to stay afloat. There are lots of single moms who may not have a high school diploma. Some are undocumented. So I can't be surprised that, when we have meetings with parents of struggling students, the moms often just nod along with everything we say, too tired or worried to rock the boat. Or that when we held a meeting in early 2020 for families of students whose first language isn't English, despite the coordinator reaching out in multiple ways and languages to more than 300 parents, only 14 parents participated. Or that during Open House night at my school in fall 2021, when I invited the parents of all 150 students in my music classes to attend, just eight showed up.

There are some challenges inherent in our American education system because of circumstances outside our control and because of choices we've made as a nation. While some countries are more selective with who they allow to immigrate, in some cases requiring higher incomes or education levels or other skills, the United States has chosen to welcome "your tired, your poor, your huddled masses yearning to breathe free." The pros and cons of such policies are outside the scope of this book. But I've also seen firsthand how in places like Vietnam and India, persistent poverty and low education levels of generations of parents has not held these nations back from building top-notch education systems. And while places like China don't have as many immigrants as the United States, that doesn't mean there are no language barriers in schools, with many different dialects spoken across the country.

Besides, the lack of parental support and appreciation for the intrinsic value of education is certainly not just a problem at U.S. schools that serve predominantly poor or immigrant families. In fact, thanks in part to good ol' American exceptionalism, many teachers will tell you it has perhaps been even tougher getting support from home at more affluent schools, where students aren't used to being made to do work they don't like and where parents don't appreciate what they see as being told how to raise their kids.

Solid safety nets for families are a common thread among nations with top-performing education systems, even when those countries' value systems, cultures and philosophical underpinnings appear very different. In western countries with high quality education systems, such as Finland and Canada, there is a strong sense of egalitarian values. That means, despite the high value placed on individualism, there also are numerous social welfare and education programs in these social democracies that are aimed at making citizens more equal. In eastern countries that score high on international tests, such as Singapore and South Korea, meritocratic values dominate, where individuals are expected to achieve through their own abilities. But those countries also have a strong sense of collectivism, drawn from traditional Asian philosophies such as Confucianism, which promotes individual achievement for the broader good of the community. These eastern nations know that their economic success depends on the success of all individuals, and they recognize such achievement won't be possible without programs that level the playing field for everyone. So while these western and eastern philosophies might seem to be diametrically opposed, they have the same result: a wide range of public programs that support young families and strong early childhood education.

What became clear to me as I visited hundreds of classrooms around the world is that family support can't be a one-way street. As the saying goes, you get what you give. The United States simply doesn't support parents and young kids in the same way as other countries with highly successful school systems, so U.S. families don't have the motivation or capacity to support us back. We've become so accustomed to this dynamic that we don't have the high expectations for parents that are a baseline standard in many countries with top-performing education systems. And as every teacher knows, people tend to live up the expectations you set for them.

Addressing this issue, more than any other I'll tackle in this book, would of course require sweeping changes beyond the public school system to better support new parents and improve early childhood education. That's for politicians to worry about, right? But such sweeping changes don't happen without loud and consistent feedback from those of us who vote those politicians into office. You have to know about a problem to care about it, and you have to care about it to make a difference.

Some of those concepts also have become highly politicized, especially in these partisan times. Policies also are changing in the United States even as I write this text, with proposals introduced at the federal level and in some states that would start to tackle some of the issues raised in this chapter. But to radically improve education in the United States, we must make long-term, systemic changes that reach beyond the classroom.

To get there, we need to first set aside our own political biases, our own doubts about what's feasible or what fits with our preconceived world views. Next, we need to take a dispassionate look at data showing what actually works. And the research and evidence I gathered are clear: Most countries with top-tier education systems offer more support *for* families *outside* the classroom, which leads to better support *from* families *inside* the classroom. That support from home is a key element in building successful schools. So I'm convinced that unless we can look past partisan notions about support for American families and early education, then take cues from nations that are outperforming us and put our money where our mouths are, we won't be able to establish the foundation needed for the educational changes discussed in coming chapters to stand a chance of succeeding. These changes need to come from policymakers. But unless regular people like you and me educate ourselves and sound the alarm, nothing will ever change.

Support for New Parents and Families

Most Americans couldn't even find Estonia on a map. And they certainly wouldn't guess that Estonia scored better than any other western country on the most recent PISA test. Nearby Finland gets all the attention, with schools there so overwhelmed by requests from educators around the world that when I showed up they initially, quite literally, closed the door in my face.

But when I first contacted Estonia's Ministry of Education in 2018 about visiting public schools there, they said they primarily heard from educators in Asian countries and had only had one other visitor from the United States in as many years as they could remember. So they welcomed me with open arms, eager to show me how their comprehensive system of support for students—from the womb until adulthood—has created one of the best education systems in the world.

When a woman gets pregnant in Estonia, she gets 140 days of fully paid maternity leave that can be taken up to two months before the baby is born. The father also gets 10 days of paid paternity leave to bond with his new baby. And after maternity leave is up, the new parents get another 435 days of paid leave to divvy up between them as they see fit, with compensation based on an average of their two salaries.

Giving parents time to guide their children's early years has long-term benefits for student success, Margo Sootla, director of the Vaatsa Pohikool basic school for grades one through nine in a rural area of central Estonia, told me as we sat in his tidy office in March 2018. Most families take full advantage of the leave programs, Sootla said, with workplaces required to hold parents' jobs open for them for up to three years.

While that's one of the most generous family leave policies of any nation in the world, among countries with top-performing education systems paid family leave is essentially a given.

When I visited Germany, Frank Eberth and his wife, Michaela, both had successful, demanding careers with healthcare companies. But the couple—who I'd met in the United States through a mutual friend, and who graciously agreed to take me to four schools their children had attended in their Bavarian village—said they'd taken advantage of their country's parental leave programs when their kids were born without any hesitation about how it might impact their careers.

Michaela Eberth said expectant moms can take leave eight weeks before their due date. They then get 80 percent of their pay from the government for the equivalent of one full year after giving birth, which they can choose to spread out over the first three years of their child's life. Their job also must be waiting for them when they return, which she said relieves a great deal of pressure for new parents while allowing new moms to stay in the workforce.

In China, where PISA scores show the average student is the equivalent of four years ahead of the average American student in math, new moms get at least 98 days of maternity leave. In Canada, which scored a No. 8 PISA ranking and produces students who average one year ahead of American students in math, women get up to 15 weeks maternity leave plus another 35 weeks of parental leave. And Finland, which ranked No. 10 on PISA and produces students on average half a year more advanced than American students in both reading and science, gives new parents a combined 14 months of leave.

Meanwhile, the United States is one of the only developed nations in the world that doesn't mandate paid family leave. A handful of states have their own family leave programs, offering from four to 16 weeks of time off for parents to bond with new babies. But most Americans are left to fend for themselves.

Some of the nations with top-performing education systems don't stop at paid family leave, either. They also support new parents by offering one-time or recurring payments to help parents adjust to the new, more expensive reality of a growing family.

In Singapore, which nabbed the No. 2 slot on the last PISA exam, all parents get an $8,000 cash gift when their first baby is born. For a second or third baby, they get another $10,000. The government also will deposit $3,000 into a Child Development Account, which can be used to pay for childcare, early education programs, health care and more. And it will match each dollar parents add to that account up to $15,000 and until the child turns 12.

Many countries with top-tier education systems also offer universal child benefits or child allowances, which are tax-free monthly payments to all parents, often with no conditions attached.

In Finland, parents get from 94 euros a month for one child up to 182 euros for a fifth child and beyond until they reach 17 years old. The Finnish government also gives all new moms a "baby box" with clothes, sheets, toys and other supplies. The box itself can also double as a crib, which researchers say has helped keep Finland's infant mortality rate low.

These policies have typically come about due to concerns over declining birth rates. The trend of fewer children threatens national economies, since it means there won't be enough people in coming generations to grow or even maintain the workforce. So governments are incentivizing their citizens to have children by offering financial support. The United States for decades was one of the only developed nations that remained immune to the trend of falling birth rates. That's now changed, with birth rates falling for the sixth year in a row in 2020 to levels that may soon mean there aren't enough babies to replace older generations. That alone is prompting some American political leaders to push for paid leave, baby bonuses and child allowance programs.

The United States government for the first time in 2021 approved sending American parents who made less than $75,000 each a year monthly checks of up to $300 per child. But the payment was a tax credit, not a simple cash payment. And the rebates were temporary, triggered by needs due to the COVID-19 pandemic. California also started experimenting the same year with the first state-funded guaranteed income plan in the nation, to send monthly checks to pregnant women and to young adults aging out of foster care. But it's up to local governments to apply for and run programs to distribute the money, meaning the support for expecting moms still isn't universal in my home state.

Though such changes are often driven largely by a desire to stabilize the population, mounting research shows that policies supporting young families also improve health and financial outcomes for parents and children. That's because they do everything from allowing new moms to breastfeed longer, to easing stress that can trigger mental health issues, to generally creating stronger bonds within new families. And studies show that the positive impact of those changes extends long after parents return to work.

After California enacted the first mandated paid family leave program in the United States in 2004, for example, a study from the Journal of Policy Analysis and Management found kids ages 5 to 10 were less likely to be overweight, have hearing problems or suffer from attention deficit hyperactivity disorder—all of which can hamper their success as students. Some data also suggests that mandated family leave programs can improve student test scores, reduce high school dropout rates, increase rates of college attendance and increase wages earned once students enter the workforce.

Many top-performing nations give all residents additional benefits that can improve the health and financial stability of families, such as universal health care that's not dependent on employment and access to free or cheap college programs. Each financial burden that's lifted from parents' shoulders decreases the likelihood that they'll need to work multiple jobs or long hours, which may leave them with little time to read to their children, check their homework or form meaningful partnerships with their teachers. It also decreases the odds that they'll face financial ruin or that they'll forgo important medical care for their children, which could pose serious problems for the future health of those kids and their ability to reach their full potential in school. The ripple effects of these benefits are difficult to overstate. But all of these programs help set students in top-performing countries up for success before they've even set foot in a classroom.

Early Childhood Education

So we've established that most nations with highly successful education programs offer substantial support to new parents through such programs as paid leave and one-time cash payments when babies are born, plus recurring monthly payments or other benefits as children grow. We've also looked at research and anecdotal evidence I picked up directly from people living in countries that benefit from these systems about how such programs help students thrive in the years to come. However, countries that score at the top of the PISA scale don't stop there. Many also offer subsidized daycare followed by high-quality early childhood education programs.

There are key differences in these programs among top-performing countries. Some mandate early education, while it's optional in other places. Some pay all fees for these programs, while others only offer potential subsidies. But here's what they all have in common: Nations outperforming the United States on international tests at the high school level spend more on early childhood education and have higher standards for early childhood curriculum and teachers. Therefore, a vast majority of parents send their children to these programs.

Poland, which ranked No. 11 in the 2018 PISA exam, offers a free state-run preschool system called *Wychowanie przedszkolne* for all kids aged 3 to 6. Parents aren't required to send their kids, but a majority do, taking advantage of free high-quality care so they can continue working while giving their children a jump on social education.

In South Korea, which scored the No. 7 slot on the most recent PISA test, the government guarantees subsidized childcare and early education for all children until they reach 5 years old. Same goes for the consistently high-scoring nation of Finland, though their programs are guaranteed free for everyone regardless of income until kids reach 7 years old. And in Belgium, preschool is free for kids starting at 2 and 1/2 years old until they go to free kindergarten at 5 years old.

In Germany, all parents have a legal right to send their 1- to 3-year-old children to a nursery program. When German kids reach the age of 3, nearly all go to preschool, which prepares them to start first grade in public school at age 6. Fees for nursery and preschool programs are subsidized based on family income, how many hours kids attend and where families live. For poorer families who qualify, these programs are free.

"In Germany, the government says all children—if their parents are rich or if they don't have a lot of money—all of the children should have the same chance to get good jobs and go to college," said Frank Eberth, whose mother taught kindergarten in a small village with a creek that ran alongside the classroom. He and his wife said there's very little resentment from higher-income residents about subsidizing those in need. Such a system is just "normal," they said, with widespread acceptance that leveling the playing field for all students benefits the entire nation by helping Germany stay competitive in the global economy.

In the United States, children become eligible for public kindergarten at 5 years old. Before that, it's up to parents to find and pay for daycare, preschool or pre-kindergarten programs.

Data from the Organisation for Economic Cooperation and Development shows the United States spends less than most other developed nations on educating and caring for kids under 5 years old. Paying for such programs isn't cheap. But there are volumes of research to show that every dollar invested into high-quality early childhood programs yields a return estimated between $4 and $12 by doing everything from improving the quality of the workforce to lifting income levels late in life, while also decreasing crime rates and reducing prison costs.

Leaving the financial burden on parents means that they—and particularly mothers, as evidenced by the number of women who fled the workforce during the COVID-19 pandemic—often give up jobs that could help their families' future financial position because they can't afford to pay for daycare now. Only around 55 percent of American kids ages 3 and 4 attend formal preschools, and they largely come from wealthier families. That's far below rates for other developed nations, which tend to hit 90 percent attendance or higher and encompass all income groups.

The lack of universal preschool in the United States causes problems for older children as well. Over the years, I've had many students who could not participate in my after-school music ensemble programs because they had to get home to take care of younger siblings. They're forced to babysit as soon as they get home, leaving them little time for homework, let alone extracurricular activities.

For American kids who do make it to preschool, they won't encounter set curriculum standards or much in the way of educational standards for instructors. Some programs only require a high school diploma for teachers, plus a simple certificate program. And the median salary for an American preschool teacher in 2020 was $31,930. That means the quality of such programs can vary widely, with little government oversight beyond basic background and safety checks.

By contrast, Finland has an established national curriculum that covers all early childhood education and care for kids from 18 months old up to age 6. After that, all students are required to attend a government-funded kindergarten, which they call preschool, before they start primary school in first grade at age 7. But while there are standards for these early education programs and high expectations for instructors, there also is a noteworthy amount of playtime built in.

As soon as I entered a public kindergarten for 3- to 5-year-olds in Seoul, South Korea, I saw neatly stacked shoes that kids had swapped for sandals as they entered. But far from feeling overly regimented, the school felt full of joy. Students walked in under a large, lovely artificial tree, passing rows of real plants and aquariums housing fish and lizards. Each classroom had its own piano, since—as Principal Kim Mi Sook explained—music was such an integral part of their learning. After a healthy lunch of fish, soup, rice and vegetables, with water to drink, students all brushed their teeth before returning brushes to a cabinet that cleaned them with ultraviolet light. They then returned to their class-rooms for differentiated learning, with some doing art projects and others doing educational play activities.

In Canada, many kids start kindergarten as early as 4 years old. They do teach basic English and math literacy, but a kindergarten teacher who guided me around her classroom at Monsignor Fee Otterson Public School in the Edmonton region explained that they focus more on teaching students to think and how to turn an idea into action. Many Canadian parents also choose to send kids to junior kindergarten when they are as young as 3, though the programs aren't free for most students. But even at the junior kindergarten level, all programs are taught by fully credentialed teachers.

Canada also doesn't wait until kids get to kindergarten to start trying to help students with special needs. I toured the 100 Voices Early Childhood Learning Center in Edmonton, Canada, which is located inside a recreation center filled with hockey rinks and other activities for the community. The center offers junior kindergarten classes for children 3 to 4 years old who need extra help. Students have either tested positive for a learning disability, such as autism or speech delays, or they don't speak English as their primary language. My host explained that out of 395 students enrolled in the program at the time of my tour, 255 were English language learners.

Each of the classrooms at 100 Voices—named for the Loris Malaguzzi poem *The 100 Languages*, which inspired the Reggio Emilia educational philosophy about the many ways students communicate—had one highly trained teacher, one student teacher from a nearby university and one facilitator on hand to help the children. Edmonton Catholic Schools, which hosts the program, had sent a team to an international conference in Italy to learn about the Reggio Emilia philosophy and bring it back to their early learning centers. Inspired by that experience, classroom lighting was dim, so as not to overstimulate children who might have heightened sensitivities. They were surrounded by options for hands-on activities, specially chosen to give them options for guided play with learning built in. Rather than buying commercially produced calendars, students made their own. It was more impressive than any preschool I'd seen in the United States, and it was completely free for all students who qualified.

In Estonia, I observed impressive kindergarten classes at a public school in Peetri. There, kids can attend kindergarten from 3 to 6 years old. They learn letters and numbers along with music and art. There's also plenty of time for play and naps, with kids sleeping on staggered tiers of wooden beds that opened like drawers as I walked through on a whispered tour led by Luule Niinesalu, director of the Peetri Kindergarten School. Estonian kindergarteners are taught by instructors who have bachelor's degrees at a minimum, Niinesalu explained. The program isn't free, but the monthly fee is nominal. And if parents can't afford it, local governments have funds to subsidize them. So most Estonian parents choose to send their kids to such programs, giving them a boost before they start first grade.

Making such programs universally available, rather than forcing parents to foot the bill, is a key component of Estonia's efforts to help families break out of the cycle of poverty, according to Gunda Tire, national project manager for PISA in Estonia. Sootla, at Estonia's Vaatsa Pohikool basic school, said in his incoming class of 25 first graders the year we spoke, 23 of them had been through kindergarten programs for one to three years. "Of course they are playing a lot there," he said. "But there is also curriculum for them for preparation for school." While such programs help parents get back to work by functioning as affordable daycare, Sootla said he also believes they help students arrive ready to learn and reflect the value parents place on education.

In China, children also attend kindergarten from 3 to 6 years old. All kindergarten teachers must have college degrees in education. Chun, a kindergarten teacher who hosted me at her school in the city of Qingdao, explained that all her colleagues can play the piano, since they use music so often to teach the children lessons. She introduced me to 5- and 6-year-olds who could recite their ABCs in English; early bilingual education is common in many of the top-performing nations.

Singapore has become a bit obsessed with trying to get all families to send their kids to preschool programs even if they're not mandatory. That's because they've seen the benefits of such programs in helping kids succeed as they go through school and join the workforce. So even though they were already at 99 percent participation in 2013, they were spending public funds to look for children not enrolled in preschool or with poor attendance to encourage them to go.

All of that combines to put American students—and therefore the nation's future workforce—behind many of their international peers before they've even started first grade. That's why it's not at all surprising to hear American companies complain that they can't find enough skilled workers to staff their businesses, forcing some to either import workers or outsource work. And it's why business leaders are some of the most vocal proponents of early childhood education programs.

The United States has tried to compensate for these gaps by creating programs such as Head Start, which has existed since 1965 to offer early education and support services to kids 3 to 5 years old who are living in poverty. But Head Start instructors don't need to be credentialed teachers. These programs also are stretched to focus on helping kids with meals, health care, social services and other needs. A number of studies have shown Head Start programs have been more successful in meeting kids' physical needs than in helping them advance academically. Head Start also isn't universally available, even to all qualifying poor families, with funding only available to serve roughly a third of American kids in need.

My son was briefly in a Head Start program in Los Angeles when he was young. When I think back and compare my visits to his Head Start class with visits to preschools at top performing countries, the differences are stark. The environment in my son's class was not engaging. Teacher turnover was high and learning was low. Play equipment wasn't high quality, snacks weren't very nutritious and kids took naps on a rug on the floor, rather than the attractive stacked beds I'd seen at that preschool in Estonia. Despite the best intentions of those behind Head Start, there's simply no comparison between the quality of that program and what other countries are providing.

Another proposed U.S. solution has been pre-kindergarten or transitional kindergarten programs. But unlike in other countries, where such programs are attended by 97 percent of the population, America's Pre-K programs are far from universal. There aren't enough teachers or classrooms to offer these programs to everyone, even in places where funding and demand exist. That means kindergarten teachers are left trying to juggle classrooms filled with small numbers of students who went to pre-K and arrive knowing how to read, plus a larger swath of students who haven't yet learned their letters, which creates inequities from the first day of school.

There is much research to show that once students start off behind the curve, it's very difficult to catch them up, despite substantial U.S. investment into such programs. That's one reason why, at my middle school, a majority of students still read at a third-grade level. Students who fall behind from a young age are more likely to drop out of high school and earn less as adults. Some data even suggests it's possible to predict future incarceration rates based on how well students are reading in the third grade.

If we want to set American students up for success and put them on competitive footing with their peers from nations that boast top-tier education systems, we can't keep turning a blind eye to the importance of everything that happens before these kids reach kindergarten. It's time to take cues from places such as Singapore, Finland, Germany and Estonia. It's time to provide better support for families, so they're equipped and capable and motivated to become true partners in their children's education.

Supported Parents Give Back

Even the best education systems in the world have problems and room for improvement. But one complaint that I hear frequently from American teachers never came up in my conversations with dozens of teachers at more than 170 public schools in top performing countries: lack of parental support.

I have many students whose parents I never speak to all school year. They don't come to school functions, despite multiple invitations in different languages. They don't return calls or reach out. Often, I feel as though these parents believe educating their child is my job alone, and I shouldn't burden them with requests for information or supplies or support of any kind. Then we teachers hear complaints from parents about the public school system, how we're not doing enough, we're failing their kids and public schools should lose funding.

By contrast, from Estonia to Ireland to Singapore, teachers told me their students' parents largely felt like their partners in education. The value of education and the role of the public school system are consistently emphasized at home from an early age, with a better universal under-standing of how competitive the global economy is and what it takes for young people today to succeed. So expectations are set high, and parents generally stay involved to ensure those expectations are met by regularly communicating with teachers, checking their children's homework and participating in school functions.

Expectations aren't only high for students, either. In Teru Clavel's book *World Class*, which looks through a mother's eyes at ways to bring the best of Asia's education policies to the United States, Clavel recounts how parents in Tokyo were drafted by lottery to participate in rigorous, time-consuming PTA programs. "Moms were expected to serve on the PTA for at least one full school year for each child they have in the school," she wrote. "Your enthusiastic participation is a sign you value the education the school provides."

There are complicated cultural factors contributing to parental involvement in some of these countries. At the Qingdao #58 school in China, for example, a veteran teacher named Liz told me parents push their children very hard in part due to lingering effects of the nation's long-held one-child policy. While that policy officially ended in 2015, many parents still have put all of their eggs into one basket, so to speak. If that one child is well educated, Liz said, parents believe he or she will have a better shot commanding a good salary and helping them as they age.

Chinese teachers play a role in that dynamic. Liz said teachers pressure parents when their children aren't doing well, making them fear potential consequences of the children's academic failure. A common practice that she used with parents was showing the scores of their child versus others in the class. The parents listen to the teachers, since teachers have high status in China. And so parents continue applying pressure to their children to study harder and catch up.

Of course, such expectations on parents and students can go too far, leading to inequities and mental health issues.

A common practice in China, as in many Asian countries, is for parents to contract with a private tutor or to send children to a "cram school" to help boost their grades. In China, more than 60 percent of primary school pupils are tutored outside the classroom in subjects such as English, literature and math. In large cities like Beijing and Shanghai, 70 percent of primary school students attend cram schools. Due to the fierce academic competition in the public schools, Chinese parents spend an average of 120,000 yuan (roughly U.S. $17,400) a year on extracurricular tutoring for their children, according to a National Education Association report. But for low-income students, this means they may fall further behind.

In South Korea, many parents also invest thousands of dollars each year to send their children to hagwons, which is that country's version of private, for-profit programs that offer additional learning for kids outside the school day. At a high school in Seoul, I asked a classroom full of students how many attended a hagwon, and almost every hand went up. One of the few hands that didn't go up belonged to a young man asleep on his desk after studying so hard.

I saw entire multi-story shopping centers filled with hagwons for different subject areas. At one of these cram schools, I spoke with a student in a navy-blue uniform blazer who said he studied math and English at the hagwon for an average of four hours every day. In some places, I learned, they've even had to create a police force to sweep the hagwons and make sure students go home at a reasonable hour rather than study through the night.

Such heavy pressure on kids to excel certainly raises concerns. But there must be a happy medium between the low parental involvement and pressure that's common in the United States and the level of pressure that's driving kids in South Korea to study until they can't stay awake in class the next day. And my hope is that reading about how involved and dedicated families are to the learning process in other countries will motivate more American parents to step up and become partners in their children's education. We teachers can't do it without you. And unless this first piece of the puzzle falls into place, with increased support for and from families, we're shortchanging our kids by sending them out to compete in a global economy when they've been behind since the day they were born.

What can I do?

Improving the quality and consistency of family support for schools by overhauling support systems for families at home is, of course, a daunting task. But you don't have to be a member of Congress to make a difference. Here are 10 steps everyone can take right now to help set the wheels in motion, with space to jot down notes on plans for accomplishing each step or how it went once it's completed.

- Write a letter to your state and federal representatives asking them to support policies that offer paid parental leave and other financial safety nets for new parents, plus high-quality subsidized daycare and early education programs for all residents.

____

____

____

____

- Start a conversation with family members, friends and colleagues about what support for young families and early education looks like in nations with top-tier education systems. Try an opener such as, "Did you know the United States is one of the only developed nations in the world that doesn't offer paid leave for parents?" Or, "Did you know that almost every child in Singapore attends a formal preschool while only about half of American students attend one?"

  ____

  ____

  ____

- If you're a parent, make a list of what you might have done differently in the first months and years of your child's life if you had guaranteed paid leave from work, monthly payments to help with expenses and access to affordable early education programs. If you're not a parent, talk to a family member or friend who is one and ask them how such programs might have helped them.

  ____

  ____

  ____

- Submit an editorial to your local newspaper sharing what you've learned about what support for families looks like in other nations and what you'd like to see happen in your community.

  ____

  ____

  ____

- Talk to a preschool teacher in your neighborhood. Ask them about the training and support they now receive and what they feel would help them better do their jobs.

  ____

  ____

  ____

- If possible, visit nations that score high on the Program for International Student Assessment test. Talk to parents, kids, educators and policymakers there about how they've made parental support and early education programs work. If you can't go in person, visit virtually. Videos of my tours of early education programs in many countries are posted on my website, KeithBallard.org. Then bring ideas from what you've seen back to your community.

- Volunteer in a local preschool or transitional kindergarten program. Take note of how such programs compare to what you've seen in countries with top-tier education systems.

- If you're a parent, commit to attending open house nights, keeping a current phone number on file with your child's school, returning teachers' phone calls, checking your child's homework and generally being an active partner in your child's education. If something is holding you back from fulfilling this role, talk to your child's school and see what help is available. If you're not a parent, consider offering to help a family member or friend with these duties.

- Make a list of what you think is blocking support programs seen in nations with better-performing education systems. Then brainstorm a solution to each obstacle. Share those ideas with policymakers and people you know.

- Push for your local school district, city or county to implement elements of family support or early education programs while you continue advocating for national change. Do this by speaking out during the public comment period at local meetings, writing to local government officials to advocate for these changes or running for local office yourself.

"The top performers have built their systems around high-quality teachers; we have built ours around cheap teachers."

Marc Tucker,
Leading High-Performance School Systems

Author Keith Ballard sits with Finnish teachers in a "pod" inside the teacher's lounge at Gradia Jyvaskyla Lyseon, an upper secondary school in Jyvaskyla, Finland.

Chapter Two

High Standards for Teachers

In Canada's major cities, it's not uncommon for 10 fully qualified, aspiring new educators to apply for every *one* teaching slot that's open in their schools. And when Canadians can't get into their own competitive teacher training programs or land a local job straight out of college, they told me during my visit to local schools that some cross the border into the United States, where it's much easier to become a teacher.

Meanwhile, in my native state of Arizona where I started my teaching career, districts are recruiting teachers from the Philippines who are willing to work for the pay and conditions they offer. They're also dropping credential requirements and other standards to fill open positions with just about anyone who has a college degree and is willing to stand in front of a classroom full of kids.

In South Korea, elementary teachers come from the top 5 percent of high school students who go on to college. I spoke with teachers there and in other top-performing PISA countries who had aspired to their careers from the time they were children, studying hard to make it into competitive training programs and fighting for limited positions so they'd have the honor of being teachers.

In the United States, studies show that half of U.S. teachers come from the bottom third of their university cohort, often graduating from large state schools spread all over the country. Former New York City Mayor Michael Bloomberg took this point a step further and asserted at a press conference that teachers are drawn from the bottom 20 percent of graduates. Keep in mind, our students already are graduating high school with lower levels of average academic achievement than students in these top performing countries, which means drawing our teachers from the lower cohort of U.S. students is equivalent to pulling from an even lower sector in places that excel on international testing benchmarks.

Students who go on to become teachers also often start university training or even graduate with degrees in other fields, but switch to teaching after discovering the other program or job market was too challenging. As a result, many Americans would agree that the United States has a serious problem with both the quality and quantity of applicants in the K-12 teaching profession. And with the COVID-19 crisis, the situation has gotten worse. That's all led to the persistent and derogatory cliche: "Those who can, do; those who can't, teach."

In Finland, starting teachers aren't paid exorbitant salaries. But they're paid roughly the same as, say, a starting engineer, making those fields equally attractive from a financial and status perspective. All Finnish teachers must have master's degrees, but don't have to pay out of pocket for these programs. They also receive high levels of support once they're in the classroom, with hands-on experience under a mentor's guidance and then time each school day throughout their careers to work together on lesson planning, training, and other development. As a result, it's challenging to get into Finland's limited teacher training programs. And once teachers are hired, they tend to stick with the profession until retirement.

In the United States, the average starting teacher's salary is $41,163 while the average starting engineer's salary is $59,662. So of course America's university engineering programs are much more competitive than its teaching programs, attracting a higher volume of more highly qualified candidates. U.S. teachers often are saddled with student debt when they graduate and are then happy to accept full-time jobs on emergency credentials, with only four-year degrees and some other basic requirements met. Once they have a foot in the door, they complete a limited and shallow on-the-job training program that doesn't have much oversight, with some mentors just signing off on benchmarks for new teachers as if they're doing them a favor. In the seven schools I have worked in over the course of my career, I received no help or training from my school or district related to my subject area. As I tell new teachers coming into the profession, "It's pretty much sink or swim. If you can't beg, borrow and steal, you probably won't make it."

Meanwhile, a significant percentage of the American public—buoyed by leaders on the right, in hyper-partisan times where everything has become political—has started to vilify teachers' unions and public schools at large. Of course teachers themselves, who make up those unions and staff those schools, are caught in the middle. They feel disrespected and derided by the very families they're trying to help, who should be partners in educating children as discussed in the first chapter of this book.

Is it any surprise, then, that U.S. districts have to continue dropping their standards to fill their teaching positions? Or that some 51 percent of public-school teachers surveyed in the United States said they felt unsatisfied with the state of their profession, according to the 2020 Teacher Confidence Index? Or that U.S. schools have a turnover rate for teachers that's unheard of in high-performing counties, with more than half of American educators typically leaving the profession within the first five years?

I'm a teacher, so I know it's easy for some people to write off my handwringing in this area as self-interest. But improvements to the field of teaching of course don't just benefit teachers. As PISA test results show, everyone benefits from having schools led by teachers who were selected from among the best of the best graduating high school and college each year, who are held to the highest standards and stay around year after year as their experience and expertise grows.

When it comes to trying to improve teaching in the United States, the vast majority of proposed solutions in recent decades have focused on changing specific techniques teachers use with students inside the classroom. I've lost count of the number of times over my 28 years as an educator that I've been forced to leave my students with a substitute teacher to attend a mandatory day-long training on the latest and greatest silver-bullet curriculum program or pricey technology tool that was supposed to revolutionize what happened in my classroom. These programs are often expensive for districts to implement and more complex than one day-long training can cover. Still, we teachers are forced to incorporate this new strategy into our lessons, sometimes replacing tried and true methods we've proven over years in the field. And often, a few years later, that transformative idea gets bumped for an entirely new one, and the disruption starts again.

Some attempts also have been made in recent years to raise the standards for teachers. But those plans have largely focused on linking teacher pay to students reaching certain benchmarks on standardized tests, then punishing teachers whose students don't hit that mark. We'll tackle problems with America's reliance on high-stakes testing in chapter five. But no matter the measuring stick, if we only try to raise the standards for teachers without also improving factors such as the preparation, support, status and salaries teachers receive, and the freedom they have to put their expertise to work in their classrooms, we're just going to keep ending up with fewer teachers rather than a larger pool of more highly qualified candidates who stick around. Then we have to lower our standards again to get teachers back in classrooms. And research shows that lowering the standards for teachers over time makes shortages worse, since the prestige of the profession falls, attracting fewer new candidates, while frustration grows among current teachers who weren't properly vetted and trained, driving more educators away from the field.

Marc Tucker, founder of the National Center on Education and the Economy in Washington, D.C., sums it up well: "The top performers have built their systems around high-quality teachers; we have built ours around cheap teachers."

To understand how we got here, a quick history lesson is helpful.

There was a time in the late 19th and early 20th century in the United States when teachers were "among the best educated people in their communities," Tucker explained both in his book *Leading High-Performance School Systems* and in conversation with me. While most people didn't go beyond elementary school at the time, teachers had two years of higher education. That meant they often ended up with more education than all but top-level professionals in their towns, such as doctors, lawyers, and ministers, which led to widespread respect and support for educators from the community.

But as colleges offering bachelor's degrees were built all over the country in the early and mid-1900s, teachers with two years of training were no longer the best educated members of their communities. More jobs required four-year degrees and those university programs got more competitive, Tucker notes. "So, step by step, teachers went from being among the best educated in their communities to being engaged in one of the lowest-status occupations requiring a college degree."

At the same time, the U.S. education system was rapidly expanding, creating high demand for teachers. But districts weren't paying teachers what architects, doctors, accountants and engineers were earning. That meant that "the status of the school of education kept sinking in the academic hierarchy," Tucker writes. "Over time, at these institutions, the teachers' colleges were widely viewed as the professional schools you could get into if you could not get into any of the other professional schools, because the admissions standards were low and the academic demands on the students modest." One might assume that lower standards would mean a wider pool of teaching candidates. But with programs easy to get into, teaching became viewed as a less prestigious career, and the number of students who aspired to a teaching career dwindled. So, while of course many skilled and dedicated people still became teachers, the field began to suffer regular shortages. And we simply accepted the fact that those who did enter the profession, on average, did not come from the top tier of high school or college graduates.

The United States has done nothing of significance to disrupt this cycle that began more than a century ago, even as the gap between the achievement of U.S. students and other top nations has grown.

But countries that have built high quality education systems have made major changes in the past few decades to how they treat the field of teaching. While there are differences in how these standards play out from country to country, top-tier education systems generally share these nine principles:

1. There is a focus on recruiting top-tier high school students to teacher training programs.
2. Teaching programs are limited to research universities, where admission standards are strict and programs are rigorous.
3. Barriers to entry for teaching jobs are kept high, often requiring advanced degrees, regardless of what hiring obstacles districts may face.
4. New teachers are paired with experienced mentors who provide constant, hands-on support during early years.
5. Teachers are compensated in line with other professionals who have similar levels of education.
6. Teachers have paid time each day for professional development and collaboration with colleagues in shared offices, allowing them to help develop curriculum and programs.
7. There are clear pathways for teachers to take on leadership roles and make more money based on expertise rather than just years of service.
8. District office staffs stay small, with resources and expertise kept in classrooms.
9. Struggling teachers get extra support and coaching instead of getting fired.

I spoke with teachers at each of the more than 170 schools I visited during my trips around the world, asking them about everything from their path to the classroom to how they use their day to how they feel about their profession. Here's a closer look at what I learned about how top-performing countries view, educate and support their teachers, and how we can implement those same strategies at home.

Prestige Problem

When I walked into Itaewon Primary School in Seoul, South Korea, I remember seeing a row of framed photos on the wall showing all of the school's teachers. I asked my host about the photos, and she said most schools in South Korea proudly display their teaching staff for everyone who enters. Estonia does the same thing, with formal, professional photos mixed with casual photos of staff members working together. In fact, I cannot recall any school within the Asian countries that I visited that did not display photos of its teaching staff prominently at the front entrance of the building.

In the United States, it's common to see photos of students and their work hanging around the school. But I have yet to visit a U.S. school where I've seen a display highlighting the teaching staff together for all to see. I recommended such a display to the principal at my own school but heard things like, "It would be expensive, and perhaps the teachers would not like it." To me, that simple distinction speaks volumes about the professional respect and esteem the school and community at large have for teachers, and it highlights the expectation of teamwork and collegiality among teachers in those top-performing countries.

Perceptions of teachers in the United States seem to fall into one of two categories. They're either seen as heroes who were called to teach and therefore have an almost supernatural passion that makes them willing to use their own money for school supplies, work long hours outside the school day, and accept that issues such as low pay and discipline problems come with the territory. The other option is to see them as lazy adults who couldn't cut it in another field, and who get to enjoy summers off and tenure that keeps them employed, almost no matter what they do. Neither one is a particularly attractive picture to paint if we want to lure our best and brightest to pursue teaching.

I regularly ask students in my middle school and high school music classes to raise their hands if they are considering becoming teachers as a lifelong profession. Often, not one hand in the room goes up. When I ask why, they tell me things like, "I want to make more money," or "It's boring." Some make jokes about not wanting to deal with kids like themselves. It seems my students as young as 12 understand that the teaching profession is fairly low status and not something they care to aspire to do.

In countries with top-performing school systems, teachers are consistently regarded as highly qualified professionals who play a key role in the well-being of the nation and who are trained, supported, compensated, and respected accordingly. That makes it much easier for schools to encourage the most talented to consider teaching as an option.

China regularly ranks at the top of surveys that look at the level of respect a culture has for its teachers. But it wasn't always that way. David, the English name for a 26-year veteran teacher I spoke with just outside his classroom at Qingdao #2, a top high school in Qingdao, China, told me teachers used to be treated like any other blue-collar workers in the years before the county opened up to the western world. But as China started working to compete in the global economy, it began upping the standards and pay for teachers. Since then, David said, teaching has become one of the most respected professions, with incomes for experienced educators that put them in the upper middle class.

As more than 40 uniformed middle schoolers piled into a classroom I observed at Qingdao Middle School #51, they chatted with each other and joked around. But the entire class fell quiet and stood as soon as their teacher Ms. Ding entered the room. They bowed to her as she greeted them, then said "good morning" back to her in English. That is how they start every class, with a bow and greeting of respect for their teacher. And students continued to give Ms. Ding their focused attention throughout the entire 45-minute lesson.

Teachers at Seoul High School in South Korea told me that the profession was so highly honored by society that competition for positions remained high even before they started raising salaries to make educators' compensation more competitive with other professions.

That respect for teachers can take a different shape in western countries, proving it's not just about performative measures. In Finland, for example, at Normaalikoulu Upper Secondary School & Teacher Training School in Jyvaskyla, students in every class I observed were highly respectful to their teachers in terms of paying attention during lessons and exhibiting no discipline issues. But English teacher and teacher trainer Pirjo Pollari said she'd "faint" if one of her students called her Dr. Pollari. In Finland, and in several other western countries I visited that perform well on PISA exams, it's common for students to call their teachers and even their administrators by their first names. Pollari explained it's not a lack of respect. Instead, she said it's about having mutual respect and not creating distance between them or power dynamics that might hamper communication. But Outi, a university student and future English teacher who was practicing lessons at Normaalikoulu, told me teaching is absolutely considered an honored profession in Finland and was something she'd aspired to since she was very young.

Just as students often rise to meet our expectations, countries with top-tier education systems seem to understand that having high expectations and esteem for teachers also can push them to raise the quality of the teaching they offer. Sharon Chen, a teacher at Affiliated Experimental Elementary School in Taipei, Taiwan, told me that communitywide expectations for her school are so high that it pressures teachers to work harder, improving the quality of education students are receiving.

The ripple effects of this simple fact could help address a number of issues plaguing U.S. education.

When the community holds teachers in high esteem, that makes it a desirable profession, which attracts the best candidates to the field. Right now, roughly half of U.S. teachers come from the bottom 25 percent of the university cohort. If the teacher pool instead was primarily the upper end of the university cohort as it is in places like South Korea, Tucker says that single change would trigger vast improvements in the U.S. education system. It would elevate the level of education students are receiving. It also would help address the teacher shortage problems that have created instability and lowered standards in U.S. schools for years.

The community attaching prestige to teaching also helps keep teachers around longer, which again helps with shortages and the quality of education. I didn't start hitting my stride as a teacher until year six. By then, statistics show, roughly half of U.S. teachers have already quit. While many teachers see the profession as a calling and therefore accept conditions they might not encounter in a different job, others can only stand the negatives—such as discipline problems in the classroom and making less money than people in other fields with similar levels of education—for so long when they're hearing their community blame them for the ills of society, demonize their unions and recommend moving away from public schools entirely.

In more than 20 years of teaching at her school in Finland, Dr. Pollari said she thought perhaps she could recall one or two teachers who had simply quit. Otherwise, she said turnover only happened when a teacher retired or took time off to be a parent or pursue further studies before coming back to the classroom. When I told her that the year before, at my school in San Diego, a third of our teachers quit at the end of the school year, she grimaced.

We try to compensate for the lack of high-quality teachers—or any teachers at all—willing to work at schools with the neediest students through programs such as Teach for America. The program, launched in 1990, sends new graduates from top universities to teach in low-income schools for at least two years. Participants go through a special summer-long training program, and they receive an extra stipend on top of their starting teacher salary. For a couple of years, I was on the San Diego Chamber of Commerce's education advisory committee. Members would talk about Teach for America with reverence, enthralled by good-hearted Ivy league graduates who were willing to come teach our poorer students. The program has excellent goals and has shown modest gains in boosting student outcomes. But with most teachers leaving after four or five years, I struggle to understand why a superintendent would promote that program as a solution in his or her district. At best, it's a temporary fix. At worst, it puts inexperienced teachers willing to accept starting salaries in positions where experience and expertise are most needed.

Parents holding teachers and education at large in high esteem means teachers can have true partners in educating their children, as discussed in the first chapter. If parents respect teachers, they will support them more when it comes to both academic and discipline issues. They'll also encourage their children to have more respect for teachers and to value the education they're receiving from those professionals.

Students holding teachers in high esteem helps eliminate many of the discipline problems that plague American schools, driving some teachers away and worsening the quality of education for everyone in the classroom. It means students are more willing to listen to teachers, which means they will learn more from their lessons rather than staring at cell phones or otherwise tuning them out. And it makes them more likely to consider teaching as a potential career for themselves, if they view it as an honorable profession.

So how do we raise the prestige of teachers in the United States? Well, for starters, money does talk.

There's a reason we pay doctors so much: They have lots of education and a skillset others don't have, while providing a service that's considered crucial to society. If we want teachers to be viewed in the same light, shouldn't we apply those same standards and then compensate them accordingly? Instead, starting teacher pay in many U.S. states is quite low, often allowing teachers to qualify for low-income housing. (We'll talk more in chapter eight about inequities between American schools.) So why would the best students in U.S. universities become teachers or stick around in the profession?

But it's not just about throwing more money at teachers. In fact, in many top-performing nations teachers don't make much more than American teachers. One key difference is that there isn't such a gap between what teachers make and starting salaries for professionals in other fields with similar levels of education. It might take state or national legislation to force that change, raising teacher salaries to be more competitive so it's viewed as a viable career path with the same prestige as, say, engineering or accounting.

Teacher pay in most of these other countries also increases based on merit, with a clear career path to advance. David, the veteran teacher in Qingdao, China, told me he's one of 15 teachers at his top-ranked school who receives a generous annual bonus for the level of expertise and experience he brings to the classroom. In Shanghai, trained master teachers can earn the same pay as principals, removing one incentive for the best teachers to leave the classroom.

In the United States, teacher pay typically increases based on years of service and additional education, which doesn't have to be in the field that person teaches. Sometimes, as has often happened in recent years in my home state of Arizona, even those annual increases are delayed if the state doesn't have the money to cover them. And while other nations often offer stipends to teachers serving vulnerable communities, we typically leave it up to those communities to find ways to offer higher pay that might entice more teachers to come or deal with the consequences if they can't.

Another key financial difference is that in most of these other countries, university training programs for teachers are free or highly subsidized. That means teachers aren't saddled with student loan debt when they start out, which in essence lowers salaries for U.S. teachers even more and could lead them to leave the profession for higher-paying jobs that better cover their bills.

Money aside, there also is an intrinsic respect for teachers in many top-performing countries that's much tougher to pin down. Those types of conversations of course start in the home, with parents teaching their children to value education and respect teachers.

In some Asian countries, educators told me they believe widespread prestige for teachers stems from Confucianism, which teaches respect for elders and social responsibility. In some European countries, they talked about a renewed value on education and educators after World War II turned everything upside down, forcing them to rethink who they were as nations.

In Finland, Ville Ylianunti, principal of Mikkolan Koulu basic school in Vantaa outside Helsinki, told me teacher programs are among the most sought-after in universities, on par with programs to become doctors or engineers. "Many young students or high school students, they dream of class teachers' work," he said. "It's something like a myth they want to pursue." But when pressed about where that aspiration comes from, he admitted he wasn't sure. "We just value education."

Pollari, from the teacher training school in Finland, said she believes the key difference between how teachers are viewed in Finland and how they're viewed in the United States boils down to one word: trust.

In all her years of teaching, Pollari said, she'd never had to show an administrator her lesson plans or display what teaching standard she was addressing—both common practices in U.S. schools. "Everybody trusts that I know what I am doing and that I am doing it very well," she said. If she was asked to start proving that to a boss every day, Pollari said she'd likely quit teaching. "The freedom in teaching is one of the biggest rewards," she said.

I asked if she thought there would be more trust in U.S. teachers if we weren't getting them from the middle and lower cohorts of the university pool. She told me to flip the analogy. She believes we would get higher quality teachers if we gave them more freedom and autonomy, and if we treated them like professionals who deserve some level of prestige in society.

That's not to say that none of the top PISA countries ever face teacher shortages.

Estonia, for example, is facing a serious problem with an aging teacher population. They have a cohort of veteran educators who know how to get results but are nearing retirement.

"It is not a very popular sort of aspiration for the young people," Gunda Tire, national project manager for PISA in Estonia, told me. They are working on ways to make the field more attractive for young people. And what's their first step? Increasing teacher salaries, which haven't seen the same boosts or leveling with other professions as in other high-performing countries.

If the United States undertakes a similarly serious effort to make teacher salaries more competitive and finds other ways to reward them, such as giving them more trust and freedom while modeling respect for educators at home, we can start to raise the prestige of the profession. That will start attracting the best of the best to aspire to be teachers.

Then we must teach those teachers how to be great.

Educators Get Educated

In Singapore, which ranked number two in the world on the last round of PISA exams, there is only one place in the country where teachers can get training and earn their credentials: the National Institute of Education. Admissions requirements to that university are stringent, with only the top applicants able to get in. And for those who enroll, the program is rigorous.

During my visit to the institute, I interviewed top researchers and professors who explained that the teacher training school was connected with their country's Ministry of Education. That ensured the university was giving aspiring teachers the information they needed about national education standards, and that the government had a direct pipeline to hear from educators about their experiences and needs.

The Ministry of Education and university also partner with local public schools in the area, so that teachers in training can regularly spend time in classrooms observing veterans in the field and teaching lessons of their own. When I visited some of those schools, I noticed cameras in classrooms—an idea that wouldn't sit well with most American or western teachers at large. But my hosts explained the cameras aren't used to discipline teachers, but to offer feedback on their lessons and to capture best practices to share with other teachers.

Granted, Singapore only has 5 million people, which is just a bit bigger than the city of Los Angeles. And the Asian nation is only a little larger than Rhode Island, which is geographically the smallest state in the U.S. So of course the United States, with its more than 330 million people, needs more than one place to train future teachers. But we have gone the opposite direction of places like Singapore and many other countries with top-tier public schools, which carefully control the quality of education teachers are receiving.

There are nearly 2,000 not-for-profit colleges and universities in the United States that offer teacher certification programs. Some are very difficult to get into and offer rigorous programs, such as the Teachers College at Columbia University. But for many college of education programs in U.S. universities, admission requirements are among the lowest of any program offered in the university. If you can get into the university, you can get into its teacher training program. That's why, again, about half of new teachers in the U.S. come from the bottom third of their university cohort, as measured by SAT or ACT scores. And for the students in these programs, courses and workloads often aren't anywhere near as challenging as those of other respected disciplines.

There also are many for-profit colleges training tomorrow's teachers throughout the United States, with a massive range in both admissions standards and the quality of education they're providing. Some have been plagued by scandals. The largest for-profit institution in the U.S. is the University of Phoenix, which gives students the option of attending entirely online—something unheard of for teacher training programs in top-tier countries. University of Phoenix also has fallen under criticism for recruiting tactics that promise students teaching jobs once they graduate, despite each state setting its own perimeters for teaching credentials. And many of these for-profit universities cost upwards of $40,000 a year, leaving graduates saddled with debt as they face starting salaries that can be as low as $35,000 a year in places like Arkansas.

A now-retired principal from my school district currently supervises students in their student teaching at the University of Phoenix. He recently told me all students periodically have to send in videos of themselves teaching lessons in their classrooms so he can monitor their progress. The student teachers may send in their very best lessons and make edits if needed. To make matters worse, the retired principals are paid relatively poorly so the unwritten rule is to simply not spend too much time in the analysis and push the student through. No one fails, everyone is moved along and the university continues to cash students' checks.

By contrast, all teacher training programs in Finland are at public, not-for-profit universities that don't charge tuition. In the 1990s the country took a look at its education system and decided, for both financial and quality control reasons, that it didn't want to offer classroom teacher programs at every university, explained Ylianunti, principal of Mikkolan Koulu basic school. So Finland closed about 80 percent of its teacher colleges, centralizing them in just nine institutions that are all research universities. That consolidation allows the ministry of education to better oversee the quality of the training provided, and it makes admission to these programs more competitive, ensuring the best high school students are getting into teacher training programs.

Universities sanctioned to offer teacher training programs in Finland, as in Switzerland, also help fund and run adjacent elementary and secondary schools, so that aspiring teachers can regularly visit as part of their preparation. Most teachers at those training schools must have some experience, so they can act as master teachers for the university students they are paired with. The master teachers have reduced workloads so they have time to work with young teacher trainees, sitting in the back of the room as they lead lessons and meeting with them afterward to discuss their progress. Student teachers also have dedicated space in the elementary and secondary schools to prepare lessons, review assignments and meet with their mentors. This practice is common in a growing number of top performing countries, where teacher colleges are paired with public schools the way medical schools are paired with hospitals.

Outi, who I mentioned earlier, was in her third year of studies in the teacher training program at University of Jyväskylä when I caught up with her at the adjacent Normaalikoulu Upper Secondary School & Teacher Training School. She was there to practice teaching English lessons to local high school students. In Finland, during the second year of their university program, aspiring teachers like Outi must start spending time in public school classrooms nearly every day either to practice teaching, to observe experienced teachers, or to help plan lessons and grade assignments. It's a challenging experience, Outi said, since they are being evaluated all the time. After she finishes a lesson in front of the students, her master teacher will ask her why she did something a certain way. But the program also is very rewarding, Outi said. And she was confident she'd be ready to teach on her own once she completed the university program.

In the United States, university students hoping to be teachers are typically required to observe some classroom teachers during their programs. But often they're on their own to arrange those visits, with no guarantees about the quality of the teacher they're observing. And as for actually teaching lessons, that typically only comes during a set window of "student teaching" that starts after they've completed all university courses. Each state has its own requirements for student teaching programs, with California requiring the most at 600 hours, or nearly double what's required in most other states. But student teachers aren't paid for the time they spend leading a class, which often amounts to at least half a year or even a full academic year. That means most need to either continue relying on financial aid or student loans during that time or take on a second job to make ends meet, unless they have family to support them. That of course limits the diversity of the pool of people who can jump through such hoops to become teachers, with U.S. classrooms still predominantly taught by white women.

Another key difference between teacher training programs in the United States and most countries with top-tier education systems is that many of them, from Estonia to Finland, require 100 percent of teachers to hold master's degrees. A good number of teachers in these places—such as Pollari, a teacher trainer at Outi's school—also have doctoral degrees. Pollari said teachers can ask for a leave of absence to pursue that higher degree, then return to their classroom teaching jobs.

In the United States, master's degrees are optional for public school teachers. Educators here typically only go back for a master's degree after they've started teaching because it's one way to get a decent pay raise, with less than 60 percent of public-school teachers holding such degrees. But to get that raise, the master's degree doesn't need to have anything to do with the field that person teaches. So they can be a math teacher who earns a master's degree in, say, art history and still get that salary bump. Only around 3 percent of U.S. public school teachers have doctoral degrees, and most educators who reach that level are seeking an administrative position—and the large pay increase that comes with it.

To make matters worse, due to ongoing massive teacher shortages, many states in the U.S. are frequently forced to waive their already-low requirements for teachers to get people in front of classrooms. Emergency credential options allow Americans to get teaching jobs with only bachelor's degrees. That means we have people taking over classrooms who may have never taught an actual lesson, since student teaching here doesn't start until after coursework ends. And often, these teachers are being sent to our neediest schools, which face high levels of poverty and students who don't speak English as their first language.

Brooke Staggs, the journalist who assisted me in writing this book, started out as a high school English teacher. She began teaching at a low-income school in Jurupa Valley, California, when she was just 21 years old. There was a teacher shortage, so she was brought on through an emergency credential, with only brief substitute teaching experience and no formal student teaching. She completed both her teaching credential and master's degree in education as she was teaching full time, racking up student loan debt along the way. Four years later, despite earning an award and a leadership role at her school, she'd grown frustrated with student discipline problems, a lack of support from parents and an overall system that just wasn't working. So she quit the profession, letting her teaching credential expire a few years later. Looking back, she said she can't help but wonder if she'd still be in a high school classroom if she'd had more training and support in those early years.

When I told Outi this type of practice was allowed in the United States, her eyes got wide behind her black-rimmed glasses, since this type of slapdash certification would be impossible in Finland or most other high-performing PISA countries. They simply don't offer alternative routes with lower standards to become a teacher, instead using high salaries with extra stipends for needy schools, solid preparation and other means to boost their candidate pool when shortages do creep up.

Boosting the quality of training teachers receive, and creating a system that attracts the best candidates, helps get better teachers in our classrooms. Next, we need to keep them there.

Support on the Job

Better preparing teachers before they reach the classroom certainly can help improve the high attrition rate we see among educators in the United States. But, as I learned during my studies in top PISA countries, there also is much more we can do to support teachers once they are on the job.

David and Sunny, the teachers I visited with in Qingdao, China, are one example of how top-tier educational countries better support their new teachers. In China, new teachers are paired with experienced master teachers and they work together daily for at least three years. This isn't just about occasionally checking in or having an assigned mentor to reach out to when they need help, as is common with teacher mentorship programs in the United States. Master teachers and new teachers in Qingdao stay together all day, alternating between the experienced teacher leading lessons while the new teacher looks on and the new teacher giving lessons while the experienced teacher observes and offers help as needed. I watched Sunny sit in the back of the room as David was teaching, her pen flying across her paper as she took notes on his methods. Then they'd switch places. And when they're not teaching, David said the pair will collaborate on lesson plans, student development, even checking homework. "I'm very honored to have the chance to learn from such a teacher," Sunny said, praising David's experience and expertise as one of the best teachers in the region.

If a new teacher in Qingdao is struggling, that daily paired teaching can last for more than three years. And both David and Sunny told me that, even after their formal mentorship programs end, it's common for master teachers and their apprentices in China to remain lifelong friends, working closely together to hone their skills throughout their careers.

Such programs are common in most top-tier countries. In Japan, new teachers have a one-year induction period where both they and their master teacher have reduced teaching loads so they can spend time working together. In New Zealand, new teachers are paid the same amount to teach 20 percent less their first year and 10 percent less their second year, using the rest of the time to observe other teachers, develop lessons and attend workshops.

In the United States, first-year teachers carry full course loads from day one. They are typically paired with a willing teacher who has at least some experience for mentorship after school or during limited preparation periods. And that mentor teacher only receives a small stipend for the additional work, which is piled on top of their regular duties.

Another distinction became clear when I talked with international teachers about their schedules. David said it's typical for teachers in Qingdao to teach two 45-minute classes per day. During a "free period," he meets one-on-one with students and provides extra help to those who are struggling. He has the rest of the day to work on lesson plans, grade assignments, coach his mentor and collaborate with colleagues on the best ways to teach certain concepts, reach struggling students and assess their skills.

In Japan, where only about 35 percent of teacher time is spent instructing students, they have established a practice called *kenkyuu jugyou* or research lessons. After teams of teachers select topics and set a schedule, they take turns giving a lesson they've spent considerable time developing to teach a particular skill. Other teachers observe that lesson, and it's typically recorded so other teachers can later use it as a model. Afterward, teachers get together to discuss what worked well, what could be improved and how they can incorporate the lesson into their own plans.

Such a schedule also allows for steady, comprehensive professional development programs. Studies have shown that targeted teacher development programs of about 50 hours, spread out over six months or a year, had the greatest effect on boosting student test scores. With top-tier countries giving teachers several hours each day when they're not tied to classroom instruction, they can build in these development programs to go in-depth over time, as research recommends. Many countries also pay teachers to attend additional professional development outside their regular weekly schedule. In Singapore, for example, teachers are paid for 100 hours of professional development each year on top of the 20 hours they have each week to work with and observe their colleagues.

In the United States, most professional development programs take place in a day-long blitz during the regular school year, after teachers have scrambled to prepare substitute teacher plans since they miss a day of instruction to participate. Secondary school teachers typically get one "prep" period a day for lesson planning and grading. Otherwise, they're typically teaching five classes of roughly an hour each. And at the elementary level, they typically teach all day, with breaks only for brief lunches and recess. All lesson preparations and grading must be done after school and on weekends, greatly extending the teacher workday. On average, American teachers spend 80 percent of their paid time in front of students, leaving little time for their own work or for steady professional development.

Given those circumstances, is it any wonder that most teachers I know in the United States dread professional development days? We'd simply rather spend the time in the classroom with our students. Meanwhile, most teachers I talked to in top countries around the world spoke highly of their collaboration time and credited it with contributing greatly to their success in the classroom.

So how do other countries get away with letting teachers only instruct a couple of classes each day? Such a system would seem likely to lead to more teacher shortages and increase staff costs significantly. But places like China achieve it by making another change that currently isn't popular in the United States: increasing class sizes. While the U.S. has focused on reducing class sizes, particularly at the primary level, it's common in Chinese secondary schools to have 45 or even 60 students in each class, explained Maryanne, a teacher from northeast China who I interviewed while she was in my district teaching Mandarin on an exchange program. That allows each teacher to educate nearly the same number of students even if they're teaching half as many classes. And then China makes up any additional costs in other ways, including with lower turnover since its teachers are less burnt out.

Such a major shift in how teachers spend their time is not just about having dedicated hours each day to develop lessons and do other work. In top-tier countries, the physical workspace is designed to encourage and facilitate collaboration. That leads to less isolation, which can be particularly tough on new teachers. And it prompts better teaching, since two minds, or 20, are always better than one at coming up with innovative and tested strategies.

One major difference Maryanne noted between how teachers work in China vs. the United States is that in her native country, teachers spend hours each day working in a large communal space with desks for everyone. There are no walls in those spaces, and they're all packed with learning materials. Maryanne said that helps fellow teachers collaborate and feel like a family.

I saw similar setups for teachers in just about every top-tier country I visited. In the teacher's space at Gradia Jyvaskyla Lyseon, an upper secondary school in Jyvaskyla, Finland, guidance counselor Jussi Lounassalo lounged on one of many large couches as he talked about how teachers there use the common space. It was entirely open, sparsely but attractively decorated in typical Nordic style. But within the open space, there was a tent-like structure around a table, where teachers could gather a bit more intimately. When I was there, a group of teachers were crowded in the indoor tent, enjoying lunch together. There also was a pod within the space with clear walls, which Lounassalo said teachers can use to make a phone call or have a more private conversation. Teachers gather in the space before and after school, during breaks between classes, and during lunch, he said, building a sense of collegiality and constantly brainstorming ideas for their classrooms.

American teachers, on the other hand, typically have desks in their classroom and often do almost all of their work there throughout the day. Unlike back home in China, Maryanne said, at her school in San Diego there weren't many chances to work with or even meet the other teachers outside monthly faculty meetings. I can attest that it's common in my district to only see colleagues in passing or when you need to make photocopies. Teachers often even eat in their classrooms or cars. There's very little opportunity for new teachers who might be floundering to get noticed before it's too late. That lack of dedicated time and space also is a challenge for veteran teachers, who might feel even more embarrassed asking for help if they encounter a new bit of technology that's not quite clicking or a student with an issue they haven't dealt with before. But if we would all gather together for hours each day, working alongside each other in a communal space, there's a much greater chance someone will be there to help before these struggling teachers give up.

Many other countries also seem to have more compassion for teachers who need to work alternative or reduced schedules for some period of time. In Liechtenstein, Principal Eugen Nagele, head of the notable Liechtensteinisches Gymnasium, said about 40 percent of his staff was teaching part time. Often it was because they had young children or had a personal issue that made a full-time schedule difficult. That system is challenging for administrators like him to manage, Nagele acknowledged. But he said it's important to help teachers maintain their work life balance, so hopefully they'll stick around and come back to teaching full time when they're ready. In the scheme of things, he said, it's likely easier to juggle multiple experienced teachers working part time than to be constantly searching for new ones. Indeed, there are volumes of studies to show that it costs more to recruit and train new employees in just about every field than to retain current staff, even if it means paying them higher salaries and offering other accommodations.

Back in Qingdao, David said he'd started teaching one extra 45-minute class a day to take a course off the shoulders of a pregnant teacher in the school. Sunny said the workload for pregnant teachers is typically reduced from teaching two classes per day to one, plus that collaboration time. And of course, as I detailed in chapter one, new moms there then get half a year to stay home with full pay to care for their new children.

When I told David that no such system exists for teachers who become pregnant in the United States, his face registered polite surprise. "When a lady is pregnant, she still has the normal teaching?" he asked.

Another common experience for teachers in top-tier systems is to routinely visit schools in other countries that regularly score well on PISA exams. As I mentioned in the introduction of this book, of the nine principals I interviewed in Finland, all had visited schools in at least five other countries. And I never met a teacher in Finland that had not visited schools in at least two different countries.

During summer holidays each year in Qingdao, David said, a teacher support program—funded roughly half by the government and half through donations by former students who help support the school—pays to send a representative group of select teachers to visit schools in other parts of China and in other countries, such as Singapore, to learn from educators there. And Chen, who teaches in Taiwan, recalled how her government sent her to study Massachusetts' well-respected schools.

I was told by countless Finnish educational administrators that their schools were constantly visited by education tourists from all around the world. They said groups of Chinese educators and administrators frequently visited their schools to learn how to improve the education system at home, which already is ranked as one of the top in the world, according to PISA. But only on one occasion could they recall ever meeting an American educational visitor other than myself.

You would be hard-pressed to find a policymaker, superintendent, principal or teacher in the United States who has visited schools in other states, let alone countries. On the rare occasion that such trips do happen, they are often considered wasteful, with some journalists, parents and even other school officials characterizing them as a thin excuse for an international vacation. While it's wise to guard against abusing travel privileges, other countries see the value in learning from the best of the best, who our students will be competing with in the global economy. So they see sending teams of educators abroad as a worthwhile investment.

A Glacial River Bath and a Glaring Wake-Up Call

Trotting around the globe, visiting top schools in places like Singapore and Switzerland, might sound glamorous. Those optics are surely one reason some U.S. school districts and states have rules against using public money for educators to travel internationally for educational research, despite that practice being common in most countries that outperform us on international exams.

But a favorite photo I brought back from my journey shows me, curled up in a bright orange sleeping bag in the seat of my rented, two-door MINI Cooper. I'm parked on the street in Lichtenstein. The tiny backseat is overflowing with my gear, while my suit is hanging carefully above the clutter. On the passenger seat next to me, my plaid swim trunks are still drying from one of the three times I'd bathed in the Rhine River. And let me tell you, even when I visited in June, the water in the Rhine was as freezing cold as the ice-capped Alps that feed the river.

When you're on a budget, as I was during my self-funded trip around the world, you have to improvise. I used a portion of the $25,000 I'd received for winning the Milken Educator Award to pay my way, then dipped into my own pocket for the balance. Still, the average price of Motel 6-quality accommodations in Switzerland and Liechtenstein was roughly $300 dollars a night. That was my budget for a week of expenses. So I slept in my car for three weeks while I visited schools throughout these pricey countries. Along with my three "baths" in the Rhine River, I also showered at rest stops and took schools up on their offers to shower in their vacant gyms.

I was fortunate that a principal let me stay at his house for a week while I visited schools in Belgium, where expenses also run high. I stayed with another principal in New Zealand, then with a friend in Germany. People all over the world were extremely generous in opening their doors to me and making me feel at home.

I'm an adventurous guy, as you'll recall from the intro-duction. Sleeping in a rental car is still a giant step above sleeping in a tent pitched on the side of a snowy mountain. So I didn't mind living this ragamuffin existence to complete my mission. But there must be a way we can allow American teachers to observe the world's best schools up close and in action, with some safeguards first put in place to ensure such trips don't become lavish vacations on the taxpayers' dime. Other countries have managed just fine by having some faith in their educators and by recognizing the value to the public in learning from the best of the best. If they've found a way, surely we can allow our teachers to experience the same sort of professional development that's mandatory in places like China and Estonia without expecting them to sleep in their cars and bathe in an icy-cold river.

In the meantime, if any of my fellow teachers need a recommendation on the best rest stop shower in Lichtenstein, I'm your guy!

Another support system for teachers that's criticized here but rarely demonized in top-tier countries is unions and the tenure programs that typically go along with them. Of course, unions are extremely limited in places like China, which is under Communist rule. But most nations that do well on the PISA exam also have either strong teachers' unions to fight for better pay, benefits and working conditions for their members or they have strong state educational systems, which make it difficult to terminate a teacher.

A final difference between the support teachers receive once they're on the job in the United States versus in many top-ranked countries—and the most important difference according to Pollari, who trains teachers in Poland—is that educators elsewhere often are given more freedom because they are treated like professionals rather than drones in a factory. They're asked to help shape the curriculum they teach, in line with national standards, during those daily collaboration sessions, rather than being ordered to teach particular lessons dictated by a textbook, grade-level plan or standardized test. They also often get to choose their own textbooks, at least at the school level, rather than having that decision dictated by the district, state or federal government.

"Trust is the most vital thing," Pollari said. "In Finland, I like to say teachers are really masters of their own art."

When teachers are given more trust and freedom to run their classes the way they see fit, Pollari said, it increases their motivation. That motivation keeps teachers satisfied, she said, and it can easily transfer to students. That lowers discipline issues while boosting learning and attendance, which in turn makes the classroom a better place for a teacher to be and keeps them around longer. So Pollari argues that the United States could get higher quality teachers if they were given more freedom and autonomy.

Salary, benefits, training programs and all else aside, Pollari said, "The freedom in teaching is one of the biggest rewards."

What can I do?

To improve the quality of teachers in the United States and keep them in our classrooms, we need to make sweeping changes to our teacher preparation and support programs. Here are 10 steps everyone can take right now to help set those wheels in motion.

- Talk to your own children, or children you interact with, about the value of education and having respect for teachers.

  ____

  ____

  ____

  ____

- Seek out and support books, movies and other cultural representations that present teachers respectfully rather than as clueless adults to be ignored or mocked, as we too often see on film.

  ____

  ____

  ____

- Parents, think of teachers as your partners in educating your kids. Just as you shouldn't undermine or disrespect a spouse to your children, try not to disrespect teachers in front of your kids. Instead, if you have issues or questions about something taking place, discuss those issues directly with the teacher or administrator.

  ____

____

____

- Support or spearhead legislation that requires teacher pay to be on par with starting salaries for other professions with similarly high levels of education.

  ____

  ____

  ____

- Find a local university near you that offers a teacher training program and investigate the requirements to get in and to complete that program. Compare those standards to the standards discussed in this book, then share those discrepancies on social media, through a letter to the editor in your local newspaper or using some other avenue.

  ____

  ____

  ____

- Support or spearhead state legislation that requires teacher training programs to be limited to nonprofit research universities for those credentials to count.

  ____

  ____

  ____

- Arrange a letter-writing campaign or demonstration to protest allowing teachers in classrooms unless they are fully credentialed.

  ____

  ____

  ____

- Sit down with a teacher at a local school and ask about their experience getting an education and the support they receive on the job. Ask them what preparation and resources they need to help them do their job better. Then consider sharing what you've learned. And if you are an educator, share your own experience with the public.

- Support calls for free or low-cost tuition for teacher training programs, and to forgive student loan debt for public school teachers now in classrooms.

- See if you can help arrange for a group of local teachers to visit schools in a place that performs well on PISA exams. If you can't get the district to pay for such a trip, try to seek a grant or fundraise to support the effort. If a trip abroad is out of reach, consider at least trying to get your teachers to visit top schools in Massachusetts.

"It is not the strongest species that survives but the most adaptable."

Charles Darwin

Author Keith Ballard, right, enjoys lunch with students in Japan, who typically eat in their classrooms.

Chapter Three

Restructuring the School Experience

Taiwanese students are in school for 222 days each year, while Irish students only attend 173 days.

Students in Shanghai spend an average of 14 hours on homework each week, while Finnish students might spend just three hours.

Many Japanese students are required to eat nutritious school-provided meals in primary and middle school, and both South Korea and Finland provide restaurant-quality food free of charge for all students each day. Meanwhile, many Canadian schools have no option for students to get meals at all.

Despite these vast differences in how their school days and years are structured, students in all of these countries outperform American students on international tests.

As I visited schools around the world, I knew sweeping changes were going to be needed to help us better compete in the global economy. Still, I was hoping to come back with some simple strategies my fellow teachers and I could steal and immediately start to implement. Perhaps, I thought, I'll be able to share with my colleagues the secret to how all of the top-performing schools organize their classrooms or how much homework they assign each night. But I quickly realized that in no other area is there more variety among top-performing school systems than in how they plan out their school campuses, calendars and daily classroom experiences.

There are some key differences between Western and Asian school systems in everything from the length of instruction time to how much recess is allowed to the types of meals students receive—if they're provided with food at all. There also is considerable variety in how states and districts within the United States handle some of these issues. Still, I noticed some common trends and lessons we can derive from a close look at how schools in countries with top-tier education systems do things when it comes to the school experience. By comparing what's out there and seeing how these different plans stack up against the research, the United States can selectively incorporate some of these strategies to get the best of all worlds.

Perhaps even more importantly, with such huge disparities between high-performing countries in this area, examining these practices can show us how *not* to spend our resources. If, for example, there aren't any links between countries that have longer school days and countries that perform at the highest levels on international tests, then perhaps that's one option we can eliminate when deciding where to focus our energy and funds.

This feels, then, like a good place to discuss funding for schools, which is sure to be a question hanging over many of the plans proposed in this book. The good news is that there's no evidence to suggest the United States must spend more to improve the quality of its schools. It simply needs to do things differently.

The United States spends $14,100 a year for each student it educates fulltime in elementary and secondary schools, according to the most recent data available at press time from the Organization for Economic Cooperation and Development. Only three nations spend more: Luxembourg, Austria and Norway. The average country that's monitored by the OECD spends $10,300 per student, or 37 percent less than the United States. And Estonia, which ranked No. 5 in the world and the best among western countries on the most recent PISA test, spends $7,900 per student, or nearly half as much as the United States.

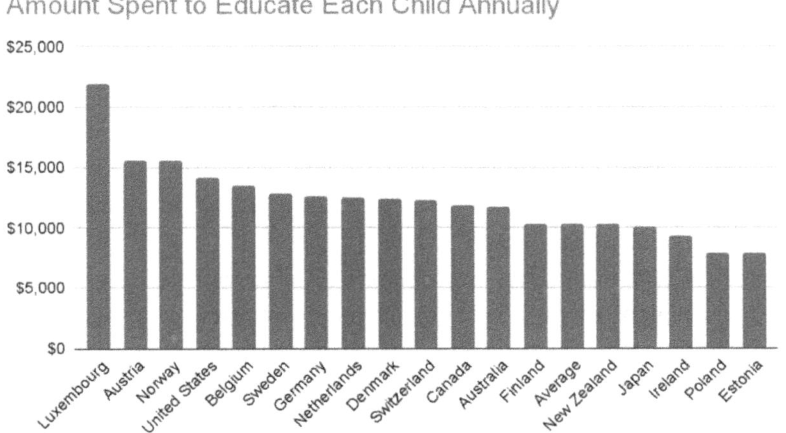

A similar gap exists when looking at education expenditures as a percentage of gross domestic product. The United States spends 6.6 percent of its GDP on all education systems, from elementary to post-secondary schools. The average among countries monitored by the OECD is 4.9 percent, while China, which scored No. 1. on the last PISA test, spends 4.1 percent of its GDP on education.

That's not to say that U.S. schools never face budget cuts and shortfalls. We'll also discuss problematic inequities between different school systems across the United States in chapter eight. But comparing budgets between different nations shows that improving public education is not just about throwing more money at our schools. It's about carefully studying best practices and seeing where that money should be spent to get the most bang for our buck.

We've established in the first two chapters that investing more to support families and to recruit, train and retain highly qualified teachers is worth the investment. When it comes to restructuring the school experience, here are some changes that my research and visits to schools around the county have shown appear to pay off:

1. Requiring at least a slightly longer school year, with shorter days for younger students

2. Starting the school day a bit later than it starts in most U.S. secondary schools now
3. Giving students more frequent breaks during the school day, with opportunities for exercise, recreation and rest
4. Keeping classroom setups simple while making the overall campus more inviting
5. Offering more nutritious meals and programs focused on teaching healthy eating *or* offering no meals at all
6. Requiring regular homework, but limiting the amount and scaling it up as students get older

While more days in school does increase learning time for students in high-performing countries, many of these changes are centered around improving the mental and physical health of students. This isn't particularly surprising, since there are volumes of studies that show how both factors are significant predictors of academic performance. But in the United States, efforts to support students in these ways often focus resources on fitness campaigns or adding counselors. Those are both good ideas. However, if we don't also make key changes to the typical school day that can build in regular, proven steps to boost mental and physical health, we are missing out on simple and effective ways to increase student focus, motivation, retention and good behavior—all of which are keys to better performance.

Time in school

When the clock struck noon during my visit to Finland's modern, bright white Mikkolan Koulu basic school, I watched as a flood of young students gathered their belongings and headed home for the day. But as the 3 p.m. hour rolled around, older students were still in their classrooms, busy studying physics and working on art projects.

The three-story comprehensive school educates first- through ninth graders in Vantaa, a large city just north of Helsinki. When I asked Principal Ville Ylianunti about the early exodus of the youngest pupils, he explained that most students start school at 8:05 a.m. each day, but that first- and second-grade students typically get out at noon. That gives them a school day of less than four hours, including breaks. That's seen as the optimum time for young students to be asked to stay on task and away from home.

Meanwhile, third- through sixth graders at Mikkolan Koulu might go until 1 or 2 p.m., for a five- or six-hour day. And seventh- through ninth graders sometimes stay until 4 p.m., for an eight-hour day to maximize their learning time.

This type of schedule, with such wide gaps in instruction time by grade levels, just isn't common in most United States schools. Each state has its own requirements for how much time students must spend in class each day. But while kindergartners here typically attend a half day, and high school students often attend a bit longer than elementary students, most U.S. students in first through twelfth grade otherwise have around six hours of instruction each day. It's been that way for more than a century, when schools were planned to start early so they could let out as the hottest part of the day approached, since air conditioning wasn't available. And they'd return to stay-at-home moms who could care for them in the afternoon until their fathers got off work.

Despite the ubiquitousness of both air conditioning and households with single or two working parents today, that schedule hasn't changed. Bus schedules, rush-hour traffic, after-school sports and a hundred other excuses are raised any time someone points at research to support the idea of shortening the day for younger students, allowing sleep-deprived teens to start school later or of extending the school day for older students. So we're forcing our youngest students to be in school longer than some research suggests is ideal while short-changing our older students by giving them less time to learn. And we're leaving it up to single parents and two-income households to figure out what to do with kids who get out of school a couple hours before they might get home from work, with research showing that kids who aren't supervised in those afternoon hours are more likely to try drugs, have sex, commit crimes and get caught up in a host of other problems that can negatively impact their education.

Meanwhile, in many Asian countries with top-tier education systems, students are in school substantially longer each day. In Shanghai, secondary students are in school for an average of seven hours a day. In South Korea, it's eight hours. In Taiwan, it's eight and a half hours. And keep in mind, as discussed in chapter one, in many of these countries a high percentage of students finish their regular school day, then go on to attend cram schools for another hour or two or more.

While the school day is shorter for young students in Finland and some other high-performing countries, students of all ages there do have a longer school year. So younger students end up with as much or more instruction time as U.S. students, without being forced to sit in a classroom longer each day. And older students in many top PISA countries end up spending substantially more time in class, with both longer school days and longer school years.

In the United States, the typical school year is 180 days. Once again, that calendar is based around an outdated model of needing to keep urban kids out of school during the hottest months while giving rural kids three months off in the summer to help their family with farming. But as research started to pour in about how much learning was lost during those long summer breaks, and how many students lost access to free lunches and other resources U.S. schools provide, there was a push starting in the early 1990s to shorten summer breaks.

Schools have experimented since then with year-round or modified year-round schedules that reduce summer vacations to, say, one or two months. But rather than lengthen the school year, most simply moved vacation days around to allow more time off around winter holidays or spring break. So here we are, in 2022, with most schools still only in session for 180 out of 365 days each year.

Estonia is the only top-performing country with students who attend a bit less school each year than the United States, with an average school year there of 175 days. Finland, Hong Kong, Germany and New Zealand are all at 190 days. At the high end of the chart is Japan with 210 days and South Korea with 220 days. So while American students get an average of 16 weeks off each year, South Korean students get eight.

This dramatic difference in educational hours puts American students at a serious disadvantage when they compete with students from these other countries to get spots in top universities or with global companies. It also handicaps U.S. companies that are relying on workers

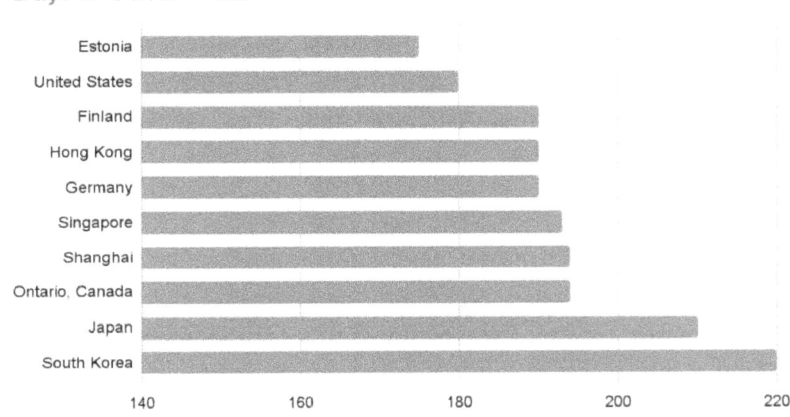

who've received hundreds fewer hours of education than workers at, say, Chinese companies.

Extending the school day and year raises two concerns: added cost and additional strains on teachers. Let's look at each concern.

As discussed earlier in this chapter, most of these other countries don't spend more money on public schooling than the United States. That means they've simply allocated their money differently, spending more to keep kids in school longer and then making cuts to offset that change in other areas. One possible place to trim was discussed in chapter two, with secondary teachers in some countries having significantly larger class sizes. We'll discuss more ways these countries save funds later in this chapter and in the chapters to come.

As for an additional strain on teachers who'd be faced with longer school days and years, survey after survey backs up what I heard from teachers in most high-performing countries firsthand: They are more highly satisfied with their jobs than American teachers. Keep in mind from chapter two that teachers in most top-performing countries spend far less time in front of a class full of students than U.S. teachers. That means they have time during the day to plan lessons, grade papers, attend trainings and do other needed work. American teachers simply do much of that work on their own time, after school, on weekends and during breaks. So their school days and years already are longer than they first appear. Plus, if teachers were more highly compensated and respected, and received more support from families at home, there would be less concern about teaching an extra 10 or 20 days a year. That's why all the changes proposed in this book need to happen in concert, since one doesn't work without the others also falling into place.

Break it up

When I entered a classroom one afternoon at Sanmin Junior High in Taipei, Taiwan, I was surprised to see the lights turned off and students completely silent, their heads resting on arms folded across their wooden desks. Some had jackets over their heads to block out the light. As I moved to the next class, the scene was exactly the same, with most preteens napping across the entire school.

It's common in Taiwanese junior high schools for every student to get the opportunity for a 30-minute nap each day—something typically only considered for kindergarten classes in the United States. A vast majority of Taiwanese students happily take advantage because the school is so academically challenging, they want to catch up on sleep and wake refreshed to continue their lessons.

I did notice a few empty desks in each class. I found those students in a communal area studying, which they'd opted to prioritize over a nap that day because they were preparing to take a major test before heading to high school.

Yes, students in most top-performing countries spend more time each day and each year in class than American students. But they also get more breaks throughout the day, which is proven effective to help students stay on task during class, better absorb the information they're receiving and cause fewer discipline problems.

It's not all about naps, though. You might recall from the first chapter that my greeting when I arrived at the first school I visited for this project in 2011 was 2,500 students lining up in strict platoon-style formations to run the track at Qingdao #58 high school in China. Rather than relegating all physical activity to P.E. classes, many Asian countries build regular outdoor exercise breaks into their school days. Some are intense, such as the running display I witnessed at the high school. Others are more fun, such as when I watched students at a primary school in Qingdao do dance routines in perfect formation, with their peers leading them on a raised platform at the front. During another break, those primary students did a series of exercises aimed at strengthening their eyes. They stood calmly in lines, red scarves tied around their necks, as they held an index finger out and swept it slowly from side to side and in and out, with their eyes carefully following each movement.

Students in many Asian countries and some European countries also get a break from learning, and a chance to get up and stretch their legs, as they do something else: clean the school. I noticed there was very little litter at a high school in South Korea, and staff explained that homeroom teachers assign students responsibilities each day to clean their own classrooms and different areas of the campus. They believe this teaches students respect for the campus, since they are less likely to make a mess if they know they'll eventually have to clean it up. It teaches them good cleaning habits for their own lives. Plus, it saves the school money on custodians. Those funds can then be funneled into covering other expenses that have a real impact on student learning.

Along with such structured breaks, in many top-performing school systems, primary students have more time to simply play, with educators there recognizing the importance of such time not only to let students get out energy but also to let them practice social skills, conflict resolution, using their imaginations and other valuable lessons learned on the playground. In Japan, for example, primary school children typically have a 10- or 15-minute break each hour. That's based on research that shows attention spans for young people start to dwindle after 40 to 50 minutes of focused instruction. And weather permitting, such play always takes place outside to account for studies showing the benefits of kids getting fresh air and sunlight each day.

Meanwhile, secondary students and teachers in other countries often have more time between classes and for lunch. In Finland, for example, it's common for older students to have 15-minute breaks between classes and then 45 minutes for lunch. At Normaalikoulu Upper Secondary School in Jyvaskyla, I watched one student use that time to play a piano in the corner of a communal room flooded with natural light and plants. Several more students were shooting pool at a nearby table, in a room that looked like it belonged in a college dorm. Others checked their phones and chatted. Teachers also had that time to relax, ask each other questions, do some quick lesson planning and do other business.

Japan: Bell Schedule for 2nd Grade

class starts: 8:30 a.m.
recess: 9:15 a.m.
second class: 9:30 a.m.
recess: 10:15 a.m.
third class: 10:30 a.m.
lunch: 11:15 a.m.
recess: 11:45 a.m.
fourth class: 12:05 p.m.
recess: 12:50 p.m.
fifth class: 1:05 p.m.
day ends: 1:50 p.m.

Meanwhile, U.S. schools have been reducing recess and other breaks over the past few decades to increase instruction time. While there are other factors at play, such as the prevalence of electronic devices, teachers such as myself certainly have noticed that students today have a harder and harder time staying focused and sitting still in the classroom.

At primary schools in the United States, there is a wide range of schedules, with some schools offering little to no recess while most offer two or three breaks a day for unstructured play. Students might, say, get a

15-minute break in the morning and 15 minutes in the afternoon, plus a 30-minute lunch. Any additional learning breaks for students, to stretch or do other activities, are left up to each teacher. Often, teachers must rotate being "on duty" during those breaks, which means they miss the breaks themselves. And it's not uncommon for teachers to "take away" recess for students who misbehave by keeping them inside, which means those who might be having the hardest time focusing get no break—and neither does the teacher.

In U.S. secondary schools, breaks between classes often are closer to six minutes. On larger campuses, that's barely enough time to get from one class to another, let alone go to the restroom, catch up with friends or do anything else to decompress. Is it any wonder, then, that so many American students walk into class still on their phones or have to leave class for restroom breaks, which takes away from learning time?

Having more frequent breaks is another reform that also has benefits for teachers, which can help to balance out proposed changes such as longer school days or years. Imagine being a high school teacher on a larger campus who needs to use the restroom. You have six minutes. It might take one minute to get all students from your last class out of the room. You need to walk across campus, do your business and get back. By the time you get there, several students are already lined up for the next class. The rush of those six minutes created more stress for the teacher, as opposed to giving them a moment to decompress or prepare for the next class. Just adding a few more minutes to those breaks, and making up for it with more time tacked onto the school day so no instruction is lost, could make a world of difference for teachers and students alike.

Classroom and campus planning

When it comes to planning classroom and campus designs, the same sort of wide variety that exists among American schools exists when comparing the schools I visited in top-performing nations. In many Asian nations, for example, it's common for classrooms to have single desks arranged in neat rows. In New Zealand, on the other hand, many classrooms have several students sharing tables to facilitate more cooperative learning. Finland similarly often has students sitting at larger desks that sometimes are curved, so two or more students can see each other and more easily do group work. But in my research and my visits to more than 170 schools worldwide, I haven't deduced a pattern in how desks are arranged that seems to have any correlation with student performance. That means this is one area where teachers can rest easy if they need to simply use what's available, or they can feel free to get creative and design their own seating plans to best suit their needs.

However, there are some lessons we still can draw from top PISA countries and potentially try to emulate when it comes to school and classroom design. I'd sum up what I've learned like this: High-quality schools tend to have clean, attractive, welcoming campuses, with places for students to gather and do activities, while classrooms are simpler and more streamlined to focus on learning.

In the United States, it's often the opposite. Aside from sports facilities, campuses tend to be rather basic, particularly after primary school. Any common spaces for students to gather are often sparse, with hard benches in the cafeteria and open quads that leave little for students or others to vandalize. Then we leave it up to teachers, both physically and financially, to make their classrooms attractive and inviting for students. Some do a fabulous job with that effort, spending hundreds of dollars of their own money each year on materials. You might find a teacher who opts to have a classroom pet or cozy reading corner. Others don't do much in this area at all, and schools can't require it if no funds are provided to make it a reality.

In other countries, the school often takes on the responsibility of creating welcoming spaces for students to gather, relax, study and recreate during their longer breaks or after hours. I mentioned above one Finnish school that had a common area with a piano, pool table, plants and other decor. At schools in many Asian countries, I saw large fish tanks and lots of plants near entrances and in hallways. These types of amenities were the norm in many schools I visited, and nowhere did they report having anything more than minor issues with students doing any sort of damage to them.

In many places, such elements also were incorporated into student learning. At Sanmin Junior High in Taipei, Taiwan, for example, there are solid rows of potted plants outside every classroom, even lining the outdoor balcony railing on the second floor. I admit the thought of such a setup at my middle school back in San Diego terrified me, because I knew it wouldn't be long before a student would knock the plants off, potentially injuring anyone in the courtyard below. But the principal said they'd never had a problem like that. She explained that students tend those plants with guidance from their teachers. They also bring in plants that attract butterflies, so they can watch them develop from eggs to caterpillars to cocoons before breaking out and flying away. The principal explained that both activities teach the students patience and how to care for something other than themselves, along with making the campus pleasant for everyone.

But at some of the most attractive campuses I visited around the world, once I got inside classrooms, they often were quite sparse. This includes from a technology perspective, with significant enough distinctions in that area that all of chapter six is devoted to the topic. Aside from some plants and perhaps some educational posters, many classrooms in both Asian and western countries have clean white or beige walls, simple desks, a board up front and that's about it. (Two exceptions to this pattern of simplistic learning spaces were at early childhood education centers, as discussed in chapter one, and at vocational schools in top PISA nations, which also will get their own detailed treatment in chapter four.)

Beyond layout and amenities, I also noticed a difference in how schools are being planned when it comes to the grade levels they serve.

In the United States, it's common to have separate elementary, middle and high schools. In some places, even primary schools are split up, with students attending one school for kindergarten through third grade and another for fourth through sixth grade. That means they may move through four different schools before graduating. The idea behind this system has been to keep campuses smaller and more personal while reducing the age gap between students on campus, which it's believed can lead to discipline problems. But such plans also are very pricey, since it's much more expensive to run two smaller schools than one larger one when you factor in everything from two cafeterias to additional bus stops.

Meanwhile, there's a push in Finland to go the opposite direction and keep both primary and middle school students together in the same schools. At Mikkolan Koulu basic school in Vantaa, Finland, they have first through ninth graders in the same comprehensive school. Principal Ville Ylianunti said that's the preferred setup for newer schools in the country, with about half of Finnish schools now using the comprehensive model. Ylianunti pointed at studies that suggest it's not beneficial for students to change schools at the sixth-grade level, having to navigate a whole new campus at such a challenging time in their development. And he said they don't have any issues with having such an age gap between kids on campus, with older students able to serve as role models and leaders in the schools.

"They have their own path and history in this building," he said, "and they respect the younger students." That's an important life lesson that's well worth teaching.

Meals: All or Nothing

At my middle school in San Diego, I watch each day as most students choose the least healthy options available for lunch and snacks. It's mandatory that students take milk, fruit and salad with their lunch whether they want it or not, if they want to eat their pizza slices and cheeseburgers, I watch as the kids throw the former items away before quickly eating the main course so they can use whatever time is left in their brief lunch break to be with friends. At my school alone, hundreds of pounds of wasted food each week is thrown away in the garbage cans. At the same time, many homeless people who live near my school can't get enough to eat. That system of course is not good for student health, which is clearly linked with educational outcomes. It's also not good for schools' bottom lines, with an astonishing amount of food wasted each day.

As I visited schools around the world, the teachers and staff and administrators who hosted me often would offer to let me pop into the cafeteria to observe or even grab some food for lunch. I learned that while some places like Finland give free meals to all students, most high-performing countries have similar systems to ours in terms of giving food for free to low-income students and at low cost for everyone else. The difference is in the quality, nutrition and portions of the food they're serving—and how the kids gobble it all down without a thought.

At a primary school in South Korea, I watched as students picked up their shiny metal trays with moderate portions of seaweed soup plus a serving of cabbage with chili powder, chopped-up anchovies with almonds, rice and tofu. After most took time to clear their plates, they returned their trays and got glasses of water, since they tend to drink after their meals in Korea. After downing the glass of water, students put their cups through an ultraviolet treatment to clean them.

I also got a behind-the-scenes tour of the school's cafeteria. The director told me she would never serve food such as pizza or hamburgers, saying, "Natural food is better." She showed me how everything was prepared in house from scratch, with no frozen or prepackaged items brought in. There had been a birthday celebration for one of the students during my visit to one school, and staff showed me a school-baked cake that was made from rice flour and had no frosting on top but tasted great.

At a public school in China, the selection of restaurant-quality food available for students to choose from each day for lunch was just staggering. There were sushi rolls, a variety of skewered meat, fish, chicken rolls, noodle soup, apples and vegetables, with water or fruit juice to drink. The food is so good, staff said, that many teachers eat school lunches each day—something that almost never happens in U.S. schools.

As lunch time rolled around back at Sanmin Junior High in Taipei, Director Li Chih-Ann showed me the large menu for that week's food. Every day, students had many choices for the types of food they could eat for lunch, though all of them were nutritious and balanced, with plenty of vegetables. Students could eat as much as they wanted and even take some home, the director explained.

In Japan, students eat similarly well-balanced meals planned by nutritionists, with baked fish, rice, vegetables and miso soup commonly served. Young students typically aren't allowed to bring meals from home. Instead, the Japanese use school lunches to teach students about healthy eating habits. There's even a word for this "food education." It's called *shokuiku*, and it's helped give Japan one of the lowest obesity rates on the planet.

Another difference in Japan is that there aren't cafeterias in most primary and middle schools. Instead, it's common for lunches to be prepared in a facility on or off campus and brought to students in their homerooms. Japanese students then have 40 minutes to eat in their classrooms before they head outside for another 20 minutes of dedicated recess.

In most of the Nordic countries I visited, I also saw lunches with smaller portions that were centered around fish, vegetables, fruit and whole grain bread. Vending machines with chips and sodas were non-existent.

At IX Liceum Ogólnokształcące im. Klementyny Hoffmanowej, a secondary school in Warsaw, Poland, I spoke with a group of a dozen students about why they think it's so uncommon to see overweight students at their schools. They told me there are lots of campaigns to encourage healthy eating and fitness. They said that like the schools, their parents also feed them lots of fruits and vegetables and give them water or tea to drink for most meals, with nutritious eating promoted at home. Eating at fast food places like McDonalds happens only from time to time, they said. Playing soccer (football to them) and jogging also are popular and working out to videos on YouTube. They called it "fashionable" to be fit.

One exception to this rule about high-performing schools providing nutritious, balanced meals is in Canada—not because their food isn't healthy, but because many schools don't provide meals at all. In Canada, issues such as whether to provide meals for students are left up to each province, which runs its local schools. Since many students can walk home for meals during longer lunch times, or bring sack meals from home, many Canadian provinces simply don't opt to spend their funds on food and food preparation. As one Canadian put it in an online forum about the topic: "Education tax dollars are better spent on education rather than catering."

It's important to find ways to make nutritious meals available for anyone who can't afford them. We saw clear evidence of how many American students were dependent on schools to get food when campuses shut down during the coronavirus pandemic. Food service workers, teachers and staff teamed up to make free bagged meals available for students to pick up each day, and there were reports of lines to get them. The question is whether schools, which already have such important jobs and face so many obstacles, are the best option to take on that responsibility. Based on what I've seen in countries with high-performing education systems, we need to either step it up by providing fresh, nutritious food in smaller portions that students are truly expected to eat or consider taking that responsibility off the shoulders of schools entirely.

Homework helps

As with other areas covered in this chapter, when it comes to how much homework kids are assigned, there is a great deal of diversity among top-performing countries. In Shanghai, 15-year-old students do an average of 14 hours of homework each week. In the United States, six hours is common. And in Finland, the average is closer to three hours a week.

That figure from Finland gets lots of attention, since it shows that it's possible to have one of the best education systems in the world while also assigning students the least amount of homework. Principal Ylianunti at Mikkolan Koulu basic school in Vantaa, Finland, said school staff regularly talk with each other and parents about how much homework students get. He said the consensus is that students have just the right amount to reinforce and practice what they've learned while still giving them plenty of time to be kids. That's in keeping with the country's overall holistic, family friendly approach to education.

At Qingdao Middle School #51 in China, I asked multiple students about how much homework they do each night. A student whose English name was Angel told me she does two hours of homework most nights after leaving school at around 5 p.m. She also takes English classes for three hours every Saturday, taking a break from education only on Sundays. Mary, wearing the same school uniform of a white zip-up jacket with a light blue collar, told me in addition to doing a couple hours of homework each night, she takes physics, math, chemistry, English and Chinese classes on Saturdays. This routine was common among every Chinese middle school student I spoke with, and no one seemed to question it. And of course, as we've discussed, students in many Asian countries also couple their regular homework with hours spent at cram schools to squeeze more learning time into each day.

With no clear correlation between hours of homework and student outcomes, the trend worldwide has been toward giving students less work to do outside the school day to help them avoid burnout and give them more time for other activities. There doesn't seem to have been a drop in achievement since that trend took off, again suggesting that lots of homework isn't necessary for students to perform well.

But before we ditch after-school assignments altogether, there is one thing every country that performs well on PISA exams has in common in this area: They do assign some homework. So while there doesn't appear to be a magic number in terms of hours required, there does appear to be a strong argument for giving students some amount of work to take home each day to reinforce what they're learning in the classroom.

What can I do?

Here are eight steps everyone can take right now to help set the wheels in motion by educating ourselves, educating those around us and pushing for real change, with space for you to jot down notes on plans for accomplishing each step or how it went once it's completed.

- Propose or support legislation that would require your state to increase the length of the school day and the number of days students must attend each year, while also requiring secondary schools to start no earlier than 8 a.m.

____

____

____

____

- Ask your child or a child in your life to keep a diary for one week of what their school day looks like. Have them make notes about how much instruction and break time they receive. Compare that information with the best practices described in this chapter.

  ____

  ____

  ____

- Advocate for your local schools to increase recess time for primary students and time between classes and at lunch for secondary students. Consider legislation to require those fixed breaks.

  ____

  ____

  ____

- Propose and develop a program for local schools that requires students to regularly help with cleaning projects in their classrooms and on campus.

  ____

  ____

  ____

- Collect funds and form a team to start a community garden or plant program at a local school. Commit to purchasing the needed items and volunteering time to help set the program up. In exchange, get the school to agree to give students time each week to tend the plants and discuss lessons that can be learned from the process.

  ____

  ____

  ____

- Collect menus with nutrition information from schools in your district. Ask the district for data on how much they spend on food each year and how much food is wasted. Share what you've learned on your social media accounts, through a letter to the editor or at your local school board meeting.

____

____

____

____

- Talk to your children or children in your life about what homework they have each night. Ensure it gets done and assist them when needed.

____

____

____

____

- Compare the amounts of homework different children in your life are doing, then compare their statistics with average hours of homework students do around the world, as discussed in this chapter. If the level of homework feels like too much, too little or not substantive enough, start a conversation with their teachers about your concerns.

____

____

____

____

"Everybody is a genius. But if you judge a fish by its ability to climb a tree, it will live its whole life believing that it is stupid."

Albert Einstein

A student in a culinary vocational program in Estonia shows off the cake she baked.

Chapter Four

Vocational Education Puts Student Choice First

Along a tree-lined street in Slovenia's capital of Ljubljana, I watched as neighborhood residents filtered into a small store selling a variety of baked goods. The counter held a case full of picture-perfect chocolate bars and fruit-topped cakes, with a glass dome full of scones next to the cash register. Loaves of fresh bread and rolls lined long wooden shelves, with the shop name, *Kruh & Cukr*, scrolled in white on a black chalkboard wall.

It looked like a typical professional bakery in Europe. Only here, student workers assisted customers as they picked out cupcakes and bread to take home to their families. Also, everything for sale was made by teenagers who attend Biotechnical Educational Center Ljubljana, a vocational high school and two-year college that's attached to the store.

Similar arrangements exist for Biotechnical Educational Center students hoping to work in other fields. An adjacent restaurant serves up meals cooked by budding chefs, for example, while students in their last year of the veterinary technician program assist the staff vet in caring for any pets brought to a nearby clinic. And all those services come at slightly discounted rates for community residents, since it's expected that student service might come with a few more hiccups than customers would get at commercial businesses—though I didn't notice any drop in quality at the student-run facilities I visited.

Slovenia, which scored No. 13 in the world in math and science on the most recent PISA exam, has one of the highest percentages of students in vocational programs, with roughly 70 percent of its student population enrolled in these courses. It's far from unique among top-performing countries in offering its students choices at the secondary level between either an academic track, bound for university after high school, or vocational programs in world-class facilities to prepare them for in-demand jobs.

In Singapore, I visited a facility where high schoolers can work on a 747-jet engine FedEx donated from one of its California facilities. In South Korea, I toured a high school where students worked on industrial robots used on assembly lines. In Germany, I toured a vocational auto-motive program that gives students the training and industry certificates they need to start full-time careers after graduation.

These types of vocational programs have been expanding in top-tier education systems over the past two decades, both in terms of student interest and government investment. And those I interviewed said that growth is paying dividends in a number of ways.

Quality vocational programs that teach tangible skills are good for the economy as a whole, advocates argue, since they can help fill in-demand jobs with trained workers and raise wages for recent graduates. That translates to more money circulating for everyone. It also helps countries with strong vocational programs such as Germany boast low unemployment rates for young people, even when those figures have risen in other places around the world.

Such programs also are good for students who may not have a passion for academia the way university-bound students do. Instead of ending up bored, causing discipline problems or possibly dropping out in high school, such students can get professional training and real-world experience in the careers of their choice. That can translate to higher-paying jobs immediately after graduation from high school or brief post-secondary programs, which sets them up for higher lifetime earnings and success. And rather than pigeonholing students, as some critics fear, my interviews and research show that giving students the option of high-quality vocational programs that might better align with their goals and talents can help solve one of the key problems plaguing American schools: a lack of student motivation.

Volumes of research show that giving students more choices when it comes to their learning boosts both motivation and engagement—particularly with tweens and teens, when those factors become increasingly problematic. While a recent Gallup poll showed two-thirds of U.S. students said they were very engaged in school in sixth grade, that interest plummeted to 34 percent by the time they reached 12th grade. Meanwhile, students in Estonia report an increase in school engagement as they enter high school, climbing from 32 percent in sixth grade to 52 percent in 12th grade. Choices to help keep kids engaged can be minor, like offering two or three options for homework assignments that focus on the same concept. They can also be major, such as letting students set their own educational goals and then go down entirely different paths at the secondary level based on those individualized goals, as Estonia allows. Along with increasing student motivation, these practices also help teach students how to make important decisions, including weighing various options and being advocates for their own lives. Those lessons help develop not just good students, but good workers, good citizens and good humans.

However, with few exceptions, the U.S. education system generally dictates what students must study. In California, for example, the high school curriculum is defined by the "A-G requirements," which are the minimum standards to be admitted into the California State University system or the University of California system. Every student is forced on a track to meet those requirements, and it's considered a success if they pass the courses, even if they only earn a D grade in the required subjects. There's not a lot an administrator can do, then, to boost student choice in the current system other than offer an array of different electives or limited Career and Technical Education (or CTE) classes sprinkled into the regular school day—if funding is available to support such programs.

This lack of choice, especially in the high school years, has led to epidemic problems with student motivation, which increases in dropout rates. It also contributes to systemic discipline problems, which impact the quality of education that students on more academic tracks receive as well.

As they get to junior high and high school, my students often tell me they feel they have no choice in their education and are stuck learning information that won't help them in the fields they hope to pursue. Some have grown up wanting to do blue collar work like many of their parents. I regularly ask students in my music classes what they want to be, and many name careers like hair stylist and mechanic and chef. I ask them if they'd feel more motivated to come to class each day if at least a portion of their day was spent doing real training for those careers instead of being forced to take classes such as algebra, and they always say yes. Thinking back to the first chapter of this book, I'd wager that many of my kids' parents also would be more connected to the work their children are doing in school if they could see clear, real-world applications. But few such programs exist in my school district, and those that are in place are nowhere near the quality and depth of what I've seen in other countries. This means that students like mine, who want to choose vocational paths after high school, will largely be stuck coming up with the money to attend community college or for-profit trade schools, which have been riddled with scandals in recent years for abruptly closing their doors or promising outcomes they don't deliver.

So how did the United States get here? Once again, a brief history lesson is helpful.

In the 1800s and early 1900s in America, most students didn't attend school past eighth grade. Those who did were generally interested in going on to colleges to become doctors, attorneys, teachers and a limited number of other careers requiring advanced degrees at the time. That meant secondary schools typically taught Greek and Latin and other liberal arts subjects that were perhaps still important then for students interested in academia, but not useful or interesting to most students who weren't on that path. It also led to a shortage of skilled labor for factories and unemployment problems in an increasingly industrialized nation.

As it became more common in the early 1900s for most students to stay in school through 12th grade, including more immigrant and low-income students, there was a push to reform secondary schools to include a curriculum that was more practical and engaging for all types of students. In his 1916 book Commercial Education in Public Secondary Schools, F.V. Thompson recognized the impact this was having on student motivation, writing: "A fundamental lack in our general high school is the failure of the high school to supply the boys and girls with an adequate motive. The general, academic or abstract cultural motive has proved ineffective; we have failed not only to meet industrial needs, but have failed to interest and hold our boys and girls."

Business and education leaders began meeting to discuss a shift to "industrial education." In 1917, President Woodrow Wilson signed into law the Smith-Hughes Act, which directed federal funds to states that developed vocational education programs aimed at preparing students for "useful employment." Programs were developed for students 14 years and up who wanted to train for careers in fields including agriculture, industry and trades, and home economics. They were required to spend half of their school time doing practical, hands-on activities that were related to their chosen field, with teachers who had expertise in each area recruited to run the programs.

The Smith-Hughes Act did successfully expand vocational education programs across the country. But problems quickly emerged. With few laws at the time to guard against discrimination based on race, gender, class or anything else, poor and non-White students were more commonly steered to vocational programs, while women were only allowed to pursue particular vocational programs such as garment making. Students who were tracked into vocational programs often started receiving little education that wasn't focused on their narrow career path, which limited their ability to make moves later or to advance in their careers if they got jobs in the field after graduation. What's more, those vocational programs often weren't well aligned with the changing needs of the business community, defeating the purpose of their original design. As a result, despite resources and hype for these programs, less than 20 percent of secondary students were pursuing the vocational path. So many states essentially threw the baby out with the bathwater, ditching rather than improving their vocational programs.

The United States has revised laws governing its vocational education programs several times since 1917, making improvements along the way. Most recently, Congress in 2018 reauthorized the Carl D. Perkins Career and Technical Education Act, which directs nearly $1.3 billion a year to career and technical education programs. Meanwhile, Congress in 2001 passed the No Child Left Behind Act, which required schools to test *all* students for basic academic achievement in math and reading. Early tests showed that students in vocational programs weren't receiving enough academic training to reach proficiency in core subject areas. So vocational programs have pivoted to also include more reading, writing and math skills, to make sure students are ready both for careers and for college after graduation. Such moves along with legal protections have helped limit racial and gender disparities in these programs.

The problem is that the American education system still hasn't pivoted to develop rigorous, high-quality, dedicated vocational campuses that can provide them with the real-world skills and certifications they'll need to get a head start in well-paying professions. Our education system, which leaves most decisions up to each state, is so decentralized that there's never been an attempt at creating national standards around vocational programs. We also clearly are not looking to other countries that have successful vocational programs as models. When I was at the top vocational school in Slovenia, administrators told me that while they regularly get weekly visitors from places such as China, Germany and Singapore, they couldn't recall an American touring their programs in the previous 20 years. As a result, there are only scattered examples of decent vocational programs in some states and districts in the United States. I've toured quality vocational schools in places such as Las Vegas, Nevada, and Mesa, Arizona, and they're doing admirable work. A study on vocational programs in Massachusetts, which is doing the best job in the U.S. in this area today, showed that enrollment in the programs significantly boosted high school graduation rates for poor students in particular without having any negative impacts to performance on standardized tests that measure more academic subjects. But unless American students are lucky enough to live near one of a limited number of programs, most are stuck relying on the few CTE classes offered as part of the regular day at comprehensive high schools.

In my school district in San Diego, I spent time touring and speaking with students in the "culinary" CTE courses offered at Southwest High School, which is located a half mile from Southwest Middle School, where I work as a teacher. While I'd seen students in places like Slovenia and Belgium working in commercial kitchens, equipped with professional-grade gas ranges and other equipment to prepare restaurant-quality food that was sold to real customers, students in the culinary class I observed in my district were making vats of macaroni and cheese on small electric stoves. Rather than wearing chef uniforms, they had simple aprons over their street clothes.

I interviewed one young man in the class who did want to become a chef. He recognized that he'd likely need to spend nearly $100,000 to attend culinary school after graduation. He'd been trying to get into the high school program and only succeeded his last semester, since the classes had been full. Meanwhile, many other students told me they were just taking the culinary classes for "fun" or to fill out their schedules.

I learned the program's teacher at the time had a budget of $4,000 a year for food, with 160 students in her courses each day. Most days, the students could not even cook due to a lack of funding for materials. So even though most CTE teachers I spoke with were committed to their programs, the overall quality suffered because these courses were too limited as well as poorly funded and designed. The overwhelming majority of the students enrolled in these programs will not be able to exit with a "school to career" skill. At best, most of these classes serve to simply help introduce students to potential professions and to spark their interest. When looking at these programs at Southwest High School vs. the vocational programs I saw that same summer while visiting more than 30 public schools in Northern Europe, there simply is no comparison, leading me to believe that many CTE programs in the United States aren't much more than marketing hype.

Things were much the same in Slovenia two decades ago, explained Bostjann Ozimek, a project coordinator for student vocational programs who toured me around Biotechnical Educational Center Ljubljana. At the turn of the century, Ozimek said, a majority of students were going to upper secondary schools that prepared them for the university track. But they found many students were struggling to find jobs in their chosen professions once they graduated from universities, without the industry demand to support so many incoming workers. And at the same time, Ozimek said many businesses couldn't find enough qualified workers to fill blue-collar jobs that required some skills and training.

So, as the European Union formed in the early 2000s, member countries such as Slovenia decided to focus education funding on building vocational programs that closely aligned with needs in the job market. The Biotechnical Educational Center Ljubljana was built in 2005, and construction was underway when I visited in 2018 on an expansion to keep up with student demand. A lot of the funding for Estonia's vocational programs came from the European Union.

Over the past decade, that investment and focus has helped Slovenia flip its dynamic. Now, Ozimek said, more students have started to enroll in vocational programs than university-track secondary schools. Vocational education is "getting the reputation back" that it had lost in the prior few decades, when there was a push for every student to strive for university enrollment after college, he said. And, while there are of course always needs in some areas of industry, Ozimek said some vocational tracks his school offers, such as veterinary technicians, have saturated the job market to the point where graduates end up continuing on to universities to pursue more advanced positions in their chosen fields, such as becoming full veterinarians. Those who go on bring training and experience in their field, and they likely were paid for their professional experience along the way.

Meanwhile, in the United States, veterinarians graduate universities with some of the highest levels of student loan debt than any other career field. That's one factor contributing to the profession also posting one of the highest suicide rates, with those numbers on the rise in recent years.

The United States is essentially in the same place Slovenia was 20 years ago. Many job fields for university graduates are saturated and don't pay enough to justify the student loan debt their programs can rack up. We also have growing shortages of trained blue-collar workers such as plumbers, electricians and mechanics, and they've only been exacerbated by the COVID-19 pandemic. I mean, have you tried to hire a professional to do improvements at your home lately? But if a student tells a U.S. high school teacher that they want to be a plumber, rather than have that choice validated, they'll likely be told they should still aim for a college degree. Following Slovenia's model, we could make a major course correction by investing serious funds into vocational education and helping students understand that taking such jobs will still allow them to make good money and be valued in our society. But instead, we simply continue to sell all students, no matter their own talents and interests, the same lines about the importance of everyone going to college.

Of course I believe in the value of education. It's my life's work, after all. And there certainly is solid data to show that U.S. students who earn college degrees have lower rates of unemployment and higher rates of income-earning potential. I also believe in setting high expectations for students and doing all we can to help every student who wants to attend college get there, no matter their background or barriers. But why are the halls of my school only lined with posters for Harvard, UCLA and Cornell universities and not also featuring, say, a list of starting salaries for electricians and detectives and other aspirational careers that don't require college degrees? It seems we've let the admirable goal of believing in the potential of every student and helping them aim high translate to the hardline expectation that every student must go to a university to succeed in life. That leaves students who don't want to or can't make it on that pricey, challenging track out in the cold, which is bound to be harmful for students and society alike.

There is another way. And I saw firsthand how the alternative is playing out with great success in countries around the world.

Built-in Choices

From the amount of unstructured play time kindergarten students have in places like Finland to the paths students get to take in secondary schools, student choice is baked into public education in many other nations in ways that aren't currently possible in U.S. schools. And much like with teachers, as we discussed in chapter two, a key ingredient missing here is trust.

In the United States, we simply assume that students are too young to make decisions in junior high about what they want to do in life. We don't trust them to have the wisdom and foresight to start carving out their own path at that age, so we try to steer all kids onto a path focused on graduating high school and going on to a four-year college, assuming that will give them the most options in the long run.

Along with a lack of trust in student judgment, there's also a fear in the U.S. that if students embark at 15 years old on vocational education paths, they've limited their options to ever go on to a university or pursue a different profession. There's good reason for some of that fear due to the history of problems with vocational education in this country. But students who've chosen vocational paths in other countries are generally free to change their minds later on. Yes, some will need to meet certain benchmarks to transition between programs, but they're not cut off from going down a different path if they choose. And in the meantime, they've been enrolled in rigorous vocational programs that have been preparing them for jobs in the real world.

Before they've even chosen a path in high school, students in a number of countries with top-tier education systems already have made a choice to be there, since students often are only required to attend school through ninth grade. In Japan, South Korea and Liechtenstein, for example, students can quit school at as young as 15 years old, while the minimum age to leave school is 16 in Finland, New Zealand and Denmark.

By comparison, there's no national minimum age to leave school in the United States. A dozen states allow students to quit high school at 16, while another 10 make students stay until they are 17 and most states require students to attend school until they are 18 years old or until they graduate. The trend around the world has definitely been toward raising the minimum school-leaving age. That's because research shows such practices significantly increase lifelong earnings and promote equity, since low-income students are otherwise more likely to drop out of school early to go to work or to care for younger siblings. But even in most countries with top-tier education systems and lower ages at which students can legally drop out of high school, the intrinsic value of education and extrinsic demands of the job market keep as much as 99 percent of students enrolled until they graduate. You could argue, then, that the required school attendance age is a difference without a distinction. But it does serve to present students with a choice to stay in school, which means those who do stick around have some combination of intrinsic and extrinsic motivation to do so.

Just looking at minimum ages also doesn't tell the full story. And this is where job training programs start to come into play. Even in some countries with higher minimum drop-out ages, they only allow students to leave high school before they reach the mandated age if they enroll in job training and apprenticeship programs, which the government helps to fund and coordinate. No such arrangements exist for students who leave high school early in the United States.

In other countries, educators also start talking to students when they're young about the choices they'll get to make, if they go on to high school, between choosing a college-bound or vocational track. In Slovenia, for example, representatives from vocational high schools visit junior high and even primary schools to start recruiting students to their programs, Ozimek explained. The lower schools have fairs, much like career fairs in the U.S., where representatives from vocational high school programs for students 15 and older can share what they offer and speak with younger students who've shown an interest in or aptitude for a particular profession. They can then start reaching out to students early about what's required to get into their programs and make sure they're on the right track. The year I visited, Ozimek said his team had done recruiting for its vocational programs at 50 different primary schools.

In Finland, students spend a couple weeks during their eighth-grade year visiting different companies to see what it's like to actually work in professions that interest them. Parents and friends help arrange many of these visits, so they're also invested in the process. And companies welcome young students because they went through the same system themselves and know they could be meeting some of their future workers. After these visits, school counselors sit down with parents and students individually to discuss possible paths in high school so they can all make informed choices together.

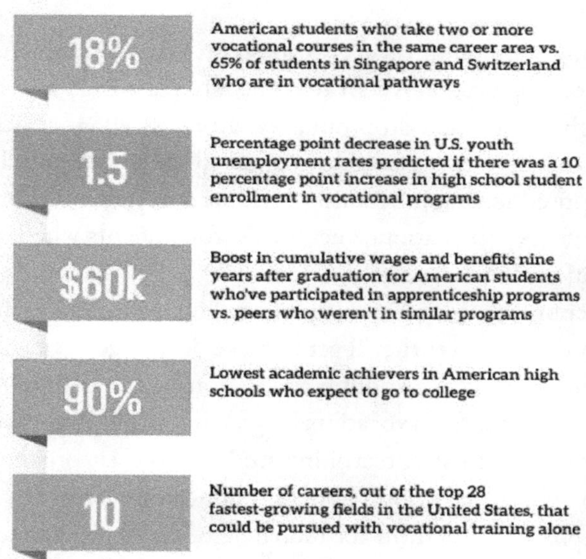

To prevent grouping students by class, race or gender, these recruitment efforts are not targeted at particular students, explained Engelbert Hillen, who is technical director of Rhein-Maas Berufskolleg vocational high school in Kempen, Germany, not far off from Düsseldorf.

Instead, he said, Germany offers the same choices to all students to pursue more academic vs. more vocational tracks—or they can take his school's popular dual system study program, where high school students can split their days between traditional academic courses and vocational courses. And for students who still aren't quite sure what they want to do, Hillen explained those students are given time to try different vocations, perhaps spending time in the auto shop, then the metal working shop, and so on until they find something that sparks their interest.

I had a student a few years back who we'll call Liliana. She was failing nearly every academic class and almost never seemed happy. I ran into her one day in the local supermarket with her mom, and the three of us started talking. Liliana, who had bright pink hair, told me she hated school. I told her I noticed she took pride in her hair and her nails and liked to try new styles, so I asked if she'd ever thought about being a cosmetologist. She responded, "What's that?" I explained the profession and Liliana immediately lit up. When I asked how she'd feel if there was a program that would allow her to start learning to be a cosmetologist while she was still in high school, both she and her mom got excited at the prospect. The dynamic of the conversation immediately changed as soon as Liliana and her mother saw hope for a path that she'd enjoy and that could lead to a solid career.

By the time students are in junior high in many top-tier countries, many have already made key decisions about their path in secondary school. At Sanmin Junior High in Taipei, Taiwan, when the regular school day ended, perhaps only a few dozen out of some 800 students actually left campus. Most stayed for free after-school programs to help prepare them for more rigorous academic programs in high school aimed at getting into college. I spoke with students who were leaving. One girl clutching a bright pink bag that stood out from her navy-blue school uniform told me she wants to be a cosmetologist, so she'll enroll in a vocational program for high school where she can start her training. Another young man told me attended a cram school at the elementary level. But by junior high, he'd decided he wanted to be a chef, so neither he nor his parents felt any need for him to stay after school or continue attending cram schools. And he couldn't wait to start his culinary training program when he went on to secondary school the following year.

Programs Abound

Students who choose to attend Slovenia's notable Agriculture Biotechnical Vocational School in Novo Mesto can learn to grow and harvest grapes at an adjacent vineyard. Then, they can learn to make and bottle wine in commercial-grade facilities. In a wine cellar located inside the school, with rough-hewn wood tables and a small bar, I got to sample a student-made white wine, which was made from locally grown apples and honey. Talk about having trust in students!

In many countries that score best each year on PISA exams, options for such high-quality vocational programs in public schools are the rule, not the exception.

New-model BMWs, Audis and Volkswagens vehicles were lined up in the brick-walled garage of an automotive program I visited at Rhein-Maas Berufskolleg vocational high school in Germany. Students were using a $20,000 diagnostic computer to analyze what was wrong with a fully loaded Mercedes-Benz CL 600 with a V12 engine, which sells for more than $200,000. The car companies had donated more than 50 vehicles for students to work on, with most less than three years old, so they could properly train for jobs servicing such cars after graduation.

Along one wall was what they called the "poison cabinet" full of carefully labeled defective car parts. The instructor selected parts and plugged them into the test vehicles one at a time without students' knowledge. The teenagers—who'd already completed coursework to learn about electronics, basic car mechanics and other foundational elements— then worked to figure out the problem, just as they would if a customer brought a problematic car to an auto repair shop in the real world.

All of the school's 1,800 students had chosen to be there, with administrators explaining that the decision is made after meetings to gather input from their parents and the school. Most students were very engaged and clearly motivated to complete the training. Since students were part of the dual system study program, they attended traditional high school two or three days a week, where they received more typical academic training, and they worked in the industry the other two or three days a week. For that work, they received wages of approximately $1,000 a month as long as they were in school and meeting the graduation requirements. They also were poised to receive solid starting salaries as certified auto mechanics when they completed high school. One student I spoke with named Manuel, who'd been in the vocational automotive program for two years, told me he expected to earn roughly $2,500 a month as soon as he graduated.

Meanwhile, in the auto mechanic program I toured at Southwest High School, many of the students in the class I observed told me they did not choose to be there. They said they were only there because the counselors could not find another open elective for them. They also normally have to work on their own cars because the school automotive program does not own any working cars. The only school-owned vehicle in the automotive compound when I first toured the program was an old, rusty 1960s milk truck. They recently replaced the milk truck with a used car, but it was quickly vandalized to the point that students couldn't open the hood to work on anything inside. So, at the time of publication, automotive students had no vehicle to work on.

Even if a student is in the Southwest High School automotive program for four years, they're taught limited automotive maintenance lessons. The only certification that they could qualify for would be as a lube and oil technician—an accomplishment administrators in my district use to brag about the program. When I asked a worker at a local oil change shop what type of training someone would need if they were hired cold, he told me it was a three-day training program, which the company generally pays for. And I learned this certification might earn graduates a dollar an hour higher than the minimum wage if they are lucky. That means students in Southwest High School's automotive program who want to work as mechanics and make solid salaries will most likely need to first attend a for-profit school, which can cost more than $50,000.

Back in Rhein-Maas Berufskolleg vocational school in Germany, spread out across a massive campus of three-story red brick buildings, I observed world-class programs to train students in everything from solar panel installation to woodworking to social services programs. I also toured a workshop that had a half-wall lined with functioning sinks and toilets that students could use to train to be plumbers. Students who complete the program will be certified plumbers, which means they can start earning decent salaries as soon as they graduate.

The plumbing workshop was empty when I was there because students were in a nearby classroom studying politics and economics as part of their traditional education. Students remained engaged in those classes, which instructors framed as helping prepare them to run their own plumbing businesses one day. But those academic courses also ensure that students graduating from the plumbing program are well-rounded and could pivot easily to other professions if they change their minds down the road.

One of the most impressive vocational schools of all those I visited was Gradia Vocational School in Jyvaskyla, a large city in central Finland. The massive campus, which was blanketed in snow when I saw it, offers 22 different three-year vocational programs (out of 43 programs recognized nationally) for students to choose from starting in tenth grade. Options include nursing, music, electrical work, marketing, photography, information technology, welding, logistics, fashion, construction and more. Student schedules include a mix of general education, vocational education and on-the-job learning. And most of these programs include real-world applications. Residents from the neighborhood bring their cars to the auto body programs, for example, knowing students have been properly trained and are supervised by certified workers. They also can order custom metalwork from student welders for their homes or businesses. It may take a bit longer than in commercial shops, but prices are lower and the quality is monitored by professionals.

Classrooms at Gradia often are set up like in university lecture halls, with tiered theater-style seating. Hallways are lined with professional display cases displaying student work in various fields and teaching students how to merchandise their products. The campus was built in 1970 but has been upgraded and modernized to include expensive, top-of-the-line equipment to train for each profession. There are locker rooms for students in the mechanics program to change into coveralls and then shower after they finish working or for culinary students to put on fully hygienic outfits so their products can be sold to the public in an on-campus store.

All of these programs are completely free. Some Gradia students must pay for uniforms, though assistance is available if needed. Unlike the German system, most vocational students in Finland aren't paid for their work. That's why a couple students I spoke to who'd taken classes in both places said they preferred the German system. But Finnish students also graduate many of the vocational programs with certificates that allow them to jumpstart careers in their chosen fields immediately after graduation or to start out at more advanced levels in college programs if post-secondary training is needed.

Gradia also had started offering adult vocational courses (similar to many U.S. community or technical college programs) on its campus shortly before my visit. Administrators explained that the trend was to incorporate both levels in the same location, so they can share resources and smoothly transition young people into further training if needed.

For students who finish ninth grade and aren't quite sure what they want to do next, or who need to catch up on skills or transition between focus areas, Finland offers pre-vocational training for six to 12 months in a program called VALMA. Such programs also are popular for immigrants who might need to learn additional language skills before enrolling in full-time vocational programs. Gradia creates individual learning plans for each vocational student, with some students completing the program in two years and others taking four years. Such offerings—coupled with the option for a dual qualification program similar to Germany, where students do vocational and general education at the same time—helps ensure that Finland's vocational program can boast "no educational dead ends" for students even if they fall behind, change their minds about career paths or want to go on to study in a university.

At Seoul Robotics High School in South Korea, students were dressed in gray wool blazers, vests and ties for their vocational training program. They were working with industry-grade equipment to train them in the world of megatronics, which combines mechanical, computer and electrical engineering to work on machines used in today's advanced automated manufacturing industry. In one classroom, they were practicing how to program computer numerical control, or CNC, machines, which are widely used to cut or move materials in manufacturing plants. In another room, they were studying electronics, with advanced circuit boards lining the walls. An administrator showed me robots students had made from scratch, from cutting the metal used in the frames to programming the robots to do simple tasks. Upstairs was a stadium students used for intense robot competitions.

I couldn't help but think of my students back home, who had told me they couldn't wait to go to cosmetology school after graduation, when I was visiting SIMA Vocational School in Aarschot, Belgium. The school offers students training in three fields: culinary arts; social services such as early education and senior care; and aesthetics, including massage therapy and cosmetology. I toured classrooms that look like working hair salons because they are! When students in the program are 15 and 16 years old, they'll primarily practice cutting and styling the hair of wigs on mannequins. Then when they are 17 and 18 years old, they'll start to work on real customers who come in from the neighboring village to get their hair done at a reduced price. They take these courses in conjunction with traditional academic courses. And when they graduate, they can start working in the field or go on to further training.

The closest thing I've seen to such a program in the United States was at East Valley Institute of Technology, a public vocational school in Mesa, Arizona. From the moment I entered the school, I could sense that the students were more mature than most students at my local high school. They had chosen to be in these programs, all with clear goals in mind. Cheesy as it might sound, I really felt I could see the difference in their eyes, which weren't glued to cell phones but were engaged in what they were learning.

Other than some supply fees of perhaps a few hundred dollars, the programs are free for juniors and seniors (and some qualifying sophomores) to attend. Students can be bussed over from 11 surrounding school districts to study in one of more than 40 occupational programs, learning about everything from 3D animation to aviation, barbering to dental careers, early childhood education to interior design. Some of these programs offer certificates at the end. Students also can opt to do dual enrollment with a nearby community college to start any additional coursework they'll need to practice in their chosen field.

Leanna was a senior in the cosmetology program when I visited the Arizona school. She wore an apron over her street clothes, combing hair on a mannequin as she talked to me about the program. They get to work on real customers a few days a week, she said. At the end of their senior year, they can take state board exams and graduate with a cosmetology license to work in the fields of makeup, hair and nails. Leanna said she plans to go on to college after high school but saw the cosmetology license as a way to earn good money doing something she enjoys while she continues her education. Other students in the program wanted to immediately start full-time work as makeup artists or in hair or nail salons.

Sabrina, who was wearing green scrubs, was in the first semester of her senior year of the veterinary assistant program. Next semester, she said, she hoped to start interning at a nearby veterinary clinic. Such internships aren't mandatory, and it's up to students at the Arizona school to arrange them. But if they do, students in some programs can spend a couple days a week in class and a few days interning in their program, much like the German apprenticeship system.

Over in the law enforcement program, first-year student Lathan carried an airsoft gun in his belt loop and students did drills, moving down the hallway with their "guns" drawn to sweep it for "suspects." Students also were doing classroom training on laws around everything from DUIs to petty theft. If they want to become police officers, they'll of course need to go on to a police academy. But the instructor explained that they partner with large companies such as Sam's Club and Walmart to prepare students when they graduate at 18 to start in jobs such as security and loss prevention. Lathan and his peers told me the program motivated them to come to school each day, which they were certain they wouldn't feel at a traditional high school.

The East Valley Institute of Technology is impressive, as are the programs at Western Maricopa Education Center or West-MEC in nearby Glendale, Arizona. Both schools are close to being on par with some of the top programs I visited in other countries. The problem is that they start a bit too late by bringing in students who are juniors and seniors, rather than freshman and sophomores as other countries do. Also, they are just two high schools in a nation with roughly 15 million high school students. Though both have been greatly expanding and evolving, they haven't been scaled up. And there have been few efforts to replicate the EVIT or West-MEC models in other school districts and states.

Businesses Buy In

A key reason vocational programs in other countries have been so successful is that their public education systems typically have developed close partnerships with their local business communities. They consult with industry leaders and trade unions from various sectors about their evolving needs, then align school program offerings and curriculum to ensure students are meeting those demands.

This idea often doesn't sit well with many Americans. We have a fierce sense of independence and don't like the idea of private industry or unions (which are controversial in some American circles) dictating curriculum just so schools can churn out "worker bees" who'll conform and make those businesses more profitable. What will that do to innovation? And to the value we place on teaching kids to be creative and think for themselves?

I'd counter that our fear of industrializing education has sent us too far in the other direction. As a result, in the United States there's a clear disconnect between what students are learning in school and the skills they need for most modern jobs. Only 49 percent of employers surveyed for the Job Outlook 2020 report from the National Association of Colleges and Employers said that recent hires came to them with proficient oral and written communication skills. Employers also said a majority of recent graduates lacked a work ethic, leadership skills and multicultural fluency. The current American education system isn't meeting the needs of American businesses today, and they know it.

Yet the U.S. business world still hasn't risen to the challenge of fighting to better tie public education to their needs. When I got back from visiting my first round of countries, for example, I contacted the San

Diego Business Journal to do a story on what I was learning about how other nations were preparing students for the workforce. The chief executive of the publication told me, "We don't do educational stories." He just couldn't see what's so obvious to people in the business world in so many other countries, that private industry and education systems should be working together.

Meanwhile, our kids are learning about this disconnect the hard way after graduation. It's a disservice to kids to *not* prepare them for careers that are in demand and offer more than minimum wage salaries, to not make them aware of which fields are growing and which are shrinking, or which ones require particular skills even for entry-level workers. And we're shafting kids if we tell them we're preparing them for careers in the real world when we're not even staying in touch with those industries to update our equipment and lessons to ensure students have the basic skills to start out in those professions.

This doesn't mean we stop offering paths for the academics and the dreamers, those who want to ask the big questions, turn industry upside down or avoid it entirely. No country I visited with strong vocational programs had in any way weakened its university-track programs as a result. Quite the opposite, in fact. When those programs weren't trying to be everything to everyone, and didn't have to deal with the discipline problems that come with having loads of unmotivated students, they were more effective for the students who wanted to be there.

It's a win-win-win. When vocational programs are aligned and connected with industry:

1. Businesses get the skilled labor they need to keep our economy moving forward.
2. Students are able to easily find jobs in high-demand fields that offer salaries above minimum wage, potentially lifting their families out of poverty for generations to come.
3. Schools get access to professional-grade equipment, free training and mentors still working in these fields, which can make state-of-the-art vocational programs affordable for public schools.

The focus on megatronics at Seoul Robotics High School is an example of this alignment between industry needs and student training in action. Wages in South Korea, as in the United States and most western nations, are too high to make many manufacturing jobs cost effective for companies. But not all manufacturing jobs are getting outsourced to places with cheaper labor. In fact, recent research has shown that many more jobs in high-wage countries are being replaced by automation than by outsourcing. Recognizing that trend, South Korea started training its young people not to work on manufacturing lines, but to program the robots that are increasingly running those operations.

That way of thinking is paying off. One wall in each program area at Seoul Robotics High featured small photos of students from the last graduating class, with information about where they'd been hired to work immediately after graduation. Many of the country's top companies were represented on those walls.

The robotics school also got its principal not from the top education program in Seoul, but from one of the largest tele-communications companies in South Korea. Principal Tae Seok Ro had been the No. 2 executive in a major telephone company before he was recruited to bring his real-world industry knowledge to the school. And when developing Seoul Robotics High's programs, Ro said he looked largely to one place: Germany.

Few places partner schools and industry quite like Germany. Germany's *meister* system, which requires craftspeople to do lengthy apprenticeships under a master in that field before they can be allowed to practice on their own, dates back to the Middle Ages. While much has changed about that system in recent decades, Germany is still one of the only top-performing countries that essentially outsources part of its vocational education system to private employers.

In Germany, rather than have the school provide all vocational instruction, students sign contracts with outside companies to do apprenticeships several days a week. The company is obligated to provide the student with on-the-job training, based on national standards. While parents used to pay masters to apprentice their children, their taxes now fund these vocational programs. And companies now must pay modest wages to the students they employ. Then, if it's a good fit, students may be offered jobs with those companies after they graduate.

At Rhein-Maas Berufskolleg vocational school, most students apprentice with small mom-and-pop businesses that might have workshops with between three and 20 people, Hillen explained. The school and employer stay in regular contact. If the student isn't behaving or performing as expected on the job, the workshop can call the school. But it works the other way as well. Schools call employers if students aren't meeting their obligations in class, and businesses can pressure students to step it up or lose their positions. Either the student or the business can end the contract at any time; Hillen said about 28 percent of his school's apprenticeship contracts get canceled before the end of the school year.

The school also takes care to make sure businesses aren't over-working students. About once a year, Hillen said, they have an incident with a student who calls in sick, then they learn that student was actually working longer hours instead of attending class. But that can trigger a sizable fine for the company, so Hillen said it's rare.

One major advantage to this system is equipment, Hillen said. No school can afford to continually purchase the latest state-of-the-art tools and technology used in the field the way private companies can. They might make big investments in new machines every 10 years or so. But in some fields, equipment that's 10 years old is nearly obsolete, which means students will need additional training on newer gear once they finish those vocational programs. Businesses, on the other hand, must continually upgrade their equipment to stay relevant, Hillen noted. So if students are doing their training in the real world, they'll be working with the latest tools and staying up to date as their field evolves. And when schools are training the workers that businesses need, they're often happy to share the latest gear, which is how Rhein-Maas Berufskolleg has dozens of new, top-of-the-line cars for its automotive students to work on at any given time.

Teachers at the school also benefit from industry partnerships. Hillen explained that teachers are given up to 10 paid days off each year to do training programs in the field they focus on, to ensure they also are staying up to date on industry developments. Companies in those in-dustries typically provide these training sessions to teachers for free. So teachers from his school, for example, might spend 10 days getting training from Mercedes-Benz on the features and changes to the latest models of their vehicles so they can pass that information along to students.

Along with these partnerships, German vocational programs regularly expose their students to information about what the job market looks like. Hillen said the state's labor agency, which helps unemployed and underemployed residents find work, sends consultants to the schools to talk to students about what fields are in demand and to help them find jobs. Trade groups from various industries, such as commerce and agriculture, also send representatives to schools to present options for careers within their profession.

Similarly, in Slovenia, Ozimek helps with a mobility project that's funded by the European Union. It encourages young people in particular to move to places where the job market indicates their skills are needed, rather than only seeking a job in their field locally or giving up and doing something else.

Other countries are taking cues from Germany and looking to increase partnerships between their vocational education programs and the business community. Finland, for example, passed laws in recent years to increase the amount of on-the-job training required for its vocational students, explained Seija Ala-Ruona, guidance counselor at Gradia Vocational School. Evidence of those partnerships is sprinkled around the school, such as the Hyundai stickers on the windows of one auto shop classroom I toured. And Ala-Ruona said she'd seen firsthand the benefits of such partnerships.

She recalled one student who was extremely shy and reserved. He clearly wouldn't have done well in a job interview, she said, since he struggled to answer simple questions when she tried to talk to him about his career path. But the student's vocational program had helped him land an apprenticeship position with a company for on-the-job training. He'd developed a relationship with the company and they got to see that, while he might be shy and quiet, he could perform very well. So they hired him for a well-paying job in his field of interest immediately after high school graduation.

I can't help but think of what would happen to that student in the United States, where there are so few built-in options to help our teens discover and pursue alternative paths to successful lives. We can do better by them. We must do better.

What can I do?

Overhauling our education system to give students more choices through high-quality vocational programs is key to improving motivation while they're in school and ensuring they have solid, realistic options once they graduate. Here are 10 steps everyone can take right now to push for that change, with space for you to jot down notes on plans for accomplishing each step or how it went once it's completed.

- Do an honest personal assessment of your own stance on the debate over whether every student should aim to get a college degree after high school. Where did that expectation come from? Can you find research to back up your views? What happens if students fall short? Try journaling, talking to trusted friends or starting conversations on social media about these questions.

  ____

  ____

  ____

- Make plans to visit vocational schools in some of the top countries in the world to see for yourself what these programs can look like. If you can't get out of the United States, try to make it to East Valley Institute of Technology in Arizona, or a vocational school in Las Vegas or Massachusetts, to see some solid examples closer to home. And if that's not doable, watch videos on my YouTube channel from these programs around the world so you have a good sense of what's possible.

  ____

  ____

- Share what you've learned about vocational education programs with your community by posting examples on social media, writing a letter to the editor of your local paper and speaking at local school board meetings.

- Teachers, talk with your students about different careers related to your subject area. Do your research and be honest about fields that are expanding and contracting so students understand *real* career prospects. Then share requirements to enter those careers and information about starting salaries, so students can make informed and realistic choices.

- Ask your child, or children in your life, what their career interests are. Help them research those interests to see what the career prospects in will look like in the future and to help them understand what training is needed. Then do research to see if there are any programs in the local or nearby school district that fit with the child's interests.

- Organize a career fair in your local community. Take care to recruit representatives from a wide variety of industries. Ask them to bring materials about the skills and education that are needed to get jobs in each field.

- Join your local chamber of commerce and start conversations with the business community about the benefits of partnering with local schools to develop and support vocational education programs.

- If you have a business, reach out to the local school district about forming a relationship. Consider offering new or used industry equipment for the school to use and providing training for local teachers. In exchange, see if you can get student workers to train in your company as part of their vocational program. And if they're a good fit, consider hiring them full-time after graduation.

- Start a petition and lobby your local school board about creating a world-class vocational program in your town. Volunteer to do the work to help get the program going.

- Write to your state and federal representatives asking them to support laws that would fund and govern quality vocational education campuses.

"Sometimes the most brilliant and intelligent
students do not shine in standardized tests
because they do not have standardized minds."

Diane Ravitch

*Students at a high school in South Korea discuss how much time they spend
studying and preparing for a single high-stakes test.*

High-Stakes Testing with Different Stakes

On the third Thursday of each November, most businesses in South Korea don't open until 10 a.m. Even the stock market delays its starting bell that morning, to ease commuter traffic and ensure students have clear paths to testing centers.

If something goes awry and students are running late, they can dial a three-digit phone number and get police escorts with sirens blaring.

As students arrive at testing centers, they're flanked by lines of younger students and parents who stand like fans waiting along a marathon route. These cheerleaders dole out words of encouragement and sticky treats, to help the right answers "stick."

Once students are inside testing halls, silence descends. Parents head to temples to pray. Planes are grounded or rerouted. Nearby military exercises are delayed. And teachers monitoring the testing hall trade their dress shoes for soft-soled sneakers, in hopes of keeping all noise and distractions to a minimum.

Then, for the next eight hours, students who want to go to a university after high school take a test known as *Suneung*, or the College Scholastic Ability Test. The exam consists of several sections that measure student knowledge of Korean language arts, math, English language, Korean history, science or vocational education, and a second foreign language. Students get a score from 1 through 9, with 1 being the highest. That score determines whether students will get into top universities and, to some extent, what their futures might look like.

Stakes couldn't be much higher for South Koreans choosing to take the *Suneung*. That's why students and their parents prepare for that day—along with, to a lesser extent, the day they take one other high-stakes test to get into high school—almost from the time they're born. The system has led to growing concerns about how such pressure impacts students' physical and mental health, with South Korean students facing higher rates of both depression and suicide than teens in most other countries. Flags also are being raised about inequities created by this system, since wealthier families can pay thousands of dollars a year for private tutoring in cram schools. With a mantra of "sleep five hours and fail, sleep four hours and pass," I watched as South Korean students who'd been preparing for this exam dozed off during their regular high school classes. The test itself is facing growing criticism, too, for focusing too much on rote memorization, with most of the exam consisting of multiple-choice questions.

These are all valid concerns that deserve careful attention. Those red flags are why most folks who study comparative education, including myself, don't recommend trying to replicate the South Korean testing system as it stands in the United States.

However, it's also clear that having students so invested in preparing for this one optional standardized test, where they are personally impacted by the results, has helped make South Korean students highly motivated to succeed. And that's driving high academic performance, with South Korea scoring No. 7 in the world when math, science and reading scores are averaged from the most recent PISA exam.

On the opposite end of the spectrum when it comes to high-stakes testing is the United States. High-stakes testing happens much more frequently here, but the "stakes" couldn't be more different. The result is lots of time and money expended with little to show for it.

While students in South Korea take just two standardized tests throughout their school careers, with results used to judge students and help them advance along different paths, studies have shown that American students have taken well over 100 standardized tests by the time they're seniors in high school. Dozens of hours and hundreds of millions of dollars are spent on these exams each year. Yet, with a vast majority of these tests, American students couldn't care less about the results. That's because students generally have no stake in the results. So I've watched as American students have used the answer bubbles on standardized tests to draw pictures, or quickly fill in random answers so they can use the rest of the testing time to nap, with nothing to motivate most of them to perform well on test days, let alone to study hard to prepare for these exams.

Rather than having test performance impact students, standardized exams in the United States are primarily used to judge schools and teachers. Results are posted online and in local newspapers, with schools and teachers subject to public shaming if scores aren't high. Schools can also lose autonomy and teachers can lose their jobs, despite decades of research that shows doling out punishments for educators based on student test scores doesn't help anyone.

There seems to be growing acceptance that the United States' obsession with high-stakes testing has proved wasteful and negative for administrators, teachers and students alike. But so far, little has changed in the past two decades, since we started in earnest down this path.

Standardized tests have existed in the United States for decades, but concerns about how often they're given and how they're used is a product of the 20-year-old No Child Left Behind movement. The motivation behind No Child Left Behind (NCLB) was admirable. The program grew out of nearly two decades of research and discussion around how, much as I've discussed in this book, the United States was no longer internationally competitive academically. The reform focused on how standards-based learning might improve the quality of education for all students, with accountability built in. When President George W. Bush signed the No Child Left Behind act in 2002, his Secretary of State Rod Paige said the focus was "to see every child in America—regardless of ethnicity, income, or background—achieve high standards."

The issue was in how student success at meeting those standards would be measured and what would happen if they fell short. The law required states to give third- through eighth-grade students standardized tests every year to assess their progress in reading and mathematics. The law required those results to be made public, so anyone could track the performance of any school across the country. Schools had to demonstrate that disadvantaged students were improving their scores each year. Otherwise, districts were threatened with corrective action, which could range from allowing students to transfer to other schools to having outside powers potentially take over and replace all administrators and staff. Regardless, all students were supposed to be showing proficiency on the exams by 2014.

The system snowballed. With such high stakes imposed by the federal government, states and districts started adding additional tests in between the nationally required assessments, to make sure students were on track. That's on top of all U.S. students already taking the National Assessment of Educational Progress test in fourth, eighth and twelfth grades. They must also take the PISA exam, whose results are a focus of this book. And students who want to attend college typically must take entrance exams, while top students often take Advanced Placement tests for college credits. Only those last two tests have potential impacts for students, while the rest have mainly been used to measure teacher and school performance.

The system has changed little through three different administrations. President Barack Obama dialed back some punitive elements of No Child Left Behind in 2011, but he maintained the level of testing and even put more emphasis on tying scores to teacher evaluations. More minor revisions came under Obama in 2015, but studies showed they did little to decrease the amount of testing taking place. Neither President Donald Trump nor President Joe Biden has cheered high-stakes testing, but neither has done anything significant to reduce the penalties or frequency of these exams.

The results of 20 years of this system are discouraging. Not only has the United States failed to make progress on producing more globally competitive students since this obsession with high-stakes testing began, but there have been other negative effects for students, educators and the public school system at large.

Students have been forced to spend dozens of hours each year preparing for and taking tests that have little to no impact on their lives. In many cases, standards measured by these tests are quite low, which means instruction centered largely around test preparation comes with lowered academic standards. Meanwhile, students have seen a reduction in options to take classes in subjects such as arts (which we'll cover in chapter seven), along with history and foreign languages, since these aren't subjects measured by most standardized tests.

At the same time, teachers have grown more unhappy, with pressure to "teach to the test," threats to their careers if students don't perform and demonization of their profession by many parents and lawmakers. And public schools have felt the same shaming and demonization, triggering the modern push for charter schools that we'll discuss in detail in chapter eight.

It's clear something needs to change.

While I'd argue that nearly every country that outperforms the United States on PISA exams is doing a better job than us at navigating the issue of standardized testing, I don't know that any one country has struck the perfect balance when it comes to frequency and stakes of these exams. So we have to ask, what improvements can we make by implementing positive aspects of testing systems in places such as South Korea without also importing the flaws such systems might present?

Based on what I've learned from studying how top-tier countries around the world handle high-stakes testing and comparing it with what U.S. schools do, here's what I'd recommend:

1. We should test students much less frequently, with no more than six total standardized tests throughout their school careers and ideally closer to three.

2. We should start testing students later, with the first exams given no earlier than third grade.

3. We should use most of these tests only for internal progress checks, with results made available just to teachers and administrators.

4. We should turn the results of those tests around quickly, so teachers can remediate and adjust their strategies as needed while those students are still in their class.
5. We should make at least one of these tests have real-world impacts for students, so they are motivated to prepare for it and to take the test seriously. And we should all help make that test a big deal, following the model of other countries that emphasize the seriousness of that exam by adjusting schedules around it.
6. However, we should not make student futures entirely focused on any one test. In terms of college placement, for example, we should maintain the U.S. system of having institutions also consider grades, recommendations and other performance measures alongside test results.
7. We should take standardized test development and administration out of the hands of private corporations and put it into the hands of educators who make simple, cost-effective materials.

Remember how in chapter three, when we compared how much countries spend on education, the United States spends more per student than many top-tier PISA countries? This is one key example of where some of that misdirected money goes, with a 2012 study estimating the nation spends $1.7 billion on standardized testing each year. That is a fraction of how much is spent on education overall. But given the hundreds of millions of dollars that would be saved through a dramatic reduction in testing and a pivot away from pricey private testing contracts, we still could spend that savings on strategies proven to truly help boost student achievement as discussed in other chapters of this book. That includes more support for families, higher pay for teachers, more days in school each year, developing comprehensive vocational education programs, a renewed emphasis on arts education and more equitable school funding.

Sounds good, right? So let's dig in on how and why we should make these changes to our standardized testing system happen.

Frequency of Testing

As I look ahead at my middle school's calendar each year, it's filled with an alphabet soup of tests. There's such an ever-changing roster of test acronyms—from STAR to CAASPP to PFT—that it's hard to keep track of all of them, let alone plan my teaching syllabus around these exams. And I'm a music teacher!

Just how extreme testing culture has become in the United States was laid out in stark terms by a 2015 study from Council of the Great City Schools, a coalition of America's largest urban schools. The study found that students in America's largest urban school districts on average would take 112 mandatory standardized tests from the time they started pre-kindergarten until they finished 12th grade. Eighth graders spent the most time testing, the study found, with an average of 4.22 days each year used to take exams. And the total doesn't include optional tests, such as college entrance exams, or diagnostic tests for struggling students or teacher-designed classroom tests.

Many of these tests were redundant, the study found, testing the same concepts over and over again. Even worse, many also weren't aligned with college and career preparedness, which meant they weren't measuring much that was useful for students' futures. And since tests are often given in the spring, with results taking two to four months to come back, teachers often don't hear anything until those students have left their classes, eliminating any chance at remediation.

Testing also starts young, the study found. Testing dictated by No Child Left Behind doesn't have to start until third grade. But some states and, more commonly, districts start testing students in pre-kindergarten and continue such tests each year.

All told, researchers found no correlation between the amount of time spent testing and how students performed on a national assessment given in grades four and eight.

By way of comparison, students in most high-performing PISA countries might take three standardized tests throughout their entire school careers. That's three elsewhere vs. 112 here. They also start such testing later, with tests typically given no earlier than third grade and often not until the end of middle school.

China, which was No. 1 on the last PISA exam, has a very similar system to South Korea. Chinese students take just two optional high-stakes tests during their school career. The first is the *zhongkao*, given at the end of junior high for students who want to attend high school. Then comes the challenging *gaokao*, a two-day test that will determine whether students can get into universities of their choice. If students in China opt against taking the *gaokao*, they will have only taken one standardized test during their school careers.

Finland and Estonia have similar testing systems to each other. Assessments are given to students in third, sixth and ninth grades. But they're not given to everyone, with only a random sample of students selected to take tests. Then, students have the option of taking a challenging exam at the end of high school if they want to go on to college. That means some students in these countries might never take a standardized test at all.

Canada is similar to the United States in that, like our states, each province determines most of the rules about standardized testing in schools. But that's about where the similarities end. In fact, teachers in the Canadian province of Ontario handed me an entire flier called "Top reasons you can't compare standardized testing in Ontario and the United States."

Ontario tests students in third, sixth, ninth and tenth grades, for a total of four standardized tests. The lower-level exams test students in reading, writing and math while ninth-grade tests focus on math and a 10th grade exam called the Ontario Secondary School Literacy Test covers a range of subjects. All told, they spend an average of six hours testing every three years. And while the U.S. spends around $55 per student on testing, Ontario boasts that it spends closer to $16 per student.

Michael Fullen, who Ontario educators told me is widely credited with helping transform the province's school system into one of the best in the world, has been advising U.S. educators for more than a decade about how to push our system in a similar direction. Some of Fullen's key recommendations have included giving standardized tests less frequently and changing how results are used, which we'll dive into in the next section.

The only other high-performing PISA country that has anything similar to our frequency of standardized testing is the United Kingdom. The U.K. showed solid performance on recent PISA exams, tying with Slovenia for the No. 13 spot when math, science and reading scores were averaged. But I did see some of the same problems we've seen here creeping into the U.K. system, with teachers expressing unhappiness at the frequency of testing and the periodic publication of results for public scrutiny.

Still, there remains a key difference between testing in the U.K. and the U.S., and it all comes down to the stakes.

Different Stakes

When I spoke with a teacher in the United Kingdom about high-stakes testing, he said, "We hear what's going on in the United States. We don't want that here." I got similar comments from educators in Canada, Finland, Estonia and elsewhere when discussing the topic of high-stakes testing during my visits to schools around the world.

Our reputation clearly precedes us in this area, and not in a good way.

Every country says standardized tests are used to assess student progress. But no nation that scores in the top tier on PISA exams systematically uses standardized test results as a basis for doling out punishments to teachers and schools.

Brooke, who helped me write this book, saw the impacts of such a system firsthand when she was a high school teacher in a Southern California school district from 2002 to 2006. The state was trying to adjust to the new No Child Left Behind law, with efforts to implement its doomed High School Exit Exam. When early results on the exam were dismal, potentially leaving a number of students behind, Brooke and other core subject teachers were increasingly pressured to factor test outcomes into their instruction. Despite the teachers' hard work, her school also was failing to meet its annual growth targets dictated by NCLB. Soon, they became a "state-monitored school," on the watchlist for a potential state takeover. They were told they could lose their jobs, no matter how strong their evaluations might be. Teachers had to start coordinating lesson plans with each other by grade level, to align with standards as they'd be assessed on the tests. The changes brought with them a looming sense of doom and sucked all of the joy out of planning lessons, which had been one of Brooke's favorite parts of teaching. By her fourth year, she realized with dismay that she'd actually substantially dumbed down her lessons, focusing less on challenging writing assignments or projects that encourage student creativity and spending more time on memorization. Frustrated, but unsure how she could change this dynamic, she left the profession after her fourth year.

Even using student test scores to positively impact teachers and schools is problematic for multiple reasons. For starters, rather than inviting collaboration, it encourages competition. If the teacher with the highest scores gets a bonus, what motivation do they have to share best teaching practices with colleagues? Students in the other teachers' classes lose out in that scenario.

Basing teacher pay, positively or negatively, on student test scores also encourages teachers to teach to the test. It can even motivate teachers to cheat, as has happened in some states where they can see substantial raises or bonuses based on test results.

Some schools have resorted to bribery to try to create some incentive for students around these tests. A former principal at my middle school, for example, offered to let the students shave his head if the school's scores increased by so many points.

Then there's the student factor. What if a teacher does an excellent job at preparing his or her students for an exam, but then the top student in the class is out sick the day of the test? What if a couple of others get test anxiety, one got no sleep the night before because his parents were fighting, and a couple more blow off the test and use the answer bubbles to make pictures? The teacher's scores will reflect those conditions. Should they miss out on promotions or raises as a result? Such situations only exacerbate the high teacher dissatisfaction and turnover we discussed in chapter two.

Perhaps most importantly, tying teacher pay to student test scores simply doesn't help improve student achievement. Study after study has shown no difference in scores for students in places where teachers are rewarded or punished based on standardized test scores. One example was a $575 million project funded largely by the Gates Foundation that aimed to evaluate teachers based on student test scores. The project was declared a flop in 2018. So we're getting all the negative results listed above without any real benefits for students.

In Canada, educators point out that no teacher can lose his or her job based on how students perform on standardized tests. Results don't directly affect teacher pay or job security, and they aren't ever discussed in teacher evaluations. Strong unions, which include teachers and administrators side by side, help ensure that's the case. And while some results are publicly released, it's never with labels that suggest a school or teacher is "failing," as the United States has done.

The only test scores made public in Estonia are on final exams, when students are leaving high school. Interim tests are only reported to the schools themselves, according to Gunda Tire, the national project manager for PISA in Estonia. She said this is intentional because they don't want to shame schools or turn the test into a competition. Instead, they want to focus on growth, or what Tire said they call "value added" to student progress over time.

The system is similar in Finland. Administrators explained that tests given to random groups of students at the third, sixth and ninth grade levels are just used as metrics to see how kids and teachers are doing. Administrators get the results so they can gauge performance. But principals and teachers alike told me results are not shared publicly and are not a big deal. They don't track kids using those scores and they don't demonize teachers based on the results, which they feared would harm morale for everyone. Finnish educators referenced the American system and how they've heard it impacts teachers, pitting them against administrators and pitting schools against each other.

Along with those randomized tests at three intervals, Finland has one other standardized test—and it's a doozy. The Matriculation Examination students must take if they want to get into university is a half-dozen day-long exams, equaling 40 hours of testing. While we discussed in chapter three how Finnish students often are only assigned 30 minutes of homework a night, students preparing for the Matriculation exam often spend much more time studying as they near the end of high school. The test contains multiple open-ended essay questions that give students a chance to demonstrate critical thinking, with prompts like this: "Some politicians, athletes and other celebrities have publicly regretted and apologized for what they have said or done. Discuss the meaning of the apology and accepting it as a social and personal act." Pressure to do well on this challenging test is high, since any student who wants to get into a competitive program to become a doctor or teacher needs to do well on this exam. And if they don't do well the first time around, many will study and work for a year or two after graduating high school before taking it again, then starting at a university when they're ready.

Stakes are high for that test. But unlike with standardized tests in America, stakes with the Finnish Matriculation test are high for *students*. That motivates them to do well on an important test they've chosen to take so they can pursue their goals. (By the way, there's simply no comparison between the Finnish exam and optional SAT or ACT tests American students who want to attend universities might take. We'll talk more about the state of those exams in the last section of this chapter. But in terms of the difficulty level and the weight they carry, they pale in comparison to Finland's university entrance exam.)

Germany had long turned up its nose at most standardized testing, relying instead on student grades, teacher recommendations and conversations between students, parents and teachers to track kids from as young as 10 years old. After criticism over how immigrants and poor students were being heavily tracked, or grouped, into the lowest-level programs, Germany developed its own set of national standards and corresponding tests to measure student achievement in grades three through eight. The program was developed shortly after NCLB took effect and might at first blush sound similar. But test results in Germany aren't used to penalize schools or teachers, and scores aren't publicized at the school level the way they are in the United States. Instead, administrators there use the scores to help target resources at schools that need help. The country's PISA scores have gone up, as has its equity ranking, which we'll discuss more in chapter eight.

In China, the first high-stakes test students take comes at the end of middle school and determines which level of high school they'll be able to attend: A, B or C. A would be the university-bound track, which is where my friend Spencer went. B high schools would be for students who likely want to attend college, but perhaps not the top universities. And C schools are largely for vocational education students. But make no mistake, even C-level schools are rigorous and disciplined.

Then, at the end of high school comes the all-important *gaokao* test, which is taken over two six-hour days. The test assesses students in Chinese, English, math and a choice of either sciences or humanities. Students get a three-digit score which dictates if and where they will go to university, with admission based entirely on those test results. As in South Korea, given the importance of the test, families start preparing kids for the test when they're young and the entire community rallies to support them on the day of the exam. And if students don't do well the first time around, their families try to pay for extra tutoring so they can retake the test again the next year.

With those kinds of stakes, there are reports of drones being used to make sure students aren't cheating on the *gaokao*. Parents and society at large pressure teachers to ensure students are ready for the exam, which has led to concerns over teaching to the test. Still, China doesn't go after teachers by tying their pay or status to students' results. And the country doesn't find fault with public schools when kids don't do well on the exams.

Japan has a very similar system, including high school and college admissions tests. The National Center Test for University Admissions, and the cram schools to prepare for it, haven't been quite as intense here. It's also not difficult to get into *a* university, with the country's declining population leaving plenty of room at most institutions. But it's still extremely tough to get into a *top* university, which is vital to landing a well-paid job with a top corporation or government ministry.

Singapore is rare in requiring high-stakes testing for students as young as third grade. Standardized tests at that level are used to route students into gifted programs. A few years later, exam scores are used to send students to different middle schools, high schools and universities, with extremely high levels of stress for that final exam. Students who don't take the college entrance test or score poorly might go to a vocational school. The next level up would be a polytechnic school, for careers that require an advanced degree and training. The best scores get students into competitive universities where they can pursue top-paying and higher-prestige careers.

Singapore has the highest number of high-stakes tests among top PISA countries. But there are still far fewer standardized tests given in Singapore than in the United States. And while the stakes are high for students, they don't impact teachers or schools.

Corporatization of Testing

Another key difference between how standardized testing works in the United States vs. most high-performing countries is who makes the tests. Ontario lays it out in the flier I mentioned above, noting that "standardized tests in the United States often are developed by commercial testing companies," while tests in Ontario are "created by qualified Ontario teachers with input from international testing experts."

In the United States, research has found that 89 percent of the estimated $1.7 billion states spend on testing materials goes to just six private vendors. Pearson Education alone accounts for some 39 percent of that money, followed by McGraw-Hill Education with 14 percent and Maple Grove at 13 percent. But some of that research is based on data that's several years old, without the transparency about total costs that would allow states and anyone who wants to keep tabs to assess the efficiency of these programs.

We do know that testing companies aggressively market new exams. Much like pharmaceutical companies courting doctors and policy makers to promote their drugs, test companies have their own lobbyists and offer retreats for education officials to learn about new options.

These vendors don't just make testing materials either. If a state or district wants to use their tests, then wouldn't it also want materials to help prepare students to succeed on those tests? Many of these same companies land deals to sell test preparation materials and pricey textbooks to the schools that buy their tests, raking in hundreds of millions of dollars more in revenue.

Companies do design their tests and textbooks around state and federal standards. But there's of course a lot of room for differentiation in how those standards are taught and what else does or doesn't get included. In that way, these private companies play a significant role in dictating what students in our public schools learn.

Critics of this arrangement say it applies a corporate mentality to education in ways that just don't make sense. Businesses are about clear, measurable results and holding people accountable when goals aren't met. Apply that philosophy to schools and it's clear why there would be a push for more and more testing, with black-and-white penalties when scores don't measure up. But schools aren't businesses, kids aren't clients and teachers aren't corporate employees.

By way of comparison, teachers develop the tests randomized groups of Finnish students take a few times in their school careers. The tests also can vary from school to school, since they're developed internally with national standards in mind. And the all-important Matriculation Examination is created by teams of educators who are subject matter experts and administered by an external board, which is appointed by the Ministry of Education and Culture. No private companies are involved.

It's also teachers who develop that all-important *Suneung* test in South Korea. A panel of roughly 500 professors and high school teachers are selected to spend a month together in a secluded location each year creating revised versions of the test. They have to give up their cell phones and cut off contact with the outside world while they work on the project. They aren't even supposed to tell anyone what they're doing, with panelists giving family members and coworkers excuses about mysterious business trips to explain their absence.

The test they create, along with test prep materials and even South Korean textbooks, are typically much simpler and less expensive than the pricey, hefty packets of full-color photos that American students get. "Textbooks" are often bundles of paper that staff has photocopied and stapled together, which means kids can write on them. And they're thrown away at the end of each year, so they don't become worn out or outdated as we've seen happen in disadvantaged districts in the United States.

It's much the same in China, Singapore, Japan and just about every other top PISA country I visited. Educators develop and administer these tests using simple materials. Results are turned around quickly. And while the development process is shrouded in mystery in some countries, others are transparent about methods, costs and changes to the tests each year. That's because there is no proprietary company information involved, unlike with American tests.

Change Afoot

For all of the reasons discussed in this chapter, there's been some level of pushback by researchers, educators and parents ever since No Child Left Behind triggered the current testing environment in the United States two decades ago. States have launched and then dropped a number of high-stakes tests in recent years, such as California formally abandoning its High School Exit Exam in 2017. And political figures as diverse as Democratic Sen. Bernie Sanders of Vermont to GOP Gov. Brian Kemp of Georgia have been leading the call to end high-stakes testing, saying it's a waste of resources that doesn't improve student outcomes.

Former Assistant Secretary of Education Diane Ravitch, who championed No Child Left Behind in its early days, has been speaking out since 2009 against how standardized testing has been used to penalize schools and teachers. In a 2016 video for the nonprofit she co-founded called Network for Public Education, Ravitch encouraged parents to have their kids "opt out" and refuse to participate in all standardized testing that year—a move she insisted would send a powerful message to policymakers. Hundreds of thousands of families skip tests each year, threatening to push testing levels below the participation threshold needed to meet federal standards. If that were to happen, Ravitch said, the government would be forced to reconsider its current systems.

Such efforts have picked up real momentum—triggering at least temporary change and potentially causing the long-term collapse of high-stakes testing culture—during the coronavirus pandemic. With permission from the U.S. Department of Education, states canceled standardized tests during the pandemic. Now state officials are looking around and realizing their students are still there, still learning and proving themselves via grades and teacher evaluations and college admissions. So there's a strong push by many policymakers and educators to convert temporary reductions in high-stakes testing into permanent changes.

A similar change is already afoot when it comes to SAT and ACT exams, which students have had to take for decades to get into most colleges and universities. Resistance to basing college admissions on these exams had already been building, with research showing inequities in the tests among low-income and diverse students, and that they weren't a good indicator of how students would perform in college anyway. So some colleges opted to stop looking at SAT or ACT scores for a few years as an experiment while they considered accepting other exams instead or designing a new assessment. But with some students unable or unwilling to take the usual pre-college tests during the height of the pandemic, more universities agreed to at least temporarily stop requiring them. In November 2021, the massive University of California system agreed to indefinitely stop considering results of SATs, ACTs or any potential replacement test as part of admissions. Instead, they'll focus on qualifiers such as grades, difficulty of high school courses taken, extracurricular activities, special skills, recommendations and application essays. After the first year without basing admissions on test scores, the UC system reported its largest, most diverse and, notably, most qualified applicant pool ever.

As research and attention around these issues grows, other countries also are reconsidering some of their standardized testing practices. In Japan, for example, criticism has mounted over how emphasis on the traditional university admissions exam has led to high rates of student depression and a lack of creativity and decision-making skills in students, since the Center Test was focused on rote memorization. So Japan rebranded its college admissions test as *Daigaku Nyugaku Kyotsu* and focused questions on assessing students' critical thinking skills, judgment and expression.

To be clear, after studying how these testing systems work in countries that perform the best on PISA each year, I didn't come away calling for the elimination of all standardized tests. After all, this entire book is based around results of a standardized exam, PISA, that measures higher-level skills and provides a useful framework for assessing global competitiveness. Research from places such as Finland and Canada shows a limited number of low-stakes standardized tests, developed by teachers, can provide valuable input. And I did witness how having one high-stakes test where the student, rather than the school or teacher, would be impacted by the results gave students motivation to study hard and perform well. If we can combine the best of these worlds, keeping in mind lessons that places like Japan have learned along the way, I'm confident we can reform our standardized testing system to make it a more cost-effective and useful tool to help drive the educational outcomes we need to be globally competitive once more.

What can I do?

Many decisions about standardized testing in the United States are made at the state and local levels, which makes it easier to change how those systems work. Here are 10 steps everyone can take right now to help set the wheels in motion, with space for you to jot down notes on plans for accomplishing each step or how it went once it's completed.

- Write letters to the editor and post on social media about your support for limiting standardized testing in U.S. schools to no more than six exams throughout students' school careers.

____

____

____

____

- Contact your state and federal representatives and tell them you support eliminating any policies that tie standardized test results to consequences for teachers, administrators or schools.

  ____

  ____

  ____

- Call for a ban on any standardized testing before grade three.

  ____

  ____

  ____

- Parents, opt your students out of all standardized testing this year. In doing so, send a letter to school leadership to explain why you don't think the current testing system is helpful for your child.

  ____

  ____

  ____

- Start a petition and collect signatures to present to your local school board that calls for a thorough review of all tests administered locally. Demand that results of that review be shared with the public and that repetitive or ineffectual tests be eliminated, that testing starts no earlier than grade three and that the number of tests be scaled back accordingly.

  ____

  ____

  ____

- Make a public push for companies that sell testing materials to be more transparent with past tests, how exams are developed, costs and other information that might help inform future decisions about exams. Call these companies out by name on social media, in letters to the editor and in public forums.

- Push your state representative to pass a law requiring that all standardized tests be developed by current teachers and other educators. And ask them to dedicate funds to that effort.

- Focus on alternative ways, other than standardized testing, to assess student progress in school. Ask your child, or children in your life, to regularly show you their work and talk with their teacher about their progress. Ask the teacher about projects and portfolios that can demonstrate achievement of certain skills.

- Teachers, if your school still uses high-stakes tests, resist the temptation and pressure to teach to the test. Instead, focus on teaching higher-level skills such as critical thinking and problem solving, and on instilling a love of learning. Have confidence that those skills will not only ensure solid performance on tests, but—more importantly—will produce students who are better equipped to be successful in college or careers.

"Technology is just a tool. In terms of getting the kids working together and motivating them, the teacher is the most important."

Bill Gates

At this elementary school and a neighboring high school in Hanoi, Vietnam, there was no technology in sight beyond the video camera the author, Keith Ballard, used to document his research.

Chapter Six

Technology is Secondary

Walking through the streets of Tokyo as an American can feel a bit like walking into our imagined future, with modern skyscrapers, high-speed trains and digital advertising all around. That backdrop makes walking into Japan's public schools feel even more like a step back in time.

There were traditional green chalkboards at the front of every general education classroom I saw while visiting schools in Tokyo's metro area, from Wada Primary School to Nanryou Junior High to Tokorozawa High School. I rarely saw computers or tablets in those classrooms. I also never saw a SMART Board, the interactive digital whiteboards that became all the rage in American classrooms a few years back. Teachers in Japan even tracked student grades in physical books, which they told me they guarded with their lives.

In short, many Japanese classrooms—and classrooms I visited in a number of countries that score the best on PISA exams each year, from Taiwan to Germany—didn't look much different than they looked a few decades earlier. That is, at least until the bell rang, triggering a Pavlovian wave of students grabbing for smartphones that had been burning holes in their pockets.

In Japan, the lack of technology in traditional classrooms is not about a lack of resources to fund digital learning tools. It's also certainly not about schools sticking their heads in the sand and not giving students the skills they need to thrive in the modern global economy. After all, Japan continues to pioneer new technologies and is routinely considered one of the most technologically advanced countries in the world. And often, the groundwork for that innovation is laid in Japan's high schools, where fundamental skills in math and science act as drivers for technology in the future.

Instead, Japan and some other high-scoring PISA countries resist making technology part of the everyday classroom experience for students at all grade levels because they recognize that such practices not only are expensive, but they also have not been proven to improve learning outcomes—and in some cases, they've even been shown to inhibit student achievement.

While we've been persuaded in the United States that educational technology can help personalize learning for students, save teachers time and equip students with digital skills they need for the modern world, there still isn't a ton of solid research around how digital learning tools such as websites, apps, online games and videos actually impact student learning. But educators who were paying attention were rocked by a 2015 study called "Students, Computers and Learning: Making the Connection" from the Organisation for Economic Co-operation and Development, the agency that developed and coordinates PISA testing around the world. The organization's landmark 204-page study evaluated use of computers and other classroom technology and the resulting student outcomes. The study found "no appreciable improvements in student achievement in reading, mathematics or science" in countries that had invested heavily in educational technology. Classroom technology also didn't help bridge gaps between advantaged and disadvantaged students as some companies and researchers had promised, according to the OECD. And most concerningly, the study found that "students who use computers very frequently at school do a lot worse in most learning outcomes, even after accounting for social background and student demographics."

Of course, improving test scores isn't the only reason to pursue particular educational practices. But while educators I spoke with in other countries cited that OECD study as at least informing their decisions related to use of technology in classrooms, it seemed to have little impact on opinions or actions in U.S. schools.

In 2019, four years after the study, a Gallup survey found most of the more than 3,000 public school teachers, principals and district-level administrators polled said they supported regular use of technology in classrooms. Many also said we need more of it, not less. Nearly two-thirds of pre-kindergarten through 12th-grade teachers, for example, said they used digital tools to teach every day, and more than half of teachers said they'd like to use educational technology even more often. There were signs in this survey that teachers, who of course see the benefits and drawbacks of such tools firsthand, were a bit less supportive than the other groups polled. Just 53 percent of teachers said they "fully support" increased use of digital learning tools, while 71 percent of principals and 75 percent of administrators held that view. But, while less than a third of people surveyed in each group said there was solid information available about the effectiveness of digital learning tools they use, more than eight in 10 agreed there is "great value" in using such tools in the classroom.

Of all the countries I visited for this project, I found none that had gone quite as full bore into embracing education technology at all levels as the United States. Here, the goal at many school districts for several years has been "one-to-one computing," where every student has access to a laptop or tablet. At the junior high and high school levels, many districts let students take those school-owned devices home with them to use for homework and studying. Some devices of course get lost or damaged. Students at my school routinely forget their laptops at home, so they don't have them to use during class. Or they forget to charge them and leave the charger at home, so they're dead by the time class starts.

The United States' approach to using technology in schools is in some ways the inverse of how places like South Korea invest in such tools, with lots of money spent on ed tech at all grade levels in the U.S. and little invested into creating cutting-edge vocational programs. Even in pre-kindergarten classes here, it's very common to see students use tablets or laptops at stations to do reading or math assignments just about every school day. And American administrators, who clearly are big supporters of classroom technology, encourage or even require their teachers to use such programs.

But despite the United States' massive investment in technology, as our scores on PISA and other standardized tests demonstrate, it has led to little or no measurable increase in student achievement. So we have to ask ourselves, is there possibly a more thoughtful approach to harnessing the promise of technology in our classrooms? And could changes in how and how often such tools are used be another way to shift educational dollars to programs that are more impactful for student outcomes?

While Japan isn't alone among top PISA countries in keeping technology simple for most students, there are several examples of high-performing education systems that do use a good deal of technology in the classroom.

One standout is Estonia, which was hosting a digital summit for education leaders from throughout Europe when I was there and continues to punch way above its weight for a country its size. Estonia was left impoverished after the collapse of the U.S.S.R. in 1991 but has transformed itself over the past few decades by positioning itself to be competitive in a global economy. Today, the entire nation relies heavily on digital tools for everything from voting to medical appointments to business operations. Gunda Tire, who is the national project manager for PISA in Estonia, told me, for example, that she hadn't signed a contract by hand in the last 10 years. And she said that same mindset carries over to education, with a decade-old nationalized system called the Estonia Education Information System. It lets teachers see student records from every year in school, so they can spot patterns and reduce administrative time. It also lets parents see their childrens' attendance records, what they're studying, what homework assignments they're working on and more, which has dramatically reduced absences across the nation. The idea, Tire said, is if both teachers and parents are aware of what is happening in school, they can take action immediately when problems crop up. That keeps them more involved, which, as we discussed in chapter one, is a key factor in having successful school systems.

As for students, it's very popular for Estonian schools to teach coding as early as first grade. There are lots of devices in schools, and Tire said students report enjoying the use of technology in their classes. But it's all about balance. "We cannot put our heads in the sand and say we'll just go with books," Tire said. On the other hand, "We have to find out how to use it reasonably."

When I visited Estonia, that meant laptops and tablets stayed in schools rather than going home with students. Teachers were careful to lay a foundation first the old-fashioned way, with pen and paper, before shifting kids to devices. Even then, they still solved math and physics problems by hand. "The computer is not the goal itself. The computer is the medium," Tire said. She cited that 2015 PISA study, which indicated that students who constantly use computers in all lessons in fact perform worse than students who use them just a bit or not at all. The focus, Tire said, is on reasonable use of digital learning tools in classrooms that's blended with traditional instruction. So although there is lots of technology used in Estonia and in some other high-performing education systems, there are a number of key differences in how and when it's used.

At the time I was finishing up this book, there certainly were more question marks punctuating discussions on digital learning tools than on any other subject we're examining, with the global COVID-19 pandemic reshaping the world of education technology more rapidly than anyone thought possible. But in reading the latest reports and talking with principals and teachers and parents I've stayed in touch with around the world, most seem to be keeping in mind the same core principles that stood out to me during my classroom visits over the past decade. If we can steal some of those best practices, my research suggests, it would help American schools use technology more efficiently while also helping American students reap more of the benefits digital learning tools can offer without so many of the potential drawbacks that we're seeing play out with our kids today.

Basics Come First

There were no computers in the eighth-grade math class I visited at the celebrated Gradia Vocational School in Jyvaskyla, Finland. The instructor told me he still believes it's better for students to read from textbooks and learn to work out problems with pen and paper first. He said he had yet to see an online math program that was as effective as the traditional method. Finnish students I spoke with said over and over that they couldn't imagine relying heavily on computers to do their math assignments, in particular, with traditional textbooks and workbooks still preferred for that type of work.

At about the same time I was speaking with those students, education journalist Natalie Wexler was making a startling discovery as she watched elementary students in the United States use technology in their classrooms to work on math. She described her findings in a 2019 article for MIT Technology Review:

> *In a first-grade classroom I visited a few years ago, most of the six-year-olds were using iPads or computers. They were working independently on math problems supposedly geared to their ability, while the teacher worked separately with a small group. I watched as one boy, whom I'll call Kevin, stared at an iPad screen that directed him to "combine 8 and 3." A struggling reader (like almost all his classmates), he pressed the "Listen" button. But he still didn't try to provide an answer.*
>
> *"Do you know what 'combine' means?" I asked. Finding that he didn't, I explained it meant 'add.'" ...*
>
> *Then I found a boy staring at a computer screen showing a number line with the question* What number comes before 84? *He listened to the instructions and tried 85, then 86, then 87, getting error messages each time. Thinking the problem was the size of the numbers, I asked him what number comes before four. "Five?" he guessed. It dawned on me that he didn't understand the word 'before'. Once I explained it, he immediately clicked on 83.*
>
> *I returned to Kevin to see whether he had been able to combine 8 and 3. But I found he was drawing bright pink lines on the iPad with his finger—one of the gizmo's numerous distracting capabilities.*
>
> *"Can you answer the question?" I asked.*
>
> *"I don't want to." He sighed. "Can I play a game?"*

Clearly, the students Wexler observed lacked the foundational reading comprehension skills they needed to understand the math questions their iPads were serving up.

One of the biggest problems I see with the use of technology in U.S. schools is that we seem to have tried to use it as a silver bullet to compensate for other gaps in our education system, from poor reading skills to overwhelmed teachers to bored students. But our lack of progress on PISA and other standardized tests—even as school use of technology has exploded—shows that just doesn't work. You simply can't make up for shortcomings such as a lack of high-quality teachers, not enough support at home or poor student motivation by handing each kid an iPad.

The inverse does appear to be true, on the other hand. Even though scarcity of resources means there are almost no digital learning tools in most classrooms in Vietnam, the country has continued to improve its scores on PISA exams. I visited 10 schools in Vietnam, including in the capital, Hanoi, and in Ho Chi Minh City, and I saw simple classrooms with green chalkboards up front in each one. Some concerns were raised (but later largely dismissed) about Vietnam's most recent test scores, so its results weren't included in 2018 reports. But in prior years, Vietnam showed rapid improvement, surpassing the United States in 2012 and 2015 despite its high level of poverty and extremely low use of technology in schools. In the most recent year with published results, when reading, math and science scores are combined, Vietnam ranked No. 11 in the world. That suggests that a quality foundation of basic skills can make up for any deficit from not having technology in classrooms, while our results show the opposite is not true.

Motivating students is one of the most common reasons I hear for why the United States is using so much technology in our classrooms. After all, ask kids and they'll generally tell you it's "fun" to use tablets and learning games in class. But in my experience, technology tools seem shiny and new, and therefore motivate students, only for a very short period of time. The excitement soon wears off and students are bored again, with the technology then serving—as it did for Kevin in the story above—as little more than a distraction.

We saw this unfold in real time in the earliest days of the COVID-19 pandemic. When students first shifted to distance learning, the devices they got to take home and the new programs we were using were exciting. Everyone logged on and was enthusiastic about the change of pace that brought some newfound freedoms, despite the chaos going on around us. But in a matter of days, I noticed the number of students logging in and working through our exercises started to plummet. Soon, very few students were regularly using the digital learning tools to stay engaged in their coursework, with as few as six out of 120 students doing the assignments on some days. Parents would ignore my emails or, when I reached them, throw up their hands and say they didn't know how to get their kids to do the remote work either. Sure, there were other factors contributing to that specific situation. But for me, that experience still serves as a good example of how technology can't compensate for a broader lack of motivation that students in top-performing countries don't experience on the same scale as American students, thanks to engrained system-wide opportunities such as more student choice and solid vocational programs.

This experience correlates with research that shows students are more motivated to answer a question, or to complete work in general, when a teacher asks them to do it rather than when they get a prompt from a digital device. It's easy to skip a question on a tablet and not so easy to ignore a teacher asking you a question. Plus students, especially in their early years, generally want to please their teachers. And increasingly as they get older, they want to look smart in front of their classmates. So there's more motivation for them to get answers right and complete assignments when there is human accountability rather than just a completion notification popping up on a tablet screen.

Along with student motivation, the other argument I commonly hear in support of increased use of technology in the classroom is that it will give our students skills they need to succeed in the "modern world." But much of our everyday use of digital learning tools in schools does little more than boost students' existing proficiency and comfort with basic digital devices. And with so many students now using smartphones, tablets and computers from a young age, most no longer need much help on that score.

This gap was demonstrated in results from the most recent International Computer and Information Literacy study, which assessed eighth graders on two digital skill sets. The United States placed No. 5 of the 14 participating countries on computer and information literacy, with Denmark, Moscow, Korea and Finland outperforming us by significant margins. For computer literacy, American students scored just slightly above average and only one point higher than Germany, which was using very little technology in classrooms at the time of the 2018 exam. When it came to computational thinking, American students scored dead in the middle and just below average. The fact that Germany did almost as well as the United States on these computer literacy tests while having much lower levels of technology use in schools suggested to researchers that strong foundational skills in subjects such as literacy and math translate to better digital skills, even with less frequent use of the digital tools themselves.

When most people talk about how educational technology can prepare students for the "modern world," research shows that what they really have in mind are programs that teach coding, programming and robotics—advanced digital skills that require specialized instruction and equipment and substantial time for students to master. That's where robust vocational education programs come into play in other countries, starting in junior high or high school. Places such as Japan and Germany keep technology simple for younger students and even many traditional classes in secondary schools, focusing those resources instead on vocational programs to ensure that digital tools are top-of-the-line when they can actually help prepare students for careers in fields dependent on technology.

I saw this approach on display at Seoul Robotics High School. While specialized classrooms absolutely had advanced, industry-standard equipment, many of the school's regular classrooms had simple white boards at the front of the room and little technology to be seen. Instructor Hyunbin Im told me he feels it's very important for students to learn to solve problems by hand first, working out solutions to programming questions with pen and paper before plugging the information into a computer to operate advanced computer numerical control, or CNC, machines. "Programming cannot solve everything," he said, arguing it's "much more important" for students to understand the basics so they'll know what to do when problems arise or the technology changes.

The dynamic was similar in Singapore. Outside of the nation's "future schools," where technology is emphasized, I didn't see a lot of computers in most classrooms. But when students got to advanced vocational classrooms, the technology there was as advanced as it gets, focused on artificial intelligence and robotics.

China to this day keeps education extremely low-tech for younger students, often not even letting kids use calculators to do math work until they reach around 13 years old. This holistic "if it ain't broke, why fix it?" approach may still be driven to some extent by a lack of resources. But teachers I spoke with said they want to be sure kids know how to do the math themselves before they start using technology to save time as they move on to more advanced calculations. Then, when students reach high school and get into vocational programs, they're using advanced technology in their classes.

That stance appears to be continuing even through the COVID-19 pandemic. When it comes to moving quickly with new programs and technology, despite the nation's massive size, few places can make changes as quickly as China due to its centralized, government-controlled system. Still, in talking with a friend who's teaching in China right now, he said more students do have personal devices and more online tutoring is taking place due to the pandemic. Otherwise, he said, the pattern of keeping education low-tech for younger students and in traditional classes remains the norm.

Whenever I discuss the high level of achievement of Chinese students with Americans, they are quick to try to deflect by insisting China is focused on rote memorization and "drill and kill" learning, rather than on producing creative thinkers as the United States does. But remember that PISA tests specifically evaluate problem solving skills, not memorization of facts. And when it comes to technology, we can see that China is now dominating one arena after another, from supercomputing to artificial intelligence. That type of innovation doesn't spring from an education system focused solely on rote learning. It's clear that China's approach to education isn't producing kids who are robots, it's producing kids who will make the robots of tomorrow.

The common thread here is that many top PISA countries are using technology less with younger students and in traditional secondary classrooms, and they're simply doing a better job at building a strong foundation of skills, support programs and student choice into their schools. We need to fix the other problems we've discussed earlier in this book first. Then, rather than relying on technology to try to motivate kids or make up for other shortfalls in our system, we can move on to implementing other key strategies I observed in schools around the world that can help us better harness the power of technology in our classrooms at home.

Slower on the Uptake

In terms of early adoption of one-to-one computing goals, use of technology with younger students and being first to pilot a number of digital learning tools in schools, The United States scores near the top of the charts. If these programs were proving effective for student learning, that would mean bragging rights over the countries that lagged behind. Instead, with those countries outperforming us on nearly every metric, I'd argue there's a lesson to learn about the benefits of being slower to embrace each bit of shiny new educational technology that comes along.

Much like with testing and textbook companies, as we discussed in chapter five, technology companies obviously have a financial interest in selling their products to schools. I can't help but think of my own career many years ago, when I used to be a salesman at a pharmaceutical company. We would show doctors studies our own company had commissioned that "proved" why our drugs were the best on the market to address a given condition. Then we would persuade those doctors to start prescribing our products, wooing them with promises of success stories or even with weekends at fancy retreats. But as the opioid epidemic and scandals around companies such as Purdue Pharma have brought to light, we all now know that drug companies can get doctors to produce studies saying basically anything you want them to say. I'm not suggesting that all educational technology companies go to the extremes that Big Pharma has. I'm just saying we should be aware of those dynamics and therefore skeptical of the promises companies make, use caution when considering new programs and rely on solid, independent research to understand how any tools might impact student learning.

Jumping back to that 2019 Gallup survey on digital learning tools, we can see that about two-thirds of administrators, or some 65 percent, said their district had stopped using a digital learning tool they had previously adopted. The most common reason administrators gave for dumping those products were that they did not improve student learning outcomes. That means most U.S. schools are spending money and class time on digital learning tools that have no proven benefits for students because they were too quick to jump at the promises of the apparent latest and greatest idea.

Never has this danger been clearer than during the COVID-19 pandemic. Dark as it may sound, the pandemic of course has been a dream in many ways for most technology companies, ed tech included. Schools reported being inundated in early months of the pandemic with pitches from companies promising to give them quick and easy ways to transition to online learning, keep students engaged, tutor kids and fill every other need highlighted by the crisis. Some companies later proved to be incompetent at best, and predatory at worst. Meanwhile, ed tech companies, which were previously the less sexy version of their Silicon Valley counterparts, saw their stock prices and investment dollars skyrocket. Ed tech was estimated to be a $107 billion market in 2015. By 2025, the industry is expected to more than triple to a new valuation of $350 billion. This could of course bring about some tremendous innovation. But it also has opened the door to even more ed tech being adopted quickly, without research to back it up or systems in place to keep new programs running optimally. That's true for countries all over the world, who were forced by the pandemic to rapidly implement technology they otherwise might not have considered for at least some time. But other countries had better systems in place before the pandemic to help avoid some of those pitfalls.

In Singapore, for example, they have long been quick to research but much slower to act when considering new educational technologies for schools. As you might recall from chapter two, the nation's teacher training programs are concentrated within a single institute at an advanced research university. Educators there study new ideas for technology as they come along, putting them through the wringer to gauge their impact on learning outcomes as well as cost efficiency, the teacher training they require and other key details. If a digital learning tool proves effective and efficient, they adopt it across all schools in the country and accompany it with comprehensive support. They also continue measuring how a given technology is working in schools and make adjustments as needed. Cameras in classrooms feed over to the National Institute of Education, not to police teachers but to assess how new programs including technology are working so they can make recommendations and changes as needed.

Rather than purchase devices for every student, Singapore found ways to implement some proven digital learning tools with students using their own smartphones. Many countries, including New Zealand, have embraced this concept of BYOD or "bring your own device." Students who don't have a personal device can borrow one from school in Singapore. But with strong support for and from parents in a country that transformed itself from largely illiterate when it gained independence in 1965 to one of the most well-educated countries in the world today, educators I spoke with said families—who, as we discussed in chapter one, get a lot of support from their government—typically found a way to provide their students with the devices they needed, without relying on schools to provide them.

To further keep costs down, education systems in Singapore and many other countries have close relationships with the business sector, which partners with them to support getting technology into classrooms. This was most evident in vocational programs, as we discussed in chapter four. Companies see this as a good investment because they're helping train potential future employees. And schools remain selective in what technology they accept, then carefully add new tools to comprehensive programs as needed.

Here in the United States, when companies such as Microsoft or Google help schools get laptops or tablets or reliable internet service, it's viewed not as a business investment but instead as an act of charity. This creates a different dynamic, with schools expected to be grateful for whatever they get and to quickly start using it in their classrooms.

But now that some of these digital learning tools have been tested over time, which ones are showing solid promise in terms of positive impacts for students and efficiency for schools outside of dedicated vocational programs? I don't want to recommend specific brand names here, so let's talk concepts.

One promising solution is platforms such as the Estonia Education Information System, which can help parents stay connected to their kids' schoolwork and help teachers cut administrative time. More schools started using such educational platforms to post and track work during the pandemic. But even before COVID-19 hit, many teachers in New Zealand posted their lesson plans on a class website so students who couldn't attend in person could see what they were doing and stay caught up. China also had two virtual learning platforms before the pandemic, which students could use when they missed a class or wanted to do additional studies. The platforms also already featured some of the best recorded teaching lessons from the prior eight years, which the Ministry of Education was using to educate other teachers. So the country was able to essentially use those lessons and beefed-up systems to let all students quickly transition to online learning as COVID-19 shuttered classrooms. Such programs, of course, take resources to create upfront, but don't take much to maintain and have very few potential drawbacks for those involved.

One other digital learning tool praised by Andreas Schleicher, who oversaw that crucial 2015 OECD study as the organization's director for Education and Skills, is "flexbooks," or digital textbooks. There are a number of potential benefits from using them. They can be quickly and easily updated as new information arises or preferred delivery methods change. They can include links to online articles and visual and audio material. They're more cost effective for schools. They're better for the environment and for kids' backs, since they no longer need to haul around hefty physical books. That's why many countries, including Estonia and Finland, have already transitioned some or all of their textbooks online.

While there are plenty of benefits, there also are some drawbacks to this digital tool, including the research discussed earlier that shows we absorb information better from printed materials than screens. And once again math, in particular, seems more challenging to fully transition to digital. That's why most places that have shifted to offering digital books still often have physical textbooks available. I watched as a student at Gradia Jyvaskyla Lyseon, the upper secondary school in Jyvaskyla, Finland, worked with a printed math textbook open in front of his computer screen. The student told me that while he was fine with digital textbooks in subjects such as Finnish and English, he preferred to use the hard copy for math—and didn't see that changing anytime soon.

I also saw promising work being done using technology to enhance foreign language instruction, so students could hear native speakers, have online chats in their new language, or record themselves speaking and get feedback. Virtual field trips can take our kids to places they might otherwise never go. And I saw a program at work in Singapore that let students text questions about whatever they were working on, and the questions would show up on a screen at the front of the room, so no one got overlooked or silenced and everyone participated.

With new tools constantly emerging, there's evidence that some high-performing PISA countries had started to speed up the incorporation of technology into their classrooms even before the pandemic hit. Finland, in particular, has come a long way in this regard in a relatively short amount of time. When journalist and author Amanda Ripley visited schools in Finland during research for her book *The Smartest Kids in the World*, she noted that classrooms there were almost devoid of technology. We discussed that phenomenon, which she said surprised her given how advanced Finnish society was at the time in other ways. But since Ripley's book was published in 2013, Finnish schools have started using digital learning tools much more as part of the regular school day. In talking with students and teachers there now, Finland seems to be nearly on par with the United States in terms of using technology to do blended learning at all levels and across a variety of classes. Still, there are several key distinctions in how they embrace digital learning tools.

First, Finland let educational technology develop for several decades before it dove in. That allowed time for research that could inform their decisions regarding how and when to use these tools. So rather than spend lots of money and time experimenting with ed tech in classrooms, they took a "wait and see" approach for years before their recent rapid increase in using such tools.

Second, as discussed in the last section of this chapter, Finland created an extremely strong learning foundation in its schools before adding a good amount of educational technology into the mix. That means it's not using digital tools to try to fill other gaps, but to augment programs already in place. And so far, this delayed approach with a solid base behind it is showing early promise for both efficiency and student outcomes.

Still, PISA scores in Finland and in places such as Australia, which do use a good amount of ed tech, have begun to stagnate or fall in recent years. And Professor Pasi Sahlberg, who studies comparative education and is a former director general of Finland's Ministry of Education, says he fears those declines are connected to students overusing technology both in and out of the classroom. There might not be much educators can do about kids increasingly staring at phones or computers rather than reading books or playing on their own time. But even some of the countries that avoided jumping on the ed tech bandwagon as quickly as the United States apparently also need to keep many of the lessons from this chapter in mind as they move forward.

Other countries, too, have made their own missteps in trying to jump on new educational technology. South Korea drew headlines for a pilot program that brought robots into kindergarten and primary school classrooms in the early 2000s, with a goal of having such robots in all of the nation's kindergarten classrooms by 2013. Robots such as Engkey and iRobi were touted as being able to help with various functions, such as taking attendance, coaching students in English lessons, reading stories to students and otherwise backing up the human teacher in the classroom.

Researchers were cautiously optimistic about the potential for these devices as long as they were overseen by qualified teachers. Some of those products have since flopped, but South Korea continues to experiment with teaching robots for young students.

One other problem that I've seen in some of the top-performing countries, along with the United States, is that some of the pressure to quickly adopt new technology in classrooms is being driven by test preparation efforts. Many high-stakes tests are now largely online, which makes it easier for administrators to distribute and score exams and to compile information about results. But that is pressuring teachers and schools to make sure students not only have the knowledge they need to answer the questions, but also the technology skills they need to do it in the digital format that's now used. One math teacher I spoke with at Finland's Gradia Jyvaskyla Lyseon said that while most students still preferred to use pen and paper to work out their problems, he had to use more technology in the classroom to ensure they were prepared to work that way on the all-important matriculation exam they'd take at the end of high school. I can't see this trend going away anytime soon, with standardized tests increasingly administered in part or entirely online. So it'll be up to educators to make sure they're not sacrificing the quality of subject matter instruction to teach to the digital aspect of those tests.

Back it Up

Another key distinction between how top-performing PISA countries and the U.S. use technology in the classroom is in the support schools provide to make these programs work.

First and foremost, teachers need solid training on how to effectively use these tools. American schools tend to talk a good game when it comes to training teachers on technology. Most, like my own, pay one teacher a small stipend to be their technology representative. That person is expected to help coordinate training and other needs for technology integration. But with U.S. teachers so overwhelmed, and with such limited investment in this area, it's a very mixed bag when it comes to how helpful such representatives are able to be. That means teachers often are left on their own to seek help and try to figure out how to use any new digital learning tools. Or, as often happens, they simply give up and don't use the fancy technology the school invested in because they just aren't comfortable with it.

As a 27-year industry veteran, I'll admit that I'm not always quick to pick up on the latest ed tech. A perfect example of this is with the SMART Boards I referenced early in this chapter. When our district started to implement these interactive whiteboards, we were told they were the way of the future and there was no going back. We're the second largest secondary school district in the United States and we put these boards in just about every classroom, using rolling versions that cost more than $10,000 apiece. The problem is, no one ever taught us how to use them. We had few trainers in our school district. And despite my requests for help, no one ever came to walk me through it until it clicked, the way we're taught to do with our own students. Instead, our technology representative just forwarded along some video tutorials. So, as district research later showed, I was among a majority of local teachers who essentially started using a $10,000 SMART Board as little more than a glorified TV screen.

By way of contrast, as we discussed in chapter two, countries that score near the top on PISA exams each year give their teachers time daily for collaboration and mentorship work with colleagues. They also regularly provide extended training opportunities. When I was in Singapore, they were hosting a conference sponsored by the National Institute of Technology. Teachers in Singapore are guaranteed the right to at least 100 hours of free or low-cost professional development annually. The federal government encouraged educators to attend the technology conference, so principals were giving teachers freedom to spend time learning about the latest tools, strategies and research around using ed tech in their classrooms.

The SMART Board debacle also illustrates another key problem with how educational technology is too often implemented in the United States: While American schools are quick to jump on buying the latest and greatest technology, they often don't set aside resources to maintain these pricey tools. When our SMART Boards started to break, the district quickly learned they were very expensive to repair. And since most of us weren't really using them anyway, we watched them get hauled out to our electronics recycling bin to get wet or otherwise damaged and then sold off in a government auction. Then, the district simply replaced them with cheap TVs from Costco.

A similar pattern unfolded with the CNC machine our district received. I heard one of our Career and Technical Education classes had one of these high-end machines. But when I went to tour the program, I didn't see the machine anywhere in sight. So I asked the instructor, who walked me outside. In an alley behind the classroom, I found this massive piece of equipment half-covered in a tarp, getting damaged by exposure to the elements. I was told no one on staff knew how to run it and the district never made efforts to maintain it, so that was where it had landed.

As with so many other problems in society, the COVID-19 pandemic shined a harsh spotlight on the lack of teacher training and technical support for digital learning tools in American classrooms. My school's principal assured us teachers we'd get full training and support with the online programs they wanted us to pivot to in a matter of weeks. In reality, I was simply told to watch some instructional videos. I ended up paying a professional out of my own pocket to help me get quickly up to speed on the new technologies we were using. Many teachers similarly reported spending more time on troubleshooting tech problems than on preparing and scoring lessons or interacting with students and parents. Some of our best schools also had their systems hacked during this time, since software was not kept updated to prevent such problems.

Since countries with top-tier education systems are typically slower and more selective about adopting new digital learning tools, they don't have as much pricey equipment to maintain. And for the gear they do buy, they generally do a better job at dedicating resources or developing corporate partnerships to ensure the tools are in working order or quickly replaced. In countries where students were expected to regularly use computers or tablets during class, for example, schools had chargers on hand for each device instead of expecting kids to remember to tote them back and forth. That's why, in touring more than 170 schools around the world, I almost never saw a laptop sitting unused because it was dead or a high-dollar piece of equipment rusting, as I saw with the CNC machine in my own district. And I did see trained teachers in places such as Ireland and Canada actively using functional SMART Boards during their daily lessons.

Find the Sweet Spot

So if schools build strong foundations before flooding classrooms with technology, if they are slow to adopt new tools until there is research to prove some benefit, if they properly train teachers to use this gear and keep it maintained, how often should teachers be using digital learning tools in their classrooms? While there isn't much definitive research to answer this question, what research exists is clear: If students don't use technology at all, their scores on comprehensive exams such as PISA are a bit lower than their peers. But if they use technology in school a lot, their scores go down significantly.

So what's "a lot?" And what's the sweet spot? The OECD's 2015 study found student test scores were highest for students who generally reported using computers in their classes "once or twice a week." Scores dropped a good deal for students who reported using them "almost every day" and fell significantly for students who said they used computers in class "every day." And in some subject areas, such as math, students who used computers even an average amount in class scored a bit lower than students who used them less than that.

The study found that of the seven countries that reported using the internet in school the most, three of them—Australia, New Zealand and Sweden—were showing "significant declines" in reading performance, while three more—Spain, Norway and Denmark—had results that had "stagnated." Meanwhile, the countries with the lowest levels of reported internet use in school—South Korea, Shanghai, Hong Kong and Japan—were among the top performers on PISA exams.

A 2019 study by the Reboot Foundation found similar results. "Fourth-grade students who reported using tablets in 'all or almost all' classes scored 14 points lower on the reading exam than students who reported 'never' using classroom tablets," the study found. "This difference in scores is the equivalent of a full grade level, or a year's worth of learning."

One reason experts believe this divergence occurs is that there are decades of research to show we absorb less of what we read on screens than what we read on paper. So even if students spend the same amount of time studying the same material on a computer, they'll retain less of the information than if they'd studied it in a textbook, handout or other printed material.

We've already discussed how technology generally doesn't provide sustained motivation. And for uninterested students, there also are more opportunities for distractions on digital devices—particularly if they have access to the internet.

Lastly, it's much easier for students to cheat by, say, copying and pasting responses and trying to pass them off as their own work. While digital tools that help teachers catch such practices also are improving, the damage from a learning standpoint will have already been done.

Aside from lowering student achievement, using too much technology in schools also has other proven negative consequences for students—which educators in other countries I visited seemed to be more concerned about than many American teachers, judging by those surveys calling for more ed tech in classrooms.

Rather than help with equity issues, for example, use of technology has been proven to exacerbate them in many low-income schools. There certainly are exceptions to the rule, and we'll discuss this topic in depth in the final chapter of this book. But research is showing that low-income schools that invest heavily in technology tend to push disadvantaged kids to spend much more time on devices than the above guidelines suggest, using tablets, for example, to make up for a lack of quality teachers or resources to serve special needs students. Those issues aren't such a problem in top-performing countries, as we discussed in chapter two. So other places aren't feeling that negative impact of technology in the same way.

This is another problem highlighted by the pandemic. Districts with more poor and otherwise disadvantaged students had the biggest problems with students falling behind and disconnecting after classes went online. If technology can help provide equity, shouldn't it have been the other way around? But COVID-19 showed that students with other obstacles were more likely to get lost when learning entirely online. They of course had more trouble with access to devices and the internet. And they were less likely to have parents with the time or energy to help them, and to be there to make them stay on task.

Low-income schools also tend to use technology with a "drill and kill" approach, where devices are used to drill students on skills such as math equations and spelling. Such programs have shown to be the least effective way to use technology in schools. So while the intentions might have been admirable, rather than helping balance out inequities, low-income schools that are heavily using technology in classrooms are very likely doing more harm than good.

Finally, there are proven negative physical, emotional, behavioral and mental health implications for kids who spend too much time on digital devices. Lots of screen time is increasingly being linked to increases in loneliness, anxiety, depression and self-harm. A study published in JAMA Psychiatry in March 2022 found a 20 percent increase in behavior problems such as aggression and difficulty paying attention among kids 12 and younger who spend lots of time on digital devices such as phones or tablets. Negative impacts do shrink significantly if kids are using devices for educational purposes or to connect with friends, the study found. But screen time still adds up. Recent research from San Diego State University found that teens who spend more than three or four hours a day in front of screens have higher rates of depression, with negative effects arising even faster for kids who are spending much of that time on social media. Such platforms are designed to hook us and keep us coming back for more. So to expect teens to use digital devices for schoolwork without sometimes getting distracted by such programs just isn't realistic. And early research is showing a significant increase during the pandemic in mental health issues made worse by too much screen time, with depression, teen suicide and other problems rising across the board. Kids need to socialize. They need good teachers looking out for them. And online connections just aren't the same.

Such research is why, when China's Ministry of Education sent out recommendations for teachers shifting to online instruction during the pandemic, it suggested limiting the online lessons themselves to 20 minutes, then giving students time to do independent work off-screen before coming back to the computer to share and discuss what they'd done.

When it comes to how much time students spend using technology in classrooms, one final distinction I noticed in speaking with teachers around the world is that, while many American teachers like me feel pressured to use more and more digital learning tools even if we don't love them or aren't trained to use them, teachers in top-tier schools tend to have more freedom to decide when and where to use ed tech. It goes back to that same single word: trust. Teachers I spoke with even in places such as Canada—which uses a fair amount of technology in classes overall, including SMART Boards and personal learning devices—said such practices generally aren't mandated. They typically do lots of blended learning, mixing technology in with other learning activities. But teachers said if they prefer to teach certain subjects or skills the old-fashioned way, they're free to do so.

That's in stark contrast to the way I and many other American teachers I've spoken to have been made to feel on this point. Here, the sense is that if you're not using as much technology as possible, then you're not doing the best for your kids. A former principal at my middle school told our math teachers to make their students work online, even though the teachers and the students told him the program they were using wasn't great. His response was that the district had bought the equipment and programs, so they needed to use them. He would similarly berate me for being a low-tech teacher, pushing me to incorporate more digital devices into my music classes. I tried to explain that my decades of teaching had convinced me that, unless they were solely focused on music production, kids needed to learn the basics of understanding and playing music the traditional way first before we could start adding in technology. That principal didn't trust me to know the best way to teach my kids, insisting that if we were going to get them ready for the future, we needed to train them on computers often and in all subject areas. I'm convinced he simply wanted to be able to tout that our students were doing "digital music" rather than taking the time to understand what methods really worked best for our students and subject matter.

Of course, we should all continue to learn new methods and update our skills, if and when our schools do make such training available. But just as research suggests that too much technology isn't great for students, it also supports treating teachers as professionals and giving them flexibility to determine what the use of ed tech in their classrooms should look like.

When it comes to technology in classrooms, there do appear to be some silver linings created by the explosion in digital learning tools that was triggered by the pandemic. For one, American teachers now report that they feel better able to use technology in their lessons, both in terms of skills and access. A whopping 87 percent of teachers surveyed by EdWeek Research Center in summer 2020 said their technology skills improved during the pandemic, perhaps helping to close some of the gaps created by our previous shortcomings in properly training teachers. Students have much greater access to devices and to internet service now. We have better systems in place to track students and capture those who can't or won't attend class to keep them from falling behind. There is also much greater access to consumer ed tech products, such as online tutoring programs that supplement classroom learning or fill in gaps when students are out of school.

However, I'd argue that the pandemic also has proved what other countries have long seemed to recognize more than the United States has: online learning doesn't benefit students as much as being in a classroom, learning from a highly trained teacher and their peers. The pivot to remote learning was an abject failure in my own classes, with study after study showing overall student achievement fell significantly during this time. Clearly there are kids who are great at doing independent work, but many are not. And with online learning, it's so easy to get lost or give up, with few immediate consequences for students. So even as some experts predict the pandemic has forever changed the way schools use technology, my hope is that we can all step back, assess how things went and keep the lessons of this chapter in mind as we make conscientious decisions about the best ways to incorporate technology into classrooms going forward.

What can I do?

There is ample opportunity for everyone—from parents to teachers, and from researchers to those in the business world—to have a positive impact on the way technology is used in schools. Here are 10 steps folks can take right now to help set the wheels in motion, with space for you to jot down notes on plans for accomplishing each step or how it went once it's completed.

- Demand or commission solid, independent research to support the efficacy of digital learning tools used in schools before they are incorporated into classrooms.

- Push to limit technology use in classrooms for students under 12 by supporting related legislation, speaking at your local school board meeting or writing a letter to the editor in your local paper.

- Support programs in schools that are aimed at training kids in specific technology skills, such as coding, robotics, digital photography and spreadsheets.

- Contact your local school district and insist that they have clear plans in place and funds budgeted to fully train teachers and to maintain any digital learning tools before they are adopted.

  ____

  ____

  ____

- Contact technology companies with proven products and ask them to partner with schools by providing equipment and training for teachers and students.

  ____

  ____

  ____

- Educators, outside of technology-focused vocational programs, aim for the "sweet spot" of having students use computers in class no more than once or twice a week.

  ____

  ____

  ____

- Parents, develop systems to limit screen time for your kids. Experts recommend taking all screens out of the bedroom before bedtime, delaying social media use until kids reach high school and creating a reasonable screen time budget with kids.

  ____

  ____

  ____

- Adults, observe and regularly talk to the kids in your life about their use of technology. Which programs in school are helpful and which are not? Do they ever feel depressed when spending time online? Take action as appropriate.

  ____

  ____

- Share solid research about the benefits and drawbacks of technology use in school. Start conversations about the topic with friends and family, on social media and in online groups.

- Model and incorporate "digital detox" time for students/kids. Math teachers, make one day a week a calculator-free day. English teachers, have students turn in an assignment that's handwritten for a change. Parents, turn off the GPS and show your kids how to use a map to navigate somewhere.

"I would teach music, physics, and philosophy but more importantly music, for the patterns in music and all the arts are the keys to learning."

Plato

A music instructor teaches ukulele at Mikkolan Koulu Basic School in Vantaa, Finland.

Chapter Seven

The Arts and Culture are Essential

Art classrooms at the Zespół Państwowych Szkół Plastycznych Arts School in Krakow, Poland, are all designed with walls of windows looking north. That's so budding student artists have plenty of even light throughout the day to paint their still life scenes and sculpt statues, inspired by masters of the craft.

Wooden shelves running the length of one studio wall are packed with busts students have made. The best work is offered for sale during a special art show held each year just before Christmas.

An art teacher's office is a studio within the studio, with his own work displayed alongside taxidermy birds and small mammals used as models for student portraits.

In a classroom across the hall during my visit, students sat in a circle around a table that held a kettle and other kitchen items. Each head was bent over a slanted art table, as students used charcoal to carefully sketch out their unique takes on the mundane.

Poland, which ranked No. 11 overall on the most recent PISA exam, places a high value on arts education—as do most countries with highly successful education systems in place.

In China, for example, most kindergarten teachers know how to play the piano so they can incorporate songs into their curriculum. Slovenia has a Music and Ballet Conservatory that's open to every qualified student, while all Japanese students learn calligraphy along with other art forms from specialized instructors.

These countries invest in quality arts education programs. And, unlike in the United States, they're generally not on the chopping block when budgets get tight. That's because these countries have a clear understanding of the vast benefits that come with having consistent, well-developed art and culture programs in public schools. They're not seen simply as bonus or elective courses to squeeze in for students who have space in their schedules. They're part of the core curriculum given to all students throughout their time in public school, with options for dedicated and advanced arts curriculum in vocational schools for students who want to pursue careers as musicians and painters, sculptors and dancers, graphic designers and photographers. And students in these countries aren't seen as performing well academically *despite* the time, attention and resources spent on arts education, but thanks in part to that very decision.

From an economic perspective alone, there is monetary value in providing steady, high-quality arts education. Sure, it's not easy to make a living working in the arts. But a report in 2021 from the U.S. Bureau of Economic Analysis and the National Endowment for the Arts said the arts contributed 4.5 percent to the country's gross domestic product during the last year on record. That was more than either the agriculture or transportation sectors. If we had well-funded arts programs in schools across the country, and if we encouraged or even required students to take more of these classes, it's safe to assume the sector would contribute even more to our national economy.

Arts education also is another way to help tackle one of the biggest problems with secondary students in American schools today: a lack of motivation. Unlike with technology, as we discussed in the last chapter, regular arts education has been shown to have a long-term, positive impact on student motivation to come to school. Students who are enrolled in visual arts, music, theater or dance classes have lower dropout rates than other students, for example, even after controlling for other factors.

As a music teacher, I've of course seen the power of arts education to motivate students, anchor them to school and give them a social network of like-minded friends. Remember Liliana from chapter four? She told me that my mariachi class had kept her coming to class and gave her something to look forward to each day. Once she went to high school and she no longer had access to such a program, her interest in school plummeted. And last I spoke with her, she was on the verge of dropping out.

There are emotional and mental health benefits to steady arts education as well, as scores of studies demonstrate. There's research to show art therapy does everything from reducing anxiety and depression in cancer patients to easing symptoms of personality disorders. It has also been found to build emotional awareness and empathy, as students learn to process and discuss their emotions while their peers do the same. There's a reason interest in and sales of art tools skyrocketed during the early days of COVID-19 pandemic, and it wasn't just boredom. Cognitive neuroscientists have found art helps reduce levels of cortisol, which is a marker of stress, in people's brains.

Regular arts education for all students also boosts creativity in ways that experts have found carry over to other subject areas. Something as simple as doodling has been found to help activate different parts of the brain that can enable non-linear thinking. Art can also help us get into a state known as "flow," where we're able to block out distractions, focus and think outside the box.

The creative benefits of regular arts education are evident in places like China. While China has a reputation for "drill and kill" style learning that focuses on rote memorization at the expense of creativity, former president of the U.S. National Center on Education and the Economy Mark Tucker told me his studies match mine in refuting such a black and white image. China gives all students regular access to art and culture instruction, from those piano-playing kindergarten teachers who incorporate music into daily lessons to regular calligraphy instruction to mandated painting classes. And despite the rigor of academic classes,

Tucker agreed that creativity is showing up as Chinese students pioneer in fields such as quantum computing and app development, and in the autonomous region of Macao, which is pioneering the drone industry. These students aren't sitting around, waiting for someone to tell them what to do, or simply finding ways to more cheaply produce existing products, as some would have you believe. They're tapping their creativity to pioneer new fields.

"Their creativity is off the charts," Tucker said. "So the message that there's no good reason to imitate these countries because they don't allow for creativity simply isn't true."

Last but certainly not least, arts education has a well-documented positive impact on academic achievement in so-called core subjects. Students who took four years of arts classes saw an average bump of 91 points on their SAT tests over peers who didn't take such courses, for example. Then there's a 2019 study out of George Mason University that found middle school students who had regular access to arts education performed better in school than those who didn't even after controlling for factors such as income. Other research shows arts education for younger students results in improved language and motor skills, as students practice describing visual elements and putting words to more abstract concepts.

Music education, in particular, much like foreign language instruction, has been found to actually create different physical pathways in the brain that are believed to help students when it comes to processing information in all subject areas. I like to stump my music students with a question. "What languages do you speak?" I ask them. They all say English, and most also say Spanish. "What else?" I ask. They sit, perplexed, and say, "I don't know Mr. Ballard." Then I tell them, "For the last year, you've been learning another language. It's called music, because music is the international language. You could sit down in any country in the world, see the music notation and play with people you otherwise couldn't communicate with." Their eyes light up, and it's almost as if I can see those new connections that have formed in their brains firing off.

I could go on and on with such examples, but the takeaway is clear: We can strengthen students' academic performance by supporting arts education.

Despite all of this research, whenever budgets get tight or other disruptions take place in American schools, arts programs are almost always the first to feel the cuts. I have seen this cycle play out so many times during my nearly three decades in education that, had I known then what I know now, I hate to say, I wouldn't have become a music teacher. Instead, I might have pursued teaching special education, which is federally mandated and so isn't nearly as subject to budgetary whims as music and arts courses have become.

I told a music teacher I met in China about the accolades my program and I personally had received, and she just couldn't comprehend how a school could cut such a program. In China, the teacher told me, schools honor teachers and programs that bring honor to them. But I've come to accept that music and arts education is simply considered expendable in the United States.

It wasn't always this way. In the middle of the 20th century, it was common for American public schools to have pretty extensive arts and music education programs. Some offered artist-in-residence programs, where professional artists would teach courses for a stint between working on their own projects. California, in particular, was seen as a model for arts education.

Researchers say the first dip in support for arts programs in public schools came after the historic events of Oct. 4, 1957. When the Soviet Union successfully launched Sputnik 1, which was the first artificial Earth satellite, it kicked off a space race that would last for two decades. With the United States rushing to catch up and capture the record of being first to put a man on the moon, resources and time for arts classes fell victim to a tremendous push for and interest in more science education in schools.

A similar wave of academically driven cuts to arts programs also was triggered by the No Child Left Behind era in the early 2000s, when testing culture took hold and more focus than ever was placed on reading and math instruction. The Common Core State Standards Initiative didn't help, since it emphasized "core" subjects without mentioning arts education.

There also is a clear pattern of cuts to funding for arts education when economic woes hit. We saw programs shrink massively during the recession in the early 1980s. It happened again with the so-called Great Recession of 2007 to 2009. During the 1999-2000 school year, for example, 20 percent of schools offered dance and theater classes, while 87 percent of schools offered visual arts classes. Once budget cuts due to the Great Recession kicked in during the 2009-2010 school year, only 3 percent of schools allocated funds for dance and 4 percent offered theater courses, while visual arts offerings fell less dramatically to 83 percent. And we were poised to see cuts to arts programs again as I was writing this book, due to drops in tax revenue and plummeting enrollment triggered by the COVID-19 pandemic.

Access to arts education also varies widely from state to state, according to information collected by the Arts Education Data Project. Within states, support for arts education varies depending on more localized economic and political conditions. Just 40 percent of California students were enrolled in arts education at the time this book was written, for example, with the highest percent enrolled in visual arts followed by music, theater, then dance. Enrollment was at 60 percent in Arizona and 84 percent in Ohio. And data isn't yet available in many states where arts enrollment is expected to be even lower than California.

Given those discrepancies and ongoing cuts to arts programs across the country, artists and advocates have been asking for years to have a Cabinet-level position created in the White House called Secretary of Arts and Culture. Music producer Quincy Jones famously pushed then-President Barack Obama to create such a role. Supporters say not only could such a person and their staff coordinate arts funding, unite arts groups and provide other direct support, but also to have a Cabinet position dedicated to this subject would send a powerful message about the value the U.S. places on arts education. But so far, the idea hasn't taken hold—which also sends a message.

Meanwhile, many other countries that score at the top of the PISA charts have a national figure who is focused on the arts. There's a minister of state for culture in Germany, a minister of Canadian heritage in Canada, and a minister of culture and art in Poland, for example. Clearly, the treatment of visual and performing arts, and the cultural significance they convey, is just one more distinction between the United States and countries with higher-performing education systems.

Mandatory Arts for All

In Finland, every student in third through seventh grade is required to take classes to learn the basics of music, woodworking, painting and other visual, performing and industrial arts. Once they reach middle school, they can opt to take additional courses in all those subjects. But unlike in the United States, these aren't electives Finnish middle schoolers can only squeeze in if their schedule isn't packed with a more "academic" load. Instead, while American students typically repeat the same five or so "core" classes daily, courses are different for Finnish middle schoolers from one day to the next. This allows them to have 25 different courses each week. Naturally, subjects such as math and science come around more than once. But so does art. In fact, nine of the 25 courses all Finnish middle school students take each week are dedicated to arts and industrial arts education.

It's all part of the Finnish mission to "educate the whole person" and to help students discover their passions. By and large, these programs for middle schoolers in Finland aren't rigorous, demanding arts courses. And they put little to no emphasis on endeavors such as, say, creating competitive school bands.

In the music class I visited at Mikkolan Koulu Basic School, for example, which serves grades one through nine in Vantaa, Finland, students were learning the ukulele. It's one of the easiest instruments to play, with very casual instruction and performance in the class I observed. But students were engaged and enjoying themselves.

The volume of artwork students at Mikkolan Koulu Basic School produce was evident throughout the campus, with pictures lining the walls. There even was paint decorating the glass walls of one workspace, where students had free rein to get as creative as they wanted.

I tossed on an apron and worked alongside eager seventh-grade students in a home economics class at Mikkolan Koulu Basic School. All boys and girls were learning basic cooking skills along with healthy eating habits. They told me they enjoyed the program, even if it was required—and not only because they were going to get to eat the chicken dish we were preparing.

The idea with mandated, relaxed arts courses like these for younger students is that they get exposure to a wide variety of mediums and life skills, forms of expression and tools. As you'll remember from chapter four, students also take time near the end of their middle school careers to shadow professionals on the job and try out different career paths. Then they sit down with their parents and school counselor to map out their plans for high school, with the decision ultimately left in the student's hands. And since they've had exposure to so many different forms of visual, performing and industrial arts, they can make an informed decision about whether to go on to pursue more serious, high-level vocational art programs in secondary school. But if not, instructors at Mikkolan Koulu Basic School told me, at least students will have perhaps picked up a new hobby or side hustle or skill that could help relieve stress and get their creative juices flowing as they pursue other subject areas.

Over in Japan, arts programs are taken much more seriously, even at the elementary level. And the emphasis on regular, high-quality arts education was clear as soon as I entered the halls of Wada Primary School in Tokorozawa, in Japan's Tokyo metro area.

A wide variety of student art hung on the walls, while the smell of paint and the sounds of musical instruments filled the air. Students here have two 55-minute art classes every week, with a variety of visual arts taught. During my visit, they were doing watercolor paintings in one room and assemblage art in another. Students at Wada Primary School also have two 55-minute music classes each week. Principal Shigeki Mukai said through a translator that they believe classes like these are very important, especially for the emotional development of children. While other courses such as math and science sometimes have just one correct answer, Mukai said art gives students a chance to forget the rules and be creative. So, he said, they have been careful not to limit these courses even as outside forces such as funding or test-prep pressure creep in.

At Nanryou Junior High School a short distance away in Tokorozawa, I was blown away by the attention paid to cultural tradition in education. I heard the clash of bamboo swords and the rhythmic shouts of students before I entered a dojo with a towering, thatched-roof ceiling under which students were practicing kendo. They were covered head to toe, in black jackets and loose pants, with protective gear from gloves to helmets that covered their faces. Kendo is a sport, but also an art form and an important tradition in Japanese culture, so the school created an attractive space and invested in quality gear.

Across the hall, students were wearing white robes and practicing judo in a similarly impressive setting. And a short distance away, in a more traditional classroom, students were focused as they created images in the style of manga, Japan's famous comics or graphic novels. Introducing instruction around manga is an example of how Japan has continued its emphasis on traditional art and culture education while also updating its course offerings to keep students engaged and adapt to the times.

Of course, the visit that stuck with me the most from my time in Japan was my observation of band rehearsal at Nanryou Junior High School. Music is compulsory for all Japanese students starting in elementary school. So these middle schoolers, in uniforms with white-logoed shirts and navy-blue shorts, sounded like an elite high school band in the United States. As a metronome ticked away in the background, they sat straight as rails on the edge of their seats, with every spine inches away from the back of the chair. (I can't get my middle schoolers to adopt that professional pose to save my life!) Their body movements and phrasing mimicked professional musicians, as they tackled 60-note runs in dynamic music that I'd hesitate to attempt with my advanced high school students. At the front of the room, their teacher conducted as if he were standing in front of a national orchestra.

I soon learned this class wasn't the exception but the rule in Japan, with a similarly high level of performance at other middle school music classes I visited throughout the country. It makes sense, then, that Japan qualifies each year to send a student band to participate in our prestigious Rose Parade, held on New Year's Day in Pasadena, California, each year.

There may be a vast difference between the rigor of arts programs in countries with top-performing education systems. But one thing is consistent: Almost without exception, all of these places mandate regular arts instruction in elementary and middle schools.

I can recount similar stories from just about every country I visited during this education tour. There were the students at Sanmin Junior High in Taipei, Taiwan, who during their required weekly art class practiced interior design skills by decorating tiny model rooms they'd created. There were the students in New Zealand who had mandated, respectful instruction about indigenous art, which was proudly highlighted throughout the schools. Then there were the middle and high schoolers who were putting on a choir concert while I was in Singapore. I sat and listened for four hours. Rarely have I heard the same level of quality from advanced American choir students as I heard in performance after performance from students as young as 12.

The explanation is clear: There are no required music or arts courses in most American elementary, middle or high schools. Not just "too few classes" or "not enough variety" in offerings. *None*, as in not one required arts course for most students over 12 or 13 years in public schools.

There are of course schools and districts that have created their own requirements for arts classes, and we have some fantastic art-focused schools scattered throughout the country. But there are no national or state requirements to ensure students are regularly exposed to arts and culture education as they grow up.

In California, we have state standards that discuss music education at all grade levels. However, few students get any sort of regular music education from first through sixth grade. Schools get around this by having their regular elementary classroom teachers do "mini" music lessons, such as having kids shake tambourines or train for "singathon" performances. Or they might occasionally pull students out of their classrooms for some dedicated music time. But it's rare for our younger students, particularly at more disadvantaged schools, to get any sort of regular instruction from a certified music teacher. And even at the upper grades, unless students choose to be in music programs, have room in their schedules and are in a school that has openings available, they might go their entire school careers with no exposure to music education at all.

Despite this reality, I had a principal several years back who called me into his office to ask how I was aligning my music curriculum with the state standards. I couldn't help but laugh. I reminded him that almost none of my students had any music instruction before coming to my middle school program. I tried to explain that expecting students to meet seventh-grade music standards when they'd never had any prior classes would be like expecting seventh graders to dive into algebra if they'd never had a math class before. Looking at the standards for high school music, which includes some fairly complex music theory, they'd be difficult for most students to meet even if they had some prior instruction. My principal heard me out, then simply said, "We realize all of this. But you have to be creative and try to figure out a way to align your curriculum with the state standards."

Clearly, our commitment to teach music and arts standards is another example of the American school system talking the talk without walking the walk.

Professional Instructors in House

In the United States, if a middle or high school does still offer classes in industrial arts such as woodworking, it's not uncommon for the instructor to also teach, say, physical education or other unrelated courses. Unsurprisingly, that's not because such a system is best to get high-quality woodworking instruction for students. Instead, it's a practical choice to keep those programs afloat. And for the teacher, the extra course can earn them a small stipend, which can help offset salaries that haven't kept pace with other professional fields.

At the elementary level, as we discussed, it's often the regular classroom teacher who's entirely responsible for any instruction in visual or performing arts that students might get. Unless the students are lucky enough to get an elementary teacher who happens to not only be a certified expert in teaching students to read and do math and learn every other "core" subject while also being a musician or artist on the side, those students likely won't ever have any arts instruction from someone skilled in the field they're teaching. And the amount of time those teachers spend on any sort of arts instruction is entirely up to them.

Many schools that have had to cut their in-house arts programs started contracting with outside programs once funding came back. Such offerings are surely better than nothing, and they can result in high-quality instruction and access to resources schools otherwise couldn't afford. But they're also not as integrated into the schools. They aren't required to have credentialed teachers leading them. Outside contracts are also even easier for schools to cut off when times get tight again, as they inevitably will.

Places like Finland would never allow arts courses—or any courses, for that matter—to be taught by educators who aren't credentialed, with master's degrees and training specific to the field they're teaching. Even at the elementary level, Finnish students are taking painting courses from trained, dedicated arts instructors. Woodworking classes are taught not only by credentialed teachers, but also by teachers certified and experienced in woodworking. Any other option seems nonsensical to them.

The same goes for most arts and culture programs I observed at schools around the world. In Japan, for example, those kendo classes I described earlier each had multiple professional instructors who performed the sport at the front of the classroom along with students to guide them. In the judo class, students were learning from instructors who had black belts. These courses weren't seen as frills to be covered by whatever teacher they could get to stand in front of the class that semester. They were valued, and the schools demonstrated that value by hiring trained professionals to lead them.

Remember that American cliche we discussed in chapter two about teachers? It says, "Those who can, do; those who can't, teach." Since teaching isn't considered or compensated as a particularly desirable field in the U.S., it's hard to imagine highly skilled judo experts or music conductors or painters wanting to teach elementary or middle school courses here. But since teaching is considered a competitive, well-respected field in most countries with top-performing education systems, it's also seen as a valuable place for experts in visual, performing and industrial arts to share their talents and expertise. That's why some other countries don't typically have trouble finding trained professionals for this steady, respected work.

Reliable Resources

It's problematic that we don't mandate arts education from subject-certified teachers for all students in the United States, as so many other high-performing countries do. But perhaps even worse is the fact that the limited visual, performing and industrial arts programs we do offer in most American schools are constantly at the whim of politics, education trends, economic cycles and fluctuating enrollment.

I spent time with students in an advanced arts course at Normaalikoulu Upper Secondary School and Teacher Training School in Jyvaskyla, Finland. We were in a simple but well-appointed room with student sculptures resting on the windowsills and paintings hung all around. As students told me how much they appreciated the option to take such a course, I was struck by how intimate the class felt. I learned there were fewer than a dozen students who'd opted to enroll in that particular advanced art course that semester. Still, school staff explained, they'd never dream of dropping the course.

Back home, on the other hand, recruiting students to my music courses, to ensure each one has high enough enrollment for the school to fund the course the next semester, is almost a second job.

The elementary schools that feed the middle school where I teach give students virtually no exposure to music, as I mentioned earlier. That means there's little opportunity for them to discover if they have any aptitude for or interest in taking music courses before they get to junior high. Instead, my school sends me over to the elementary school, where I might get to speak for five minutes to sixth-grade students during their regular classes and try to convince them to ask their parents and counselors to carve out a spot in their schedules the following year for one of my courses. I find myself remembering back to my career as a pharmaceutical representative. Only instead of convincing doctors to prescribe the drug I'm selling, I'm trying to convince 11- and 12-year-olds to voluntarily dedicate hours of their lives to experimenting with music.

Middle school art teachers in places like Poland and Japan never have to worry about such responsibilities. That's because their classes are a mandatory part of the curriculum for all younger students. And even when many of these courses become optional electives as students reach high school, they don't cancel classes if enrollment numbers fail to meet a certain threshold, in the same way they would never consider canceling a math course if the class size ended up smaller than usual.

Meanwhile, if not enough students sign up for arts courses in the United States, the teacher typically gets blamed and their courses can get cut—particularly if any financial challenges arise.

Parents got involved and saved the music program from cuts when I taught years ago at Point Loma High School in San Diego. But nothing could stop the cuts that hit when I was teaching at Montgomery Middle School in 2010, coming out of the Great Recession. I had 160 kids in a mariachi program who had performed for two U.S. presidents, had appeared on the show *Inside Edition* and had been on TV probably more than 50 times. The mariachi program went over a cliff overnight after budget cuts came. So the district moved me over to teach at Southwest High School, only to cut a class there in 2018 after I'd built up that program.

My biggest fight came in April 2021, when the district said it was eliminating three of my classes at Southwest Middle School and was planning to move me to another school. So I quietly got my students' parents involved and reached out to local journalists. We invited three TV stations to cover our "final concert" of the year. That's where I sprung the surprise on my school administration. I began to tell parents at the concert how the administration cut the music program without their input. The parents did not take it very well. Later that day, the parents and students from my music program eventually took over three rooms at a school board meeting, with the TV news crews following us live. After the negative coverage, the district said it was all a "big misunderstanding" and that the program would continue for the 2021-22 school year.

Still, support for music programs in our school has gotten so bad that my district stopped paying to tune the piano in my classroom. I eventually had the piano removed because it had so many broken keys and out-of-tune notes.

Once again, this isn't just a matter of spending more money. You'll recall that we spend one of the highest dollar amounts per student in the world to educate our kids. We'll discuss broader issues with school funding in the final chapter. It's enough to say here that the way we are now spending our education dollars sends a clear message about the low value we place on arts education—despite the clear lessons the world's best schools can teach us about what a difference such programs can make.

What can I do?

If this chapter has helped convince you of the need for expanded arts and culture programs in public schools, here are steps you can take right now to help set the wheels in motion, with space for you to jot down notes on plans for accomplishing each step or how it went once it's completed.

- Advocate for arts and culture programs to be considered part of the "core" curriculum in your local schools. Do this by speaking at your local school board meeting, writing letters to the editor in your local paper or even proposing legislation to require such mandated changes at the state or federal levels.

____

____

____

____

- Create regular opportunities for visual arts, music, theater and dance for the kids in your life. Look for free classes or public arts programs in your community that you can take them to. Buy or borrow cheap instruments and art supplies for them to use at home, and regularly dedicate time to work on art projects together.

____

____

- Encourage the kids in your life to take arts courses in school. Help them research what options are available and, if needed, request that more courses be added to the roster.

- Volunteer to arrange an artist-in-residence program at your local school, where the professional works alongside in-house, credentialed teachers.

- Do an inventory of arts courses offered in your local schools and see how it compares with programs described in this chapter in other countries.

- Share information about arts programs in other countries with people in your circle through conversation and social media posts.

- Demand that arts courses be taught by credentialed teachers. Consider speaking to your local political representatives about sponsoring a law to that effect.

- Advocate for a Secretary of Arts and Culture position in the White House cabinet.

- Give time, money and attention to organizations that fight for arts education in schools.

"Charter schools are a 'policy Band-Aid' when a heart transplant is needed."

Marc Tucker

All students in Finland take home economics courses like this one.

The Equity Question

If my decade-long quest to learn from the world's best schools has taught me anything, it's this: Poverty does not have to be destiny.

Nothing drove this point home for me more than sitting inside a simple, stone-walled classroom in Ho Chi Minh City, the largest city in the developing nation of Vietnam. The windows had bars instead of glass and the only decoration was a banner that declared "Merry Christmas" months after the holiday had passed. Yet, the poorest 10 percent of Vietnamese students regularly perform better than the average American student on the PISA exam.

Or consider again the nation of Estonia, which has a smaller population than the state of Maine. While Estonia isn't a poor nation, its government spends roughly half as much on education per student each year as the United States. It also has a poverty rate that's about six percentage points higher than the U.S., and a per capita gross domestic product that's nearly half the annual rate for Americans. Still, not only did Estonia crush the United States on the most recent PISA exam, coming in at No. 5 overall vs. No. 25 here, it also scored far higher on a series of metrics used to measure the all-important goal of equity in education.

The main way PISA and other organizations attempt to quantify equity in schools is to look at how easy it is to predict a student's academic achievement based on his or her income level, gender, immigration status and other background factors. Estonia is one of 11 countries—including places such as Australia, Canada, Japan and Norway—that had above-average reading scores on the 2018 PISA test but also showed a positive, below-average connection between student performance and socio-economic status. The United States scores precisely average on that equity metric, coming in just below Turkey and just above Lebanon.

The United States scores higher on some key equity metrics than several of the countries that perform better on PISA each year, including Germany, Belgium and Switzerland. And the U.S. performs better than average in terms of "academic resilience" among its immigrant students, with 24.5 percent of its lower-income immigrant students earning top reading scores vs. an average international rate of 16.8 percent and just 13.6 percent in Estonia. That's a particular feat considering we have lower barriers to immigration than most other countries, which poses a unique challenge when it comes to equity in the United States. But there still is tremendous room for growth when it comes to closing the achievement gap here between all types of diverse student groups, whether those gaps are gender-based, language-based, special needs-based or income-based.

When it comes to the overall percentage of students who are considered academically resilient, for example, the international average is 11. In the United States, it's 10 percent. In Estonia, 16 percent of the most disadvantaged students earned top reading scores.

As for the gap in reading scores between advantaged and disadvantaged students, the international average is 89 points. In the United States, there's a 99-point gap in reading scores between students in the top-third of income brackets vs. the bottom third. That translates to a difference of more than three grade levels in reading skills. In Estonia, that gap is 61 points, or two years' difference between reading levels of richer and poorer students. And in Morocco, it's just 51 points.

"The world is no longer divided between rich and well-educated nations and poor and badly educated ones," Andreas Schleicher, a director with the Organisation for Economic Co-operation and Development, which administers PISA, wrote in his report on the 2018 exam. "When comparing countries that score similarly in PISA, their income levels vary widely. History shows that countries with the determination to build a first-class education system can achieve this even in adverse economic circumstances, and their schools today will be their economy and society tomorrow. So it can be done."

That's the good news! But there's a reason we're focusing on equity in the last chapter of this book. In many ways, addressing equity issues is the culmination of everything we've been discussing for the last 200 pages. So let's take a quick look at how stealing ideas from the world's best school systems when it comes to topics we've discussed in the previous seven chapters can dramatically impact the equity of education students are receiving.

1. **Support for parents**: Families receive more support in most countries with high-performing education systems, from paid family leave to free, high-quality daycare to affordable college. Such programs benefit needy families the most, helping to offset some of the inequities students in the U.S. face before they've even set foot in a classroom.

2. **Teacher quality**: Other countries have made teaching a respected profession that attracts the best people and requires extensive training for all candidates, and they send their top performers to lead schools that struggle the most. In the U.S., teaching isn't a competitive field. Disadvantaged schools frequently must loosen job requirements to attract educators and see the highest rates of turnover, leading to more disruptions and less-experienced teachers working with the neediest students.

3. **School experience**: Most countries that score high on PISA exams send their students to school more days each year while starting those days a bit later, building in frequent breaks and offering highly nutritious meals for everyone. Disadvantaged students benefit the most, since they're more likely to be left on their own when school isn't in session and to face sleep shortages, behavior problems during long teaching sessions, and lack of

access to healthy food—all of which negatively impact their academic achievement.

4. **Vocational education**: Offering high-quality vocational programs in public schools, as most of the world's best education systems do, ensures disadvantaged students in particular have a clear path to solid careers without having to pay out of pocket for specialized training once they graduate. Such programs also improve motivation while reducing behavior problems and dropout rates, all of which disproportionately impact low-income students.

5. **High-stakes testing**: High-performing education systems rarely make students take standardized tests. And when they do, results are not used to punish or shame schools or teachers as they are in the United States. That can be demoralizing for disadvantaged communities, which already are contending with test questions centered on majority groups. What's worse, studies show U.S. school districts in disadvantaged communities tend to spend the most time on standardized tests, which takes instruction time away from the students who need it most.

6. **Technology**: U.S. schools have invested heavily in technology at all levels, with disadvantaged schools tending to use digital learning tools the most. While that might initially appear to be a positive when it comes to equity, mounting research shows that extensive use of educational technology actually lowers academic achievement. That's why there is less technology used through middle school in many countries that perform best on PISA exams each year.

7. **Arts education**: While regular arts education from trained instructors is required for all students through middle school in most high-performing countries, it's rare outside of the most advantaged American schools. That shortchanges disadvantaged students the most, as arts education has been found to boost everything from creativity to motivation to academic achievement.

See how the deck is stacked against our neediest students from the start? That's even more problematic when you consider that the United States has higher levels of income inequality and higher percentages of immigrant students than most developed nations.

If we address all of seven of these factors discussed in earlier chapters, it will go a long way toward improving the fairness of American schools. However, there are some additional lessons we can learn about equity in education from examining how the world's best schools handle issues such as funding, reaching students with different ability levels and offering options for alternative education paths. So we'll examine each of those points in this final chapter.

I've tried to steer clear of politics in this book. I'm not a political guy anyway, and the whole idea here is to look at best practices from around the world in countries with vastly different partisan dynamics at play, to see what really works when it comes to education. But I know conservatives will cheer the push for vocational education and the general criticism of our public schools, while liberals will welcome the pitch for family support programs and less standardized testing. And this chapter will touch on topics such as school funding and charter schools, which have become a major partisan flashpoint in recent years. So I challenge you, reader, to keep an open mind and see what lessons can be learned from how the U.S. is handling such issues differently than just about every country that routinely beats us on global measures of academic achievement.

Focusing on equity in education isn't just about some altruistic goal of bettering life for the neediest students and giving everyone an equal shot at success—though those are certainly worthwhile aims in and of themselves. But research into some of the best performing school systems in the world shows they got that way by focusing first on making success in school accessible to all students.

"Decades ago, when the Finnish school system was badly in need of reform, the goal of the program that Finland instituted, resulting in so much success today, was never excellence. It was equity," writes journalist Anu Partanen in an article for *The Atlantic* on the success of the Finnish school system. "Since the 1980s, the main driver of Finnish education policy has been the idea that every child should have exactly the same opportunity to learn, regardless of family background, income, or geographic location. Education has been seen first and foremost not as a way to produce star performers, but as an instrument to even out social inequality." But while academic excellence may not have been the goal of Finnish reforms, it was the result, with Finland regularly scoring near the top of PISA's global rankings.

I'm convinced that education truly can be the great equalizer. And I'm convinced that can change the future for families and entire nations, if only we can set aside our partisan disagreements and preconceived notions about what school systems should be and instead simply look at what has proven effective.

Focus on Funding

A curious thing struck me as I visited schools throughout places like Japan, Estonia, South Korea, Netherlands, Singapore and Finland. After visiting at least eight schools in different parts of each country, I noticed that while campuses might look different and offer different vocational programs or academic focuses, there was little to no difference in terms of the *quality* of those facilities or programs.

I quickly learned that, while such equity in schools all across these countries surprised me, it surprises them that the United States accepts anything else.

Gunda Tire, national project manager for PISA in Estonia, told me she's confident that one of the key reasons Estonia is performing so well on international testing is that all schools in her country get the same level of financial support. "It's not like the rich kids' schools get more and the poorer get less. Everyone gets the same funding," she said, with free lunches, for example, for everyone no matter income levels. "From the state's point of view, everyone is equal."

South Korea and Japan also frequently score highly for having some of the most equitable school systems in the world. In both places, schools everywhere, again, receive the same amount of government funding. Prefectures also pay teachers about the same no matter where they work, from schools in the priciest Tokyo neighborhoods to the poorest rural communities.

In Ireland and New Zealand, administrators told me there are some differences in funding for schools across the country. But it's the schools serving underprivileged children that get more money, rather than the schools in ritzier areas. So these nations are investing state and federal money specifically to make their school systems more equitable from place to place.

Meanwhile, in the United States, the difference in quality between schools from one state to another—or even one community to the next—is staggering.

In high-poverty states such as Mississippi, I visited schools that look like they could be in developing countries. Teachers in Mississippi and West Virginia also make, on average, nearly half as much money each year as teachers in places such as New York and California. Admittedly, there's a substantial difference in cost of living between these states. But such tremendous gaps in salaries also limits those states' ability to attract quality teachers to schools that need the most help.

In my own community, distinctions between the quality of programs, facilities and resources from wealthier parts of San Diego County to areas like the district where I teach, near the Mexican border, are nearly as stark. Same goes for schools in counties to the north, where schools in Orange County's Newport Beach look very different from schools in nearby Santa Ana and the gap between schools in Los Angeles County's Beverly Hills vs. places like Compton is difficult to overstate.

I've talked a couple times about the average amount spent per student each year to educate students in the United States vs. in other countries, noting that we're on the higher end of that scale. But simply looking at national averages does not tell the full story.

While the national average is above $13,000 per student, New York spends more than $25,000 per student each year, while Arizona spends less than $9,000 per student and Idaho spends less than $8,000.

There are communities in and around Chicago where schools in one district spend under $10,000 per student while schools in another district spend nearly $29,000. Can you imagine the difference in the quality of education students are receiving? It's the difference between struggling each year to recruit enough teachers vs. attracting the best in the field, or between having no music classes vs. having regular courses from highly trained instructors. It's the difference in class sizes, the ability to take field trips and to pay for full-time support staff such as counselors and nurses.

With such distinctions in mind, it's not tough to understand how there came to be a 99-point gap in reading scores between students in the top and bottom thirds of income brackets in the United States.

The main factor driving this extreme inequality is in how our schools are funded. While state and federal funding for schools is generally determined based on formulas that factor in student populations and needs, at least a third of school funding in most states comes from local revenue. And those local revenues are based almost entirely on property taxes. That means schools in communities with expensive homes and thriving businesses get far more money than schools in places where housing is cheap or industry is scarce. So rather than keeping funding equal everywhere, as places like Estonia do, or giving additional funds based on greater student need, as Ireland does, the United States' system of linking school funding to the local real estate market guarantees that kids at the highest socioeconomic levels have better programs, facilities and teachers while the most disadvantaged students have the fewest resources. Such a system is simply unheard of in most top-tier countries due to how it exacerbates inequities.

Tying school funds to the real estate market also opens education budgets to tremendous fluctuation based on changes in home prices. This is why our school budgets are on such a constant roller coaster, leading schools to lay off teachers when there is a recession and scramble to rehire them—often lowering teacher standards along the way—to get people back in the classroom when home prices and therefore school budgets improve. It's why music and arts programs like mine are constantly on the chopping block. And it makes it very difficult for schools to invest in new programs or facilities when they're never certain what their funding might look like in the years to come.

In countries where education funding isn't tied in any way to property taxes, schools can rely on solid levels of funding each year. Budgets can fluctuate a bit with changes in student populations, but not because the housing bubble burst.

Some states also have passed laws that pose additional challenges when it comes to school funding. In California, for example, we were a national leader in education in the 1960s and 1970s. Then voters approved Proposition 13, which caps how much property taxes can go up each year. Of course this is nice for taxpayers, and it does help a bit with preventing inequities between communities from getting worse. But arbitrarily capping the amount property taxes can go up every year was a huge hit to California school budgets. It was devastating to arts education, and it surely contributed to our system going from being one of the best in the nation to being at the middle of the pack. Discussing the merits of such tax policies is outside the scope of this book. But having education funding tied to the real estate market, which is subject to a variety of regulations and fluctuations, is simply not something that would be considered fair or wise in most countries.

This isn't just about income inequality, either. For a host of complex reasons—including redlining, which historically kept Black people out of certain neighborhoods—the idea of basing school funding on property taxes tends to have the most negative impacts on non-White students. So the system exacerbates racial inequities in the United States as well, which has led to numerous lawsuits over the past 50 years. And it has helped drive the resegregation of schools, with far more racial divides in schools today than there were in the 1980s.

As people have begun paying attention to the problems caused by this system, some states and districts have made efforts to smooth out the inequalities created by property tax funding. Districts in some poorer communities, for example, have found ways to offer higher salaries so they can attract and retain more teachers. Districts in Arizona have taken to making the school week just four days to save money and lure teachers—which is a bit like robbing Peter to pay Paul, as the saying goes, since it might attract teachers while also reducing instruction time for the neediest students along the way. Some states have started making their funding formulas less reliant on local revenue sources or using their money to offset differences between districts. That's how the United States has managed to make some improvements in how it performs on some equity metrics in recent years. But we still have a long way to go, and there doesn't seem to be any great way to address this issue without decoupling our education budgets from real estate markets.

The current funding system, believe it or not, grew out of Massachusetts colonists in the mid-1600s asking local settlers to pitch in to fund schools that would help their kids learn to read the Bible. The mechanisms have changed, but this idea of local revenues driving school funding has remained persistent for nearly four centuries. A bit has changed over those 400 years. Maybe it's time to rethink this model?

A big driving force behind U.S. funding plans that tie school budgets to local revenue sources is our ongoing preference for "local control." Most high-performing countries have education systems that are much more top-down than ours, with everything from standards for students to requirements for teachers to funding levels set at the state or, often, national level. Communities in those places typically don't have much ability or desire to usurp that authority. But a good deal of trust is placed in individual schools and teachers to execute those plans, without much micromanaging.

In the United States, there's a strong contingent that wants control over how school districts are funded and run to sit at the local level. That has translated to powerful school boards making major decisions about budgets, curriculum, facilities and more. That's true even though there are no requirements that school board members have any level of experience or expertise in such issues to get elected. Many school board races in smaller communities aren't even contested.

The harms of such a system famously played out in the late 1990s in a community on the outskirts of Phoenix, where I used to teach. As wealthy retirement communities rose up in the Sun City area, the retirees who moved in—and no longer had school-aged kids—started to complain about their tax dollars going to fund schools in the nearby Latino-majority Dysart School District. Retired residents refused to vote for any bonds to help fund school improvements. Then three of those retirees won seats and took over a majority on the local school board, and a push was made for the enclave of retirement communities to vote itself out of having to pay into funding the school district at all. Those schools had to cut programs and delay facility repairs as the fight played out, eventually losing the property tax dollars from those retirement communities but gaining a smaller community that supported the district.

Places like Estonia and Japan would never hand over control of such important decisions about their school systems, such as how they're funded, to laypeople. School boards, where they exist in other countries, generally don't have nearly the same power as ours do. And school funding remains equitable between communities, regardless of the value of homes and businesses in the area.

The Same, Then Different

Funding isn't the only thing that's largely equal between schools in countries that perform best on international exams each year. Rather than being tracked based on their ability levels, students in most of these countries also receive the same education from kindergarten all the way through middle school.

This practice goes far beyond all younger kids getting access to regular music classes, as we discussed in chapter seven. Elementary and middle school students in places like Sweden, South Korea, Norway and Japan also all generally take the same math, science and reading courses. Once they reach high school, that's when their interests and achievement levels start to dictate the courses they take, with lots of options for college or vocational programs they can pursue.

In the United States, we flip that model. Younger students often are grouped or tracked based on their abilities, with options for more advanced math or science classes starting at least in middle school. Then, high schoolers have fewer options than their counterparts in places like Germany or Singapore, with all American teens generally pushed onto a college-ready path. That explains why test results show there isn't just tremendous inequality between one school and the next in the U.S., but there's often also a sizeable gap between students of different income levels and with different challenges within the same school.

The idea of younger students being streamed, or tracked, based on their academic performance was once embraced in the United States and other countries. Schools deliberately clustered students by ability level in elementary schools and put lower-performing students, average students and high-achieving students on entirely different paths in middle school, with different courses, teachers and schedules starting in sixth grade. But in the late 1980s and early 1990s, the concept fell out of favor as studies, news articles and lawsuits pointed out that low-income and minority students were being disproportionately pushed into the lowest tracks—sometimes without any solid data to back those decisions. Findings on the benefits of the practice also were mixed, with detractors arguing the potential harms that tracking has on the self-esteem and progress of the neediest students isn't outweighed by clearly proven benefits for everyone involved.

Even after the stigma around tracking led most U.S. schools to ditch formal streaming programs by the mid-1990s, the practice continued in many classrooms and campuses in less obvious ways. There still were "gifted" or enrichment programs for younger kids. Elementary teachers still clustered students by ability level for group work in reading and math. At the middle school level, students could still opt to take more advanced math classes, such as algebra, than their peers. And research shows such practices also became more common again in U.S. classrooms by 2010, as teachers grappled with ways to reach disadvantaged students and to challenge advanced students—who sometimes have demanding parents.

For years, Germany had a strict dual-tracking system in place for students. When students were as young as 10, teachers would decide if they would go to the *Gymnasium*, which is the college-prep track, or one of two tiers of vocational school tracks. But when the shock from the country's first PISA scores hit in 2000, the country also recognized that it had one of the worst equity scores in the world, with a gap of more than 100 points in reading scores between the top and bottom economic cohorts. Many German schools started to delay tracking until the high school level, and the county's marks for equity metrics improved.

Meanwhile, the persistence of tracking in U.S. schools is the main factor Schleicher, with the OECD, points to when asked to explain why there are such large achievement gaps on PISA exams even among American students who attend the same schools. The more schools offer remedial and accelerated classes, he suggests, the more they tend to increase rather than narrow the gap in learning between rich and poor students, immigrant and native students, White and non-White students, and boys and girls.

A 2015 study across 33 countries backed that concept, with researchers finding that a full third of the achievement gap in math was due to the difference in classes students were taking, while the rest was tied to their backgrounds. Michigan State University education Prof. William Schmidt, who was lead author of the study, explained his findings this way to The Hechinger Report: "In every society, we want school to be the great equalizer, to help students overcome poverty. In effect, this study says that schooling is making things worse."

While many top Asian countries give students largely the same courses through middle school, and score top marks for equity, they do have their own issue to grapple with when it comes to an unfair advantage for richer kids. As we've discussed in previous chapters, China and South Korea, in particular, are known for having high percentages of students who attend "escalator" or "cram" schools to get further ahead and prepare for the all-important exam at the end of high school. Such tutoring programs can be costly. While I talked with many teachers and students about how even poor families find ways to get their kids into cram schools, clearly they are not within reach for all disadvantaged students. But those are issues within the private tutoring industry, not the public-school systems. And even with such programs helping more advantaged students get further ahead, the overall equity in public schooling seems to help prevent the same sort of massive achievement gaps between rich and poor students that are common in the United States.

The idea of teaching all students the same thing through middle school might sound noble—and simpler for schools and teachers, who wouldn't have to worry about differentiating lesson plans and schedules. But as a teacher and parent, I know what folks in both categories are thinking: In places where all classes are the same, which students are they designed to serve? And if it's students in the middle, as seems most logical, doesn't that mean low-performing students will be left behind while high-achieving students will be left bored?

In Finland, schools have answered this question by essentially teaching to the high end of the middle cohort of students. This challenges students in the middle without feeling too remedial for high-performing students, who still can dive more deeply into the subjects at hand. But keep in mind that the Finnish system was rebuilt around striving for equity rather than personal excellence and around cooperation rather than competition. So there isn't the same emphasis put on helping younger students, especially, to pursue more advanced paths. And Finland's test scores indicate that its approach isn't holding back high achievers. Instead, regarding that 2015 study on school tracking around the world, Schmidt says there seem to be academic benefits for top students who spend more time at the elementary and middle school levels gaining a deeper understanding of core subjects without feeling the need to rush ahead to more advanced courses.

When it comes to lower-performing students in Finland, there simply aren't the same gaps in achievement, largely thanks to the factors covered in chapter one, such as families getting more support and all students having access to high-quality early education. Places like Finland also insist on having the same support services—such as special education teachers, guidance counselors, speech therapists, school psychologists and social workers—available to all students no matter the socioeconomics of the community. In Estonia, for schools too small to support such services full-time, there are free, government-run support centers called Rajaleidja Network Centres in each community where all kids ages 1.5 to 18 years old can get help with counseling, speech therapy, bullying prevention and more.

While there are some national mandates in the United States around special education resources in particular, the quality of such programs still varies widely from state to state and even community to community. Other support services, such as school counselors, are largely dependent on school budgets. Since budgets are impacted by the socioeconomics of a community, schools in well-off areas tend to have greater access to support services, while schools in low-income areas might share such experts between several campuses or not have them at all. That reduces opportunities for these experts to work with U.S students who are struggling, or to catch problems before they start to noticeably impact achievement, when compared with Finnish students who have regular access to such services.

So when schools aren't grappling with big gaps between the lowest and middle cohorts of students, and when they aren't so worried about helping high achievers get even further ahead before they've entered high school, then teaching to the high end of the middle can work for everyone.

It's true that Finland also has a more homogeneous population than the United States, with less than 9 percent of its population made up of people born in another country while nearly 14 percent of the U.S. population is foreign-born. But in Canada, nearly 22 percent of the country's residents were born elsewhere. Still, Canada boasts higher PISA scores and better marks on equity metrics than the United States. So the mere presence of high percentages of immigrant students alone cannot be used to predict achievement and equity levels, or to make excuses for continuing to track students in ways that exacerbate achievement gaps.

Researchers such as Tucker, who have studied this issue, say the distinction isn't solely in the methods Canada uses to educate its immigrant students and support their families, but in how those students ended up in its classrooms to begin with. Canada generally has a welcoming attitude toward immigration, believing that it boosts the country's economic and cultural diversity. But aside from asylum cases, Canada also has stricter requirements around who is allowed to settle within its borders, with applicants given points based on their level of education, English proficiency, job skills and other factors that suggest they'll be able to quickly start contributing to the economy—and integrate into local schools. Canada and most high-performing PISA countries simply don't allow for immigration based strictly on family reunification, as the United States does. That policy, when combined with geography that makes us more vulnerable to illegal border crossings, means our immigrants tend on average to have statistically lower incomes and levels of education and less English proficiency than immigrants settling in places such as Canada and Australia.

I have tremendous respect for the parents of my students, who came to the U.S. trying to build a better life for their kids. It's my honor to teach these students to play mariachi music or steel drums and to try to help them find their own paths in life. But no matter your views on immigration, we can't pretend the reality of our current system doesn't impact our schools. And if we're looking strictly at how countries that perform the best each year on international exams handle issues that directly impact their school systems, we have to acknowledge that most of them are simply more selective about who they allow in.

However, even when comparing just immigrants from similar income levels, foreign-born students in Canada perform significantly better on PISA exams than similarly rich or poor immigrants in the United States. This suggests that even if we don't change our immigration policies to be more selective, replicating other things Canada is doing differently from us—from setting higher standards for teachers to focusing less on standardized tests to equally funding schools that offer the same academic programs for all young students—could go a long way toward improving academic performance and equity for everyone.

Few Alternatives Allowed

When I talked with educators at some of the world's best schools about what we're doing back home, few topics raised more alarm bells for them than the growing push in the United States for alternatives to traditional public schools such as private schools, homeschooling and, most notably, charter schools.

None of the countries with top education systems include the concept of charter schools, which are publicly funded schools that are privately run by nonprofits or for-profit businesses. Charter schools get the same taxpayer dollars as public schools but are exempt from many of the rules and regulations applied to traditional public schools. Federal laws around issues such as civil rights still apply, and the precise exemptions are different from state to state. But often, charter schools don't have to meet the same standards regarding certification for teachers, student attendance, textbook and curriculum guidelines, and class sizes. They also can tailor the student body through an application process or strict academic, attendance, behavior and parent involvement requirements to stay in the school, rather than serving all students in any given community as is the charge of traditional public schools. Supporters argue this gives charter schools more autonomy to craft education plans that fit individual communities or cater to groups of students who want to focus on certain paths, such as arts or science.

Minnesota passed the first laws allowing for public charter schools in 1991. Then, in 1994, President Bill Clinton signed a law that allowed federal funds to start going to charter schools, and nearly every state now has such laws on the books. But as with standardized testing, the roots of the current charter school movement in the United States really took off during the Bush administration's No Child Left Behind era of the early 2000s. With the emphasis on testing and accountability, and a push to punish schools that didn't make the grade when scores were published, public schools began to be vilified. Students could transfer out of traditional public schools that didn't meet NCLB standards. Those schools also could get taken over by the government or converted into charter schools. If students weren't testing well, critics said, surely it must be the fault of lazy teachers who were protected by powerful unions and tenure laws, or general bureaucracy that was holding traditional schools back.

California was the first to also pass a so-called "parent trigger law" in 2010. The law lets parents gather signatures and, if a simple majority agree, force changes at low-performing schools, including turning them into charter schools. Other states soon followed suit, with parent trigger laws on the books in at least seven states.

It's rare today for parents to try to go that route and turn an existing traditional public school into a charter school, since the process is long and often full of friction. Instead, it's become much more popular for parents to simply support new charter schools coming into their communities. Data from the National Center for Education Statistics shows that the percentage of charter schools in the United States grew from 5 to 8 percent from the 2009-10 to 2018-19 school years, jumping from approximately 5,000 nationwide to some 7,400. The percentage of public-school students who attended charter schools increased even more during the same time period, from 3 to 7 percent. And enrollment in charter schools skyrocketed over that decade from 1.6 million students in 2009 to 3.3 million students in 2018—even as the number of students at traditional public schools dropped by 400,000.

Those gaps are expected to grow even bigger when the next rounds of data are released. More parents turned to charter schools during the COVID-19 pandemic because many didn't follow the same health guidelines that shut schools down or required masks with an aim of slowing the spread of the virus. Some families also have been driven to charter schools by disagreements over how to teach concepts such as the history of racism or LGBTQ rights in the United States. So while Clinton, a Democrat, signed the law allowing federal funds to go to charter schools, and fellow Democratic President Barack Obama boosted funds for charters schools, divides over these recent issues have helped the concept of charter schools become much more partisan, with conservatives largely driving the push for "school choice" while liberals decry the inequity of having a system with different standards that pulls needed resources away from traditional public schools.

"Calling charter schools 'public schools' because they receive public tax dollars is like calling defense contractors 'public companies' because they also depend on public funding," Carol Burris, who was the 2013 New York State High School Principal of the Year, wrote in a 2017 article for the *Washington Post*.

As a veteran teacher in traditional public schools, I know some charter school proponents may dismiss what I have to say on this topic out of hand because they assume I'm biased and financially motivated to protect the system I depend on. But as I near retirement, I assure you I'm not simply looking out for my own paycheck. And as a teacher and a parent, I certainly understand the frustration with the current state of

America's public schools. That frustration, after all, is what drove me to spend a decade going around the world looking for better ideas and to spend three years compiling what I found in this book!

So, when it comes to the concept of charter schools, what did I find in countries that outperform us each year on international exams? In short, I discovered that a two-tier system like ours is essentially non-existent in most high-performing countries.

There are examples of widespread, charter-like schools primarily in two countries: England, where they're called "academies," and in the Netherlands, where they're called "particular education" or *bijzonder onderwijs* schools. (Alberta, Canada, also is the only province in that country that has charter schools, with a total of 15 spread mostly across rural areas. In 2022, Alberta's budget calls for spending $75 million dollars over the next three years to expand charter schools.)

England's "academies" are largely converted public schools, with some custom-built institutions, that are operated by nonprofits and don't have to follow the same rules as traditional public schools when it comes to curriculum and staffing. Research so far shows that while the movement has taken funding away from regular public schools, it hasn't led to broad increases in student performance.

In the Netherlands, their "particular education" system includes publicly funded, independently run schools that are based around specific religious denominations, such as Roman Catholic and Islamic schools, or distinct educational philosophies, such as Montessori and Waldorf pedagogies. This system, which sometimes gets mistakenly lumped in with private schools, has existed in the Netherlands for more than 100 years. There has been some pushback recently over public funds going to schools that promote certain religions. But unlike in the United States, the Dutch constitution doesn't require separation of church and state. Federal law would make the Dutch system illegal here, though some U.S. leaders have pushed for states to try to follow such a model.

New Zealand made a push toward charter schools, or what it called partnership schools, a decade ago. But the general public, educators, researchers and political opponents pushed back. The federal government abolished them in 2017, with unions calling them a "failed, expensive experiment" and the nation's minister of education saying they were "driven by ideology rather than evidence."

Charter schools in the United States also have been a mixed bag.

There are examples of charter school success stories. But often, even those highly touted models are not all they appear to be if you dig a bit deeper.

Take the BASIS series of charter schools in Arizona, for example, which claimed seven of the top ten spots in *U.S. News & World Report*'s 2022 ranking of the nation's "best charter high schools." These schools boast challenging curriculum and high standards for students. And BASIS schools dominate national rankings with reported graduation rates of 95 or even 100 percent and similarly high "college readiness" scores, as measured by the proportion of students who passed at least one Advanced Placement or International Baccalaureate exam.

The issue is with which students BASIS schools are—or, most importantly, are not—serving. An analysis by the group Arizonans for Charter School Accountability shows BASIS schools tend to serve a much higher percentage of White and Asian students and a much lower percentage of students with learning disabilities than public schools in the same communities. BASIS schools also reported having no students who spoke English as a second language.

While federal laws prevent charters schools from discriminating on the basis of race or disability, Burris notes in her *Washington Post* article that BASIS schools find other ways to control their demographics. One way is by not having to provide transportation or a free lunch program to their students, as traditional public schools do. And while these schools are free to attend, parents are regularly asked to volunteer and to pitch in funds for a teacher bonus program, books and other resources. Those factors make it much more difficult for low-income students to attend BASIS schools.

Even for students who do make the commitment and get into BASIS schools, there are strict attendance and academic requirements to stay enrolled, which disproportionately impact students with learning disabilities, or health issues or who aren't native English speakers. Data shows more than half of students who enrolled in BASIS schools had switched out and returned to traditional public schools by 12th grade, which helps explain why many of these schools boast 100 percent graduation rates for those who do finish their studies there.

Then there's the issue of how such schools are using taxpayer dollars. Charter schools typically don't have to follow the same laws regarding transparency, avoiding conflicts of interest and other safeguards as publicly funded systems. That means it's harder for parents, researchers and reporters to dig into exactly how public funds are being spent. Even if there's no blatant mismanagement, there is clear research to show that more taxpayer dollars go to administrative costs in charter schools versus in public schools, with principals and CEOs who are often paid disproportionately large salaries relative to the size of schools they're overseeing.

A 2016 study commissioned by Arizonans for Charter School Accountability reports that BASIS spends nearly four times as much per pupil on administrative fees as a typical public school in the state. The charter system spent $12 million on administration to serve 9,000 students in 2015, while the six largest public schools in the area spent a combined $10 million to serve roughly 250,000 students. For fiscal conservatives, this should ring all sorts of alarm bells.

Those inflated executive salaries typically don't carry over to teachers, though. Many charter schools don't require that classes be taught by credentialed teachers, and they aren't represented by unions that have fought to get decent pay, benefits and job security for educators. That also means charter school teachers often are paid less, which makes it tough to see how they could possibly attract the best in their field. So if these schools do hire credentialed teachers who have either been laid off or lured from traditional public schools by the idea of more freedom or out of the same frustration with the system that I've experienced, they often come back to traditional public schools once there's an opening. That's why charter schools tend to have even higher teacher turnover rates, which isn't good for stability, mentorship and building expertise.

Then there are the charter school corruption scandals that regularly pop up in the news around the country.

While there are problems with giving too much power to school boards at traditional public schools, those folks are at least democratically elected and therefore accountable to the community members they serve. But it's not at all uncommon for the boards of directors and charter management organizations, or CMOs, that oversee charter schools to be full of family members, friends and political allies of those involved in forming those schools. With little oversight, and with tens of millions of dollars of public funds on the line, it's an area ripe for corruption.

In my home county of San Diego, 11 people were indicted in 2019 for taking $50 million in taxpayer funds for a chain of online charter schools run by A3 Education. Authorities say they made fake attendance records to boost their public funding, then spent the extra money on real estate ventures and lining their own pockets.

Then there was Texas-based IDEA Charter Schools, which planned to spend nearly $2 million a year to lease a private jet for travel until reporters exposed the plan and a backlash ensued. Or take the ECOT system, which was Ohio's largest charter provider until the state accused the program of inflating attendance records and demanded repayment of $80 million in taxpayer funds. ECOT abruptly closed its schools in January 2018, leaving students scrambling to find new classes in the middle of the school year. There are so many such examples that a watchdog group started a popular Twitter hashtag to track them: #anotherdayanothercharterscanday.

Setting those instances of foul play aside, the main question when evaluating whether we should continue to invest in charter schools is simple: Do they produce better results for students?

We've already discussed how the vast majority of countries that outperform us on PISA tests don't allow charter schools as we envision them. But there's also mounting research from within the United States that shows, overall, charter schools do not improve student achievement.

One of the most comprehensive data sets on this issue comes from a research center at Stanford University, which supports privatizing schools and has been tracking test scores from charter students for more than a decade. The center has found that about a quarter of charter schools across the United States do boast scores that are slightly above average national scores. However, another quarter perform worse than the average student, and half of charter school students perform the same as everyone else.

What's worse, while the issues with charter schools themselves are mixed, one thing is clear: The explosion of such schools is having a detrimental impact on public school systems in the United States. Public schools get most of their funding based on the number of students enrolled. So as hordes of students leave for charter schools or other alternative options, we're seeing public schools forced to cut resources or even shut down in communities across the country.

Charter schools have gotten so popular in places like New Orleans and Detroit, for example, that there are neighborhoods with no traditional public schools left—even though the charter schools that have replaced them don't have to accept all kids from that area. And Detroit overall has the worst performance on a national exam among big-city schools in the country.

Many other countries achieve the goals American charter schools strive for without creating this sort of two-tier system. Places like Estonia have added options for public schools centered around, say, music or science. But those schools must meet all the same requirements for teacher standards, funding, transparency and everything else that applies to their traditional counterparts. That has helped them avoid corruption scandals and the types of divisions we're seeing in our country today over the charter school debate.

When it comes to homeschooling, the practice also is widely discouraged in most countries that regularly beat us on international exams. Some parents of course do an excellent job maintaining high academic standards for their homeschooled kids and are careful to find ways to make sure they spend time with other young people. But they're not required to do so, and there's little oversight over homeschooling in most countries. Educators I spoke to in other countries told me they believe regular school attendance is extremely important to help socialize kids, to ensure they eat well, to make sure they're receiving high-quality curriculum and to help guard against problems such as undetected abuse.

For all of these reasons, homeschooling is almost nonexistent in a place like Finland. A counselor at Mikkolan Koulu Basic School, which serves grades one through nine in Vantaa, Finland, told me they had one pupil in the entire community served by his school who was studying at home at the time. That's because the student had been expelled for three months due to violent behavior. That was the only such "homeschooling" case the counselor was aware of in the school's 50-year history.

In the United States, roughly 5 percent, or under 2 million students, were homeschooled before the COVID-19 pandemic took off. By fall 2021, U.S. Census data showed that figure had shot up to 11 percent. Some of that jump was likely temporary, as parents on both sides of the school closure and mask debates grappled with ways to either avoid such regulations or, on the other side of that coin, keep their kids safe during the pandemic. But some parents and kids have told reporters they don't intend to ever go back to public schools.

I interviewed some American students who switched to home-schooling during the pandemic and plan to stick with it. I asked them why and they told me things like, "We can do the assignments whenever we want." As we talked more, I found out many of them were sleeping in on school days and typically weren't spending as much time on their studies as they would in school. In short, they were being lazy. And I fear their schooling, along with their work ethic and socialization, will suffer.

The final alternative to traditional public schools is private schools. While roughly 10 percent of U.S. students attend private schools, it's tough to fairly compare academic performance between those students and public-school kids, since the cost and high standards at many private schools heavily influence their demographics. But many countries that perform better than us on PISA exams, such as Finland and Norway, have virtually no privately funded schools. "Private" schools in places such as Canada and Ireland accept substantial public funding. As a result, they don't end up looking much different than traditional public schools in those places aside from, say, limited Catholic influences. And in places like Singapore, private schools are primarily international schools catering to foreigners and expats. So I've seen nothing in my travels or research to suggest that a greater prevalence of private schools is key to higher academic performance.

A greater push toward privatizing education—and particularly any widespread voucher program, where parents could take a share of taxpayer dollars that would normally go to public schools and instead use it to pay for private school tuition instead—could well be the final nail in the coffin for many public-school systems that are already struggling. Some public school critics are surely cheering for such an outcome. But as countries around the world have shown us, it doesn't have to be this way.

We don't have to choose between either continuing to settle for a public education system that's kept us steadily in the middle of the pack on PISA exams each year or blowing up our public school system entirely. We don't have to treat schools like businesses or commercial goods, where if you don't like something, you just shop elsewhere, letting the "free market" work the problem out. Instead, we could remake our public education system, rebuilding it from the ground up over time into one that's more equitable and effective, just as other countries have done when circumstances called for drastic measures.

Japan and South Korea did it in the aftermath of war. Estonia did it after the Soviet Union collapsed. China did it after opening up to the international community. Will it take a massive world event for us to commit to sweeping change in America's education system? Or could we simply look at the facts, decide enough is enough, and start working toward real change today?

Whenever the time comes, I hope this book can serve as a blueprint to help us steal ideas from the world's best schools and build an education system those same schools will one day want to steal for themselves.

What can I do?

Building more equitable schools is a complex undertaking. But here are steps everyone can take right now to help set the wheels in motion, with space for you to jot down notes on plans for accomplishing each step or how it went once it's completed.

- Contact your representatives and tell them you support state and federal laws that prohibit school funding from being tied to property taxes. Push instead for formulas that equally fund schools across all communities, or that provide extra funding to disadvantaged schools.

  ____

  ____

  ____

- Visit a school in a wealthy community near your home. Then visit a school in a disadvantaged community. Compare notes on what you see, then share those notes with a letter to the editor in your local newspaper, in a presentation to your local school board and on your social media channels.

  ____

  ____

  ____

- Advocate for laws in your district or state that would require all schools to have the same support staff members, such as guidance counselors, speech therapists and psychologists.

  ____

  ____

  ____

- Look back over the previous chapters and identify a policy that would particularly impact equity in your local schools, such as strict standards for all teachers or more support for families. Double down on one of the tips at the end of that chapter to push for that change.

  ____

  ____

  ____

- Push to introduce or support existing legislation that would require virtually all students to take the same courses through middle school, and then to have more options once they hit high school, the way high-performing countries do.

___

• When talking with kids in your life about school achievement, emphasize cooperation over competition. Discuss ways they can learn from their classmates and what they, in turn, can teach to others.

___

• When you hear discussions about "school choice," make sure those involved understand how such efforts divert funds from traditional public schools. Commit to speaking up and sharing facts about charter schools so people can make informed decisions.

___

• Consider running for your local school board on a platform of promoting equity. If you win, take steps to implement best practices from this chapter in your district.

___

Final Four Questions

When I talk to people about this project, versions of the same four questions inevitably pop up.

The first often gets asked in hushed tones, accompanied by a wink or an elbow nudge, as if they're about to learn some big secret I've been holding back all this time. It typically goes something like this: "Okay Keith, all of this information is great. But which country *really* has the best education system?"

If I could pick any place to enroll my own son, thinking over all I've learned from my travels and research examining everything from test scores to vocational programs to teacher quality to quality of life for students, I would choose Finland without a doubt. It is a well-oiled machine that doesn't go with the "flavor of the month" in terms of educational reforms. I found Finnish education to be all about equity and student choice, which had a direct correlation to higher student motivation. The vocational programs also were world-class. And they've managed to strike that improbable balance between high achievement without driving their kids to study 20 hours a day, as I witnessed in many of the Asian countries that also outperform us on PISA exams each year.

However, Finland isn't perfect. Their scores and international ranking have slipped a bit in recent years, and there are cultural and demographic differences that would make it tough to lift the Finnish system and drop it onto American schools. I also have been floored by elements of school systems in other countries, from the arts programs of Japan and Taiwan to the vocational education programs of Singapore, Switzerland, Germany and Estonia, and from the equity of immigrant-heavy Canadian schools to the cooperative learning of New Zealand. That's why I didn't write this book focused solely on the Finnish education system. I agree with PISA founder Andreas Schleicher, who says the exams should be used less as a traditional comparison tool and more as a "crowdsourcing platform for better education practices." So I remain convinced that the path to building the best education system here is found by stealing best practices from all of these countries around the world.

The second question I often get falls somewhere along these lines: "That all sounds great, Keith. But how could school systems from places like Finland and Switzerland ever work here, given how _________?" And they fill in that blank with comments about how polarized or decentralized we are, how many more immigrants we have or some other condition they assume is distinctly American.

I hope chapter eight largely addressed that question by showing how countries like Vietnam, with far more poverty than us, and Canada, which is similarly decentralized and has more immigrants than we do, have managed to build education systems that out-perform ours. But the key here is that you can't just take one chapter of this book, try to implement that policy plan and hope students—particularly the neediest students—

will magically start performing on par with students in a country that also practices that policy. Each of the eight concepts here builds on the others. If families don't get more support, and in turn support schools more, elevating the teaching profession won't solve the problems we're facing. If we put in place plans for quality vocational programs without addressing issues with equity in school funding, the kids who need access to that vocational training the most still will get left behind. If I had to pick the two most important areas to focus on first, I'd say teacher quality and vocational education. But I don't believe we'll see our schools achieve their full potential unless we address all eight areas addressed in this book.

That's also why I didn't focus a chapter on one of the biggest challenges many teachers cite with American students: a lack of motivation. My years of studying top-performing schools have convinced me the fix for that problem is complex. It's about students being taught the value of education at home from parents who have the resources and drive to support them. It's about students learning from high-quality teachers who also are motivated to perform at their best and stick around. It's about students having a classroom and school calendar that's been thoughtfully arranged. It's about students being given choices in their education, including options for high-quality vocational education programs and regular access to arts education without us constantly trying to distract them with technology. And it's about treating students equitably, so all students are motivated to achieve, and to help their peers achieve, at the highest levels.

Yes, there are many complex socio-economic, political, cultural, historical and even religious factors in play when comparing these countries. And no, I didn't go into detail on many of these distinctions, country by country, discussing how each factor influences the various education systems. But we can either use those differences as an excuse to just keep doing what we're doing, or we can commit to real transformation and prove it can still be done.

The third question I often get falls along these lines: "Okay Keith, I get that we have room for improvement. But there have to be some things schools in the United States are still doing better than anyone else, right?"

I've racked my brain on this question and come up with one serious answer: sports and other extracurricular activities. We generally have quality, well-funded programs that are widely available to all students. No other country I visited matches us in this area. And it's not a bragging right that should be dismissed because it's not academics. As with the arts, there's plenty of research on how involvement in sports and other extracurricular activities can keep students motivated, build their self-esteem, improve their physical health, teach them leadership skills and plenty more that can help students be broadly successful. I hope that never changes. Instead, we should be looking at the way we've built up our sports programs and use it as a model that could be applied to other parts of the educational experience. One administrator in South Korea told me that if the United States could take the enthusiasm and financial support it directs at high school sports and turn that attention to academics, he's convinced we'd be No. 1 in the world on international exams.

The fourth and final question I've heard when I've spoken to people over the years about this project goes something like this: "The changes you're asking for are too big. Why don't you focus on smaller changes that individual teachers can make in their classrooms, such as how to arrange their desks or how much homework to assign each night?"

Trust me, I wish it was that simple. But the first problem is that I found no consensus on either of those issues, or on other similarly granular topics, as I compared the world's best schools. There is tremendous variety in how much homework students are doing in South Korea vs. Finland or what classroom layouts look like in Vietnam vs. New Zealand. So sorry, reader, we can't get off that easy.

The larger problem with this idea of focusing on small changes is that they'll yield just that: small change. If we want to make sweeping changes in the quality of our public schools, the achievement levels of our students and our ability to compete on a global scale, we need to make sweeping changes to our education system. So I won't back down from advocating for comprehensive reform at the federal and state levels.

The first step to solving a problem is recognizing that the problem exists. Hopefully, at the very least, this book has opened your eyes to what's possible in terms of high-performing education systems and how we're falling short. Next, we need to collectively take steps toward real change.

You may feel like that type of reform is beyond your reach. But the truth is that most major political reforms are sparked by big shifts in public opinion. When the people voting politicians into office and bankrolling their campaigns start applying pressure around a particular issue, it's amazing how quickly these problems that once seemed impossible to tackle can begin to be addressed. So I'd encourage you to look back at the list of steps at the end of each chapter that everyone can take. Create your own challenge based on your schedule and drive. You might commit to starting to work on just one of those challenges each month. Or you might be ambitious and try to tackle them all in a year. You can team up with friends or colleagues who also are reading this book and either work together or divvy up the steps. Maybe you'll brainstorm your own!

Finally, don't let perfection stand in the way of progress. Lots of small steps can become a stampede that will reverberate in the halls of your state house and in Washington, D.C. And that can lead to real transformation.

We owe it to our kids, and our country, to try.

Acknowledgements

First and foremost, I need to thank my wife Yvonne and son Anthony for their patience with me regarding the countless hours that I spent researching this project and for the months that I spent traveling throughout the world visiting schools.

Tom Teagle, my friend and former principal, has been one of my biggest cheerleaders and an inspirational force in my life.

I never could have done this book without my writer Brooke Staggs who is a fantastic person, a true professional and an incredible writer. I hit the trifecta with Brooke!

I would also like to thank Dr. Ed Brand, the former superintendent of the SUHSD for his support before he retired.

I benefited enormously from the many people who took time to share their thoughts about education. A special shoutout to Amanda Ripley, who gave me direction on my project and also helped me facilitate my school visits in Poland. Marc Tucker, former president and CEO of the NCEE, was the most instrumental researcher who helped me formulate my ideas regarding educational change in America. John Simmons, my friend and teaching colleague, always encouraged me to keep moving forward with my project, even when I had doubts. And Mike Rose, a professor at UCLA who passed away in August 2021, gave me insightful information regarding the importance of vocational education.

As I traveled around the world, Frank Eberth was gracious enough to arrange school visits for me in Germany and also invited me to stay with his family at his beautiful house. Elizabeth Ding, my friend and a former middle school English teacher in Qingdao, China, facilitated all of my school visits in China. Her son Spencer also gave me great insight about the Chinese educational system. Shirley Zhong in Toronto, Canada, also helped me better understand the Chinese educational system and culture. Michael Fullan, professor emeritus at the University of Toronto, facilitated by arranging school visits in the Toronto, Canada metro area. Arto Ahonen, a Finnish educational researcher and director of PISA in Finland, was instrumental in helping me gain access to K-12 schools in Finland. Without his help, I am not sure that I could have visited schools in Finland. Peter Klucken was also very instrumental in helping me set up school visits in Duisburg, Germany. Asada Tadashi and Dr. Noriyuki Inoue of University of San Diego were instrumental in arranging my school visits near Tokyo, Japan. Anna Silem with Innove went way above and beyond the call of duty as my host while I was visiting schools in Estonia. Caroline McKeown (director of PISA in Ireland) was instrumental in setting up my school visits in Ireland. Justin Song was my No. 1 contact in South Korea who really did a great job arranging my school visits and helping me navigate my way through Seoul. Justin's academic knowledge impressed me greatly! Guy Prenen, a retired principal, also helped arrange school visits throughout Belgium and hosted me in his house. Paul Leong, an assistant principal in Singapore, invited me to have dinner with his wonderful family and helped me greatly in visiting schools in Singapore. Robinson Devadhason, a fantastic person and my accountant in Chula Vista, California, facilitated all of my school visits in India. I would like to thank Brendon Henderson, a principal in the Wellington metro area of New Zealand, and his great family for their fine hospitality and allowing me to stay at their home house while visiting schools.

I'd also like to thank: Paul Leong. Kimmo Paavola, Veli-Matti Harjula, Janne Kaskenviita, Eerika Kantonen, Seija Ala-Ruona, Jussi Lounassalo, Pekka Ruuskanen, Pirjo Pollari, Ville Ylianunti, Janne Kaskenviita, Eerika Kantoen, Engelbert Hillen, Rudolf Schirmer, Uwe Schonfeld, Urs Kuhn, Christel Sagemuller, Meelis Kond, Margo Sootla, Gunda Tire, Juta Hirv, Meeli Kaldma, Urve Krause, Riina Müürsepp, Margo Sootla, Liisi Tomingas, Luule Niinesalu, Maie Kitsing, Meeli Kaldma, Kaie Piiskop, Gunda Tire, Meelis Kond, Martina Carmona Orozco, Maureen Orey, Carlos Navarro, Rigoberto Gonzalez, Ariel Delgado Cisneros, Dzielski Witold, Popowska Dorota, Malgorzata Holowka, Anna Zawadzka, Tadeusza Kosciuszki, Jung Keun, Dr. Ro Tae Seok, Brian Raisbeck, Hyunbin Im, Kim Mi SookLiew Beng Keong, Tenn Tann, Christine Kong, Dave Long, Amalia Trujillo, Michael Fleming, Seamus Mulconry, John Harper, Richard Bruton, Marie Therese Kilmartin, John Barry, Noreen Russell Kennedy, Caroline

Acknowledgements

McKeown, Maria Bn Ui Spring, Tommy Brown, Susan Campbell, Toru Nagahama, Tadashi Asada, Taro Tenegawa, Kumiko Somura, Yasuhiro Sekiguchi, Toshio Saito, Shigeki Mukai, Saskia Dobbelaere, Annelies Eeckeloo, Joris Debolle, Danny Steegmans, Sarah Candreva, Katleen Kielbaey, Michel Cardinaels, Ilse Scheirlinckx, Annelies Eeckeloo, Sarah Candreva, Bernadette Smith, Michele Scott, Paolo Burzese, Richard Cherry, Leslie Crossley, Michael Cohen, Paul Valle, John Glezakos, Tod Dungey, Stephen Hopkins, Marg Clarke, Karen Donkers, Jeff Foran, Leslie Crossley, Stephen Hopkins, Marcel Normandeau, Aimee Saldivar, Lori Nagy, Cindi Williams, Jennifer Allen, Marie Whelan, Jackie Flynn, Corine Gannon, Kristen Hodgins, William Moreau, Edward Brophy, Hugh MacDonald, Marcel Normandeau, William Morris, Pareekshith Abimanyu, Kalyan Kumar, Robin Lu, Anna Chiang, Taipei Economic and Cultural Office, Ms. Pang, Huichen Pan, Mr. Jin, Ms. Chou, Sharon Chen, Lichuan Wu, Li Chih-Ann, Li Chi-Hsh, Michelle Lien, Jithu U. Krishnan, Thomaz Dirickson, Ailton Aparecido Rodrigues, Conselho da Mulher, Fred Palmeira and Antonio Taliberti.

And finally, my thanks to: Carla de M. Alves, Renaldo Santos, Maria Riberio Bueno, Marcia Regina, Eva-Maria Schaedler, Arnold Kind, Rachel Guerra, Christian Weidkuhn, Eugen Nagele, Sandi Paulina, Tit Naubauer, Mojca Straus, Bostjan Seruga, Ptuj Boštjan Šeruga, Vida Hlebec, Martin Pivk, Janja Zupančič, Mojca Straus, Bostjan Ozimek, Marko Gale, Alojz Kranjz, Andrejra Psnikar, Fani al-Mansour, France Absec, Rüdiger Thierhoff, Birgit Höntzsch, Urs Kuhn, Jeff Wollentin, Darakorn Phensiri, Wongdaun Suwansiri, Chris Turvill, Chudcha Johnburom, Phaiboon Klaharn, Donald Culton, Nguyen Xuan Vang, Paula Cordeiro, Phamthanh Nghi, Margaret Petrochenkov, Vo Van Dung, Tien Dung, Nguyễn Thái Vĩnh, Tien Dzung, Can Thi Ngoc Bich, Ingeborg de Groodt, Joost Dirkwager, Amber Opstal, David Butcher, Dr. Hans Luyendijk, Ingeborg de Groodt, Cees de Groot, Hans Luyendijk, Radmilla Jovanovic , David Butcher, Henriette Boeve, Frits Welling, Joost Dirkzwager, Radmila Jovanovic, Rich Beal, Zafina Chen, Simon Cockerell, Rachel Brandon, Jan Otene, Kayleen Macnee, Deb King, Barri Dullabh, John Murdoch, Kayleen Macnee, Fiona Wain, Kayleen Macnee, Jan Oteen, Robin Lu,

Acknowledgements

Anna Chiang, Taipei Economic and Cultural Office, Ms. Pang, Huichen Pan, Mr. Jin, Ms. Chou. Sharon Chen, Lichuan Wu, Li Chih-Ann, Li Chi-Hsh, Michelle Lien, Jithu U. Krishnan.

223

Selected Bibliography

Alliance for Excellent Education in Washington, DC. "Technology Can Close
Achievement Gaps, Improve Learning: In a New Report, GSE
Researchers Identify Secrets to Successful Technology
Implementation, Particularly With Students at Risk of Dropping
Out." *Stanford: Graduate School of Education*, (September 2014).
https://ed.stanford.edu/news/technology-
can-close-achievement-gaps-and-improve-learning-outcomes
ARC. "Pasi Sahlberg - Excellence or Equity?" *YouTube* video, 11:25.
September 15, 2016. https://youtu.be/3VX0m-BcMpY
Ballard, Keith. "School Interviews Around the World." YouTube, (2011-
2018). https://www.youtube.com/user/keithballard1
Barnum, Matt. "Does England's Rapid Expansion of Charter-Like
'Academies' Hold a Lesson for the U.S.?" *Chalkbeat*, (December
2017). https://www.chalkbeat.org/2017/9/21/21100922/does-
england-s-rapid-expansion-of-charter-like-academies-hold-a-
lesson-for-the-u-s
Barshay, Jill. "Schools Exacerbate the Growing Achievement Gap Between
Rich and Poor, a 33-Country Study Finds: Rich Kids Get Steered into
More Demanding Math Classes While Poor Kids Get Less
Challenging Content." *The Hechinger Report: Covering Innovation
& Inequality in Education*, (October 2015). https://hechingerreport.
org/schools-exacerbate-the- growing-achievement-gap-between-
rich-and-poor-a-33-country-study-finds
---. "What 2018 PISA International Rankings Tell Us About U.S. Schools:
Results Point to Achievement Gaps Inside Each School." *The
Hechinger Report: Covering Innovation & Inequality in Education,
(December 2019)*. https:// hechingerreport.org/what-2018-pisa-
international-rankings-tell-us-about-u-s-schools/
Bauerlein, Mark. *The Dumbest Generation: How the Digital Age Stupefies
Young Americans and Jeopardizes Our Future (Or, Don't Trust
Anyone Under 30)*. New York: Penguin Group, 2008.
Berwick, Carly. "The Great German School Turnaround: The European
Country Managed to Raise Test Scores While Reducing Educational
Inequality. But With the Dramatic Influx of Migrants, Will its
Success Last?" *The Atlantic,* (November 2015). https://www.the
atlantic.com/education/archive/2015/ 11/great-german-scool-
turnaround/413806/

Bouygues, Helen Lee. "Does Educational Technology Help Students Learn?" *Forbes*, (June 2019). https://www.forbes.com/sites/helenlee bouygues/2019/06/ 14/does-educational-technology-help-students-learn/#1275b34a4539

Bracey, Gerald W.. *The War Against America's Public Schools: Privatizing Schools, Commercializing Education.* 1st ed. New York: Pearson, 2001.

Brokaw, Tom. *The Greatest Generation.* New York: Random House Trade Paperbacks, 1998.

Bryant, Jake, Felipe Child, Emma Dorn, and Stephen Hall. "New Global Data Reveal Education Technology's Impact on Learning." *McKinsey & Company,* (June 2020). https://www.mckinsey.com/industries/ education/our- insights/new-global-data-reveal-education-technologys-impact-on-learning

Bushweller, Kevin. "How COVID-19 Is Shaping Tech Use. What That Means When Schools Reopen." *Education Week*, (June 2020). https:// www.edweek.org/technology/how-covid-19-is-shaping-tech-use-what-that-means-when-schools-reopen/2020/06

Calderon, Valerie J., and Daniela Yu. "Student Enthusiasm Falls as High School Graduation Nears." *Gallup*, (June 2017). https://news.gallup.com/ opinion/gallup/211631/student-enthusiasm-falls-high-school-graduation-nears.aspx

Campbell, Carol et al. *Empowered Educators in Canada: How High-Performing Systems Shape Teaching Quality*. San Francisco: The Stanford Center for Opportunity Policy in Education, 2017.

Cardoza, Kavitha. "In Canada's Public Schools, Immigrant Students Are Thriving." *Education Week: Equity & Diversity*, (February 2018). https://www.edweek .org/leadership/in-canadas-public-schools-immigrant-students-are-thriving/2018/02?r=1728354129

Carter, Abi. "Digital Education: Only a Quarter of German Schools Have WiFi." *I Am Expat*, (November 2019). https://www.iamexpat.de/ education/ education-news/digital-education-only-quarter-german-schools-have-wifi

Chepkemoi, Joyce. "Countries Who Spend The Most Time Doing Homework." *World Atlas: Society*, (July 2017). https://www.world atlas.com/articles/ countries-who-spend-the-most-time-doing-homework.html

Chua, Amy, and Jed Rubenfeld. *The Triple Package: How Three Unlikely Traits Explain the Rise and Fall of Cultural Groups in America*. 3rd ed. New York: Penguin Books, 2015.

City & Guilds Group. "Case Study: The Economic Benefits of Career and Technical Education and Training in the United States." London. https://www.cityandguildsgroup.com/~/media/CGG%20Website/Documents/CGGroupUS%20pdf.ashx

Clavel, Teru. *World Class: One Mother's Journey Halfway Around the Globe in Search of the Best Education for Her Children*. New York: Simon & Schuster, Inc., 2019.

Craw, Jennifer. "Matching Training to Economic Goals." *NCEE*, (October 2019). http://ncee.org/2019/10/matching-training-to-economic-goals/

Darling-Hammond, Linda et al. *Empowered Educators: How High-Performing Systems Shape Teaching Quality Around the World*. San Francisco: The Stanford Center for Opportunity Policy in Education, 2017.

--- Chung Wei, Ruth, and Alethea Andree. "How High-Achieving Countries Develop Great Teachers." *Stanford Center for Opportunity Policy in Education ~ Research Brief*, (August 2010). https://edpolicy.stanford.edu/sites/default/files/publications/how-high-achieving-countries-develop-great-teachers.pdf

Davie, Sandra. "Students Don't Perform Better With Tech Use In School: OECD." *The Straits Times*, (November 2015). https://www.straitstimes.com/singapore/education/students-dont-perform-better-with-tech-use-in-school-oecd

Dickinson, Kevin. "Equity Made Estonia an Educational Front Runner: Estonia Has Combined a Belief in Learning with Equal-Access Technology to Create One of the World's Best Education Systems." *Big Think,* (September 2020). https://bigthink.com/thepresent/estonia-education/

Dintersmith, Ted. *What School Could Be: Insights and Inspiration from Teachers across America.* Princeton: Princeton University Press, 2018.

Downey, Maureen. "Are American Students and Their Parents Willing to Work as Hard as East Asians?" *The Atlanta Journal-Constitution*, (July 2017). https://www.ajc.com/blog/get-schooled/are-american-students-and-their-parents-willing-work-hard-east-asians/KtwhUPPAxTSJ0kNK0NrfoN/

Education International. "New Zealand: Government Announces End of Charter Schools." (February 2018). https://www.eiie.org/en/item/22365:new- zealand-government-announces-end-of-charter-schools

Edutopia. "Singapore's 21st-Century Teaching Strategies (Education Everywhere Series)." *YouTube* video, 7:44. March 14, 2012. https://www.edutopia.org/ video/singapores-21st-century-teaching-strategies-education-everywhere-series

E-Estonia. "Enter e-Estonia: e-education." (March 2020). https://e-estonia.com/enter-e-estonia-e-education/

Enchikova, Ekaterina, Cibelle Toledo, Tiago Neves, and Gil Nata. "Does PISA Help Fighting for Social Equity?" In *Education and City: Quality Education for Modern Cities,* vol 3, 1st ed, edited by Svetlana Vachkova and Sabina Shu-Chun Chiang, pp. 80-89, European Publisher, 2022. https://www.europeanproceedings.com/ article/10.15405/epes.22043.8

EQAO (Education Quality and Accountability Office). "Top Reasons You Can't Compare Standardized Testing in Ontario and the United States." (July 2015). https://www.eqao.com/wp-content/uploads/infographic -EQAO-US-comparison.pdf

European Commission/EACEA/Eurydice. *Compulsory Education in Europe - 2019/20: Eurydice - Facts and Figures*. Luxembourg: Publications Office of the European Union, 2019. https://eacea.ec.europa.eu/ nationalpolicies/eurydice/sites/default/files/compulsory_education_in_europe_2019_20.pdf

First Five Years Fund. "Head Start & Early Head Start." https://www.ffyf.org/ issues/head-start-early-head-start/

Fishman, Ted C.. *China Inc.: How the Rise of the Next Superpower Challenges America and the World*. New York: Scribner, 2006.

Floden, Robert. Interview by Keith Ballard. March 9, 2022.

Frase, Larry E., and William Streshly. *Top 10 Myths in Education: Fantasies Americans Love to Believe.* Lanham, Scarecrow Press, Inc, 2000.

Friedman, Thomas L., and Michael Mandelbaum. *That Used to Be Us: How America Fell Behind in the World It Invented and How We Can Come Back.* 1st ed. New York: Farrar, Straus and Giroux, 2011.

Fullan, Michael. *All Systems Go: The Change Imperative for Whole System Reform.* Foreword by Peter Senge. Thousand Oaks: Corwin: A Sage Company, and Ontario Principals Council, 2010.

Gallup, Inc. "Education Technology Use in Schools: Student and Educator Perspectives." *NewSchools Venture Fund*. Gallop, Inc., 2019. http://www.newschools.org/wp-content/uploads/2019/09/Gallup-Ed-Tech-Use-in-Schools-2.pdf

Gao, Henry, "Education in Finland: A Model For Equality." *The Borgen Project*, (October 2016). https://borgenproject.org/education-in-finland/

Gilchrist, Karen. "These Millennials Are Reinventing the Multibillion-Dollar Education Industry During Coronavirus." *CNBC: Startups*. (June 2020). https://www.cnbc.com/2020/06/08/edtech-how-schools-education-industry-is-changing-under-coronavirus.html

Gladwell, Malcolm. *Outliers: The Story of Success.* 1st ed. New York: Little, Brown and Company, 2008.

Goldstein, Dana. *The Teacher Wars: A History of America's Most Embattled Profession.* New York: Anchor Books, 2014.

---. "Teacher Pay is So Low in Some U.S. School Districts that They're Recruiting Overseas." New York Times, May 2, 2018.

Goodwin, A. Lin et al. *Empowered Educators in Singapore: How High-Performing Systems Shape Teaching Quality*. San Francisco: The Stanford Center for Opportunity Policy in Education, 2017.

Gray Ph.D., Peter. "Head Start's Value Lies in Care, Not Academic Training: Here's My Theory About Why Some Early Childhood Programs Help and Others Hurt." *Psychology Today*, (February 2020). https://www.psychologytoday .com/us/blog/freedom-learn/202002/head-start-s-value-lies-in-care-not-academic-training

Hall, Jim and Dave Wells. "Higher Administration Chargers of Arizona Charter Schools Cost Taxpayers $128 Million a Year." Arizonians for Charter School Accountability with Grand Canyon Institute, (Feb. 23, 2016). http://grandcanyoninstitute.org/wp-content/uploads/2016/02/AZCharterAccuntability_GCI_Policy_Paper_ChartersHigherAdminCosts2-23-16.pdf

Hammerness, Karen, Raisa Ahtiainen, and Pasi Sahlberg. *Empowered Educators in Finland: How High Performing Systems Shape Teaching Quality.* 1st ed. San Francisco, Jossey-Bass: A Wiley Brand, 2017.

Hansen, Michael, and Diana Quintero. "Analyzing 'The Homework Gap' Among High School Students." *Brookings*, (August 2017). https://www.brookings .edu/blog/brown-center-chalkboard/2017/08/10/analyzing-the-homework-gap-among-high-school-students/

Hatch, Thomas. "10 Surprises in the High-Performing Estonian Education System." *International Education News,* (August 2017). https://internationalednews .com/2017/08/02/10-surprises-in-the-high-performing-estonian-education-system/

Higgins, Lori. "NAACP Releases Report on Charter Schools, Cites Detroit and Michigan." *Detroit Free Press, (July 2017).* https://www.freep.com/story/news/2017/07/26/naacp-charter-school-report-detroit/512724001/

Hobbs, Tawnell D. and Lee Hawkins. "The Results are In for Remote Learning: It Didn't Work." *The Wall Street Journal*, (June 2020). https://www.wsj.com/ articles/schools-coronavirus-remote-learning-lockdown-tech-11591375078?mod=searchresults& page=1&pos=2

Integral. "German School System - Abitur." *Integraledu: Secondary Education*. http://www.liceestrainatate.ro/en/articles/german-school-system---abitur

Jackson, Abby. "The Poorest 10% of Vietnamese Students Performed Better on an International Exam Than the Average American Teen." *Insider*, (December 2016). https://www.businessinsider.com/poor-countries-outperform- america-pisa-exam-2016-12

Jelita, Angela. "The Downsides to Singapore's Education System: Streaming, Stress and Suicides." *South China Morning Post*, (September 2017). https://www.scmp.com/lifestyle/families/article/2111822/downsides-singapores-education-system-streaming-stress-and

Jr-keng, Tsai. "Prepare Now For Online Education." *Taipei Times*, (March 2020). https://www.taipeitimes.com/News/editorials/archives/2020/03/17/2003732829

Kagan, Sharon Lynn et al. *The Early Advantage: Building Systems That Work for Young Children*. New York: Teachers College Press, 2019.

Koenig, Rebecca. "The Post-Pandemic Outlook for Edtech." *EdSurge: Edtech Business*, (June 2020). https://www.edsurge.com/news/2020-06-11-the-post-pandemic-outlook-for-edtech

Kynge, James. *China Shakes the World: A Titan's Rise and Troubles Future -- and the Challenge for America*. New York: Houghton Mifflin Company, 2006.

Lambert, Olivia. "'A Fear of Failure': 12-Year-Old's Insane Before and After School." *Yahoo! News*, (October 2019). https://au.news.yahoo.com/i-developed- a-fear-of-failure-inside-the-worlds-best-education-system-044001062.html

Long, Heather. "By Age 3, Inequality is Clear: Rich Kids Attend School. Poor Kids Stay With a Grandparent." *The Washington Post*, (September 2017). https://www.washingtonpost.com/news/wonk/wp/2017/09/26/by-age-3-inequality-is-clear-rich-kids-attend-school-poor-kids-stay-with-a-grandparent/

Lukianoff, Greg, and Jonathan Haidt. *The Coddling of the American Mind: How Good Intentions and Bad Ideas are Setting Up a Generation for Failure*. New York: Penguin Press, 2018.

Marshall, Ray, and Marc Tucker. *Thinking For A Living: Education And The Wealth Of Nations*. New York, BasicBooks: A Member of the Perseus Books Group, 1993.

Matias, Selma. "Comparison of the U.S. and Finland's Educational Systems on Students' Academic Achievement." *Digital Commons: Capstone Projects and Master's Theses,* (December 2019). https://digital commons.csumb.edu/cgi/viewcontent.cgi?article=1684&context=c aps_thes_all

McKeever, Vicky. "Closing the Gap: Finland to Give Men and Women Almost 7 Months of Paid Parental Leave Each." *CNBC: Make It,* (February 2020). https://www.cnbc.com/2020/02/05/finland-to-give-men-and-women-equal-paid-parental-leave.html

Meier, Deborah, Alfie Kohn, Linda Darling-Hammond, Theodore R. Sizer, and George Wood. *Many Children Left Behind: How the No Child Left Behind Act is Damaging Our Children and Our Schools.* 1st ed. Boston: Beacon Press, 2004.

Messenger, Tony. "Messenger: Teach for America Changes its Focus Amid Difficult Times for Public Schools." *St. Louis Post-Dispatch,* (September 2021). https://www.stltoday.com/news/local/ columns/tony-messenger/messenger-teach-for-america-changes-its-focus-amid-difficult-times-for-public-schools/article_38a400df-8018-517e-9779-5b0aaae09c47.html

Miron, Gary, William Mathis, and Kevin Weiner. "Review of Separating Fact & Fiction: What You Need to Know About Charter Schools." Edited by Don Weitzman and Erik Gunn. *NEPC: National Education Policy Center,* (February 2015). https://nepc.colorado.edu/thinktank/ review-separating- fact-and-fiction

Montgomery, Mike. "The Pandemic Should Have Been Edtech's Moment To Shine. So Far, It Hasn't Been." *Forbes,* (June 2020). https://www. forbes.com/sites/mikemontgomery/2020/06/04/the-pandemic-should-have-been-edtechs-moment-to-shine-so-far-it-hasnt-been/

National Center for Education Statistics (NCES). "State Education Practices (SEP) Compiles and Disseminates Data on State Education Practice Activities: Table 5.1 Compulsory School Attendance Laws, Minimum and Maximum Age Limits for Required Free Education, by State." 2017. https://nces.ed.gov/programs/statereform/ tab5_1.asp

---. "Total and current expenditures per pupil in public elementary and secondary schools: Selected years, 1919-20 through 2016-17." *Digest of Education Statistics,* (August 2019). https://nces.ed.gov/ programs/digest/d19 /tables/ dt19_236.55.asp?current=yes

NCEE. "Top-Performing Countries: Canada." http://ncee.org/what-we-do/center- on-international-education-benchmarking/top-performing-countries/canada-overview/canada-teacher-and-principal-quality/

---. "Top-Performing Countries: Japan." http://ncee.org/what-we-do/center-on- international-education-benchmarking/top-performing-countries/japan-overview/japan-teacher-and-principal-quality/

Nestler, Herb. "Comparing Education in the US and Germany." *Nestler Learning and Development: Culture*, (September 2018). https://www.herbnestler. com/blog/2018/4/20/comparing-education-in-the-us-and-germany

Newberry, Laura. "More Parents are Home-Schooling. Some are Never Turning Back." *Los Angeles Times*, (Jan. 24, 2022). https://www.latimes.com/california/newsletter/2022-01-24/8-to-3-homeschooling-on-rise-8-to-3

New Media Mill. "Leading High-Performance School Systems: Lessons from the World's Best." *YouTube* video, 2:58:58. April 23, 2019. https://www.youtube.com/watch?v=lcTGfBEwA2w

Ng, Jane. "99% Pre-School Attendance is Not Good Enough." *The Straits Times*, (May 2013). https://www.straitstimes.com/singapore/99-pre-school- attendance-is-not-good-enough

Ning, Annie, and Betsy Corcoran. "How China's Schools Are Getting Through COVID-19." *EdSurge: Global Education*, (April 2020). https://www.edsurge.com/news/2020-04-20-how-china-s-schools-are-getting-through-covid-19

Oakes, Jeannie. "Keeping Track: How Schools Structure Inequality." New Haven: Yale University Press, 2005.

OECD. "Equity and Equality in Education: Supporting Disadvantaged Students and Schools." OECD Publishing, (2012).

---. "PISA 2018 Results: Combined Executive Summaries." Volume no. I, II and III. https://www.oecd.org/pisa/Combined_Executive_ Summaries_PISA_ 2018.pdf

---. "Policy Lessons for Korea," in Lessons from PISA for Korea, OECD Publishing, Paris (2014).

---. *Students, Computers, and Learning: Making the Connection*. PISA, OECD Publishing, 2015. https://read.oecdilibrary.org/education/students- computers-and-learning_9789264239555-en#page10

O'Neal Schiess, Jennifer. "Prioritizing Equity in School Funding." *Bellwether Education Partners: From Pandemic to Progress,* (February 2021). https://bellwethereducation.org/sites/default/files/Bellwether_Pandemictoprogress_SchoolFunding_Final.pdf

Partanen, Anu. "What Americans Keep Ignoring About Finland's School Success: The Scandinavian Country is an Education Superpower Because it Values Equality More Than Excellence." *The Atlantic*, (December 2011). https://www.theatlantic.com/national/archive/2011/12/what-americans-keep-ignoring-about-finlands-school-success/250564/

PBS NewsHour. "What International Teens Think About School In America." *YouTube* video, 8:20, December 13, 2016. https://www.youtube.com/watch?v=YW8FV2EKRac

Pellissier, Hank. "High Test Scores, Higher Expectations, and Presidential Hype: Should South Korean Schools Point the Way to American Reforms?" *Great!Schools.org*, (October 2013). https://www.greatschools.org/gk/articles/south-korean-schools/

Pham, Sherisse. "High Test Scores, but China Education Flawed: China's Education System Prepares Students for Tests, but Not Much Else." *ABC News*, (December 2010). https://abcnews.go.com/Politics/chinas-education- prepares-students-tests/story?id=12348599

Phillips, David, and Michele Schweisfurth. *Comparative and International Education: An Introduction to Theory, Method and Practice.* 2nd ed. New York, Bloomsbury Publishing, 2014.

Poh, Joanne. "Child Care Subsidies in Singapore 2022 - What Do You Qualify For?" *MoneySmart: Family,* (March 2022). https://blog.moneysmart.sg/family/child-care-subsidies/

Randazzo, Sara, and Christine Mai-Duc. "Oakland's School Closures Might Be a Warning Sign for California: City Decides to Close Seven Schools After Protests and Hunger Strikes as Enrollment Declines Expected to Accelerate Throughout the State." *The Wall Street Journal,* (February 2022). https:// www.wsj.com/articles/oaklands-school-closures-might-be-a-warning-sign-for-california-11644499800?st=5ceu67wohqh5lcq&reflink=desktopwebshare_twitter

Ripley, Amanda. *The Smartest Kids in the World and How They Got That Way.* New York: Simon & Schuster, 2013.

Robinson, Ken, and Lou Aronica. *Creative Schools: The Grassroots Revolution That's Transforming Education.* New York: Penguin Books, 2016.

Rose, Mike. *The Mind at Work: Valuing the Intelligence of the American Worker.* New York: Penguin Books, 2004.

Rothman, Bob. "After the Shock: The German Education System in 2017." *NCEE*, (September 2017). http://ncee.org/2017/09/after-the-shock-the-german- education-system-in-2017/

Sahlberg, Pasi. "Excellence or Equity?" Speech at Atlantic Rim Collaboratory, Reykjavik, Iceland, Sept. 15, 2016, https://youtu.be/3VX0m-BcMpY.

---. *FinnishED Leadership: Four Big, Inexpensive Ideas to Transform Education*. Thousand Oaks: Corwin, 2018.

---. *Finnish Lessons: What Can the World Learn from Educational Change in Finland? (The Series on School Reform)*. Foreword by Andy Hargreaves. Series Foreword by Ann Lieberman. New York: Teachers College Press, 2011.

---. "GERM That Kills Schools." Speech at TEDxEast, New York, May 11, 2012, https://youtu.be/TdgS--9Zg_0.

--- et al. *Hard Questions on Global Educational Change: Policies, Practices, and the Future of Education*. New York: Teachers College Press, 2017.

Salaky, Kristin. "What Standardized Tests Look Like in 10 Places Around the World." *Insider: Lifestyle*, (September 2018). https://www.insider.com/standardized-tests-around-the-world-2018-9

Sanders, Bernie. "Bernie Sanders: America Must End High-Stakes Testing, Finally Invest in Public Education: Across the Country, Teachers, Parents and Students Are Pushing Back Against an Ineffective and Punitive Standardized Tests Regime. I Stand With Them." *USA Today*, (January 2020). https://www.usatoday.com/story/opinion/2020/01/08/bernie- sanders-education-no-child-left-behind-testing-column/2827348001/

Sato, Mistilina, and Jiacheng Li. *Empowered Educators in China: How High Performing Systems Shape Teaching Quality.* San Francisco: Jossey-Bass, 2017.

Schleicher, Andreas. *World Class: How to Build a 21st-Century School System*. Paris: OECD Publishing, 2018.

--- Salinas, Daniel. "Equity in Education: Breaking Down Barriers to Social Mobility (United States)." *OECD:Programme For International Student Assessment (PISA),* (2018). https://www.oecd.org/pisa/Equity-in-Education-country- note-US.pdf

---. *PISA 2018: Insights and Interpretations*. Cyprus: OECD, 2019. https://www.oecd.org/pisa/PISA%202018%20Insights%20and%20Interpretations%20FINAL%20PDF.pdf

Schulman, Robyn. "Five Major Differences Between The Chinese And American Education System." *EdNews Daily*. http://www.ednewsdaily.com/ five-major-differences-between-the-chinese-and-american-education-system/

Spees, Ann-Cathrin. "Could Germany's Vocational Education and Training System Be a Model for the U.S.?" *World Education News + Reviews,* Vocational Education and Training, (June 2018). https://wenr.wes.org/2018/06/ could-germanys-vocational-education-and-training-system-be-a-model-for-the-u-s

Stewart, Vivien. *World Class Education: Learning from International Models of Excellence and Innovation.* Alexandria: ASCD, 2012.

Strauss, Valerie. "It Looks Like the Beginning of the End of America's Obsession with Student Standardized Tests." *The Washington Post*, (June 2020). https://www.washingtonpost.com/education/2020/ 06/21/it-looks-like-beginning-end-americas-obsession-with-student-standardized-tests/

---. "The Brainy Questions on Finland's only High-Stakes Standardized Test." *The Washington Post*, (March 2014). https://www.washington post.com/news/answer-sheet/wp/2014/03/24/the-brainy-questions-on-finlands-only-high-stakes-standardized-test/

---. "What and Who Are Fueling the Movement to Privatize Public Education - And Why You Should Care." *The Washington Post*, (May 2018). https://www. washingtonpost.com/news/answersheet/wp/ 2018/05/30/what-and-who-is-fueling-the-movement-to-privatize-public-education-and-why-you-should-care/

---. "What the Public Isn't Told About High-Performing Charter Schools in Arizona." *The Washington Post,* (March 2017). https://www. washingtonpost.com/news/answer-sheet/wp/2017/03/30/what-the-public-doesnt-know-about-high-performing-charter-schools-in-arizona/

TEDx Talks. "Germ That Kills Schools: Pasi Sahlberg at TEDxEast." *YouTube* video, 18:41. June 27, 2012. https://youtu.be/TdgS--9Zg_0

The Center for High Impact Philanthropy. "High Return on Investment (ROI): Invest in a Strong Start for Children." *University of Pennsylvania: Center for High Impact Philanthropy*, (2015). https://www.impact .upenn.edu/ our-analysis/opportunities-to-achieve-impact/early-childhood-toolkit/why-invest/what-is-the-return-on-investment/

The Hechinger Report. "Study: Homework Matters More in Certain Countries." *U.S. News*, (January 2015). https://www.usnews.com/ news/articles/2015/ 01/05/study-homework-matters-more-in-certain-countries

The Nation's Report Card. "Results from the 2019 Mathematics and Reading Assessments." https://www.nationsreportcard.gov/mathematics/ supportive_files/2019_infographic.pdf

Timsit, Annabelle. "Overhauling Japan's High-Stakes University-Admission System: The Ministry of Education is on a Mission to Save the Country's Economy--and the Effort Could Be a Boon For Kids' Mental Health, Too." *The Atlantic*, (January 2018). https://www. theatlantic.com/education/ archive/2018/01/overhauling-japans-high-stakes-university-admission-system/550409/

Tucker, Marc S.. "Asian Countries Take the U.S. to School: A Closer Look Reveals Key Differences in How They Educate Their Students and Offers Valuable Practical Lessons in Getting All Children to Achieve." *The Atlantic*, (February 2016). https://www.theatlantic .com/education/archive/2016/ 02/us-asia-education-differences/471564/

---. *Leading High-Performing School Systems; Lessons from the World's best.* Alexandria: ASCD; Washington, D.C.: National Center on Education and the Economy, 2019.

---. Interview by Keith Ballard and Brooke Staggs. Dec. 28, 2019.

---. *Surpassing Shanghai: An Agenda for American Education Built on the World's Leading Systems.* Cambridge: Harvard Education Press, 2011.

--- et al. *Vocational Education and Training for a Global Economy: Lessons from Four Countries*. Cambridge: Harvard Education Press, 2019.

---. "Why Other Countries Keep Outperforming Us in Education (and How to Catch Up): Money From the American Rescue Plan Could be Our Last Best Chance to Build the School System We Need." *Education Week*, (May 2021). https://www.edweek.org/policy-politics/ opinion-why-other- countries-keep-outperforming-us-in-education-and-how-to-catch-up/2021/05

Turner, Cory. "U.S. Tests Teens A Lot, But Worldwide, Exam Stakes Are Higher." *NPR: Education* (April 2014). https://www.npr.org/2014/ 04/30/ 308057862/u-s-tests-teens-a-lot-but-worldwide-exam-stakes-are-higher

--- Reema Khrais, Tim Lloyd, Alexandra Olgin, Laura Isensee, Becky Vevea, and Dan Carsen. "Why America's Schools Have a Money Problem." *NPR: School Money,* Heard on Morning Edition, (April 2018). https://www.npr.org/ 2016/04/18/474256366/why-americas-schools-have-a-money-problem

U.S. News & World Report. "Search Best High Schools." https://www.us news.com/education/best-high-schools/national-rankings/charter-school-rankings

Wagner, Tony. *The Global Achievement Gap: Why Even Our Best Schools Don't Teach the New Survival Skills Our Children Need - And What We Can Do About It*. New York: Basic Books, 2008.

Walker, Timothy D.. "The Ticking Clock of Teacher Burnout: On Average, American Educators Spend More Hours With Students Than Their International Counterparts—and That May Not Be a Good Thing." *The Atlantic*, (September 2019). https://www.theatlantic.com/education/ archive/2016/09/the-ticking-clock-of-us-teacher-burnout/502253/

Wexler, Natalie. "How Classroom Technology is Holding Students Back: Educators Love Digital Devices, But There's Little Evidence They Help Children--Especially Those Who Most Need Help." *MIT Technology Review: Humans And Technology*, (December 2019).

Wikipedia. "Education in Singapore." Last modified March 2022. https://en.wikipedia.org/wiki/Education_in_Singapore

---. "Education in South Korea." Last modified May 2022. https://en.wikipedia.org/wiki/Education_in_South_Korea

Winerip, Michael. "A Chosen Few Are Teaching For America." *The New York Times*, (July 2010). https://www.nytimes.com/2010/07/12/education/ 12winerip.html

Woessmann, Ludger. "Why Students in Some Countries Do Better." *Education Next*, (July 2006). https://www.educationnext.org/whystudentsinsomecountries dobetter/

Wood, Tyler Coolidge. "The Suneung." *Tyler Coolidge Wood*, (February 2017). http://www.tylercoolidgewood.com/korean-highstakes-testing

Yee, Vivian. "Grouping Students by Ability Regains Favor in Classrooms." *New York Times*, (June 2013). https://www.nytimes.com/2013/06/10/education/ grouping-students-by-ability-regains-favor-with-educators.html

Yourex-West, Heather. "Why Standardized Tests are a Controversial Subject for Alberta Schools." *Global News*, (September 2019). https://globalnews.ca/ news/5844773/alberta-matters-standardized-tests-controversy-education/

Zakaria, Fareed. "On GPS: Takeaways from PISA Education Rankings." *CNN* video, 4:45. December 12, 2016. https://www.cnn.com/videos/tv/2016/12/12/ exp-gps-1211-schleicher-kopp-pisa-education-study.cnn

Zhao, Yong. *Reach for Greatness: Personalizable Education for All Children (Corwin Impact Leadership Series)*. Thousand Oaks: Corwin, 2018.

Notes

Unless otherwise stated within the text of the book or on the following pages, the people I quote and the scenes I describe all came from reporting I did in schools around the world from 2011 to 2022. I documented many of those visits on my YouTube channel: Educator Keith Ballard. You can search country names or topics there to find interviews with particular people or to see scenes described in the pages of this book for yourself.

Introduction: Inspiration on a Mountaintop

3 *American spending*: NCES, "Total and current expenditures…"

4 *Consider these facts*: These details are drawn from analysis of PISA data by experts and me, along with a phone interview and writing by Marc Tucker.

5 *50 percent*: Estimates of how many jobs will be replaced by AI vary widely, with on United Nations study citing an estimate of up to 80 percent. However, other sources, include the Brookings Institution put the estimate closer to a maximum of 54 percent.

6 *Performed best*: For most of my discussions around country rankings on the PISA exams, I have relied on 2018 figures, which were the latest available at the time of publication. Unless otherwise noted, I used rankings that combined average performance by country on reading, math and science.

7 *Numerous surveys show*: Some 51 percent of teachers said they felt unsatisfied with the state of their profession, according to the 2020 Teacher Confidence Index. Some 52 percent of Americans said they were not satisfied with the quality of the public education system in a 2017 Gallup poll. And only 49 percent of employers surveyed for the Job Outlook 2020 report from the National Association of College and Employers felt that recent hires came to them with proficient oral and written communication skills.

Chapter One: Family Support: It's a Two-Way Street

15 *Age of 25*: Several countries, including Canada and Australia, have performed longitudinal studies that look at how student results on the first PISA tests, given starting in 2000, correlated to their success as adults. They've generally found students who scored well on the exams were far more likely to graduate from college and be employed 10 years later.

17   *18,720 hours*: OECD tracks hours in school by country, with this calculation drawn from that source and others that estimate averages across all 50 states.

23   *Mounting research shows*: To name a few… The 2011 study "The Effect of Maternity Leave on Children's Birth and Infant Health Outcomes in the United States" found decreases in infant mortality and premature birth and increases in birth weight in families with access to paid leave. The 2018 study "Did California Paid Family Leave Impact Infant Health?" showed a reduction in infant hospitalizations after families got paid leave. The 2015 study "Paid Maternity Leave and Breastfeeding Practice Before and After California's Implementation of the Nation's First Paid Family Leave Program" found a significant uptick in breastfeeding, which is linked to greater infant health.

25   *Spend more on early childhood education*: OECD tracks this data.

25   *Majority do*: OECD tracks this data, with 52 percent of 3-year-olds in Poland and 86 percent of 6-year-olds enrolled in early childhood education programs.

26   *Yields a return*: The National Forum on Early Childhood Policy and Programs estimates that, for every dollar invested, quality early childhood programs can yield returns of $4 to $9. Other studies, including a 2009 study of Perry Preschool in Michigan, estimate the return is as high as $12 per $1 invested.

26   *Median salary*: From the *U.S. News & World Report* on preschool teachers.

29   *Singapore*: The nation's Deputy Prime Minister Heng Swee Keat announced in 2020 that Singapore intended to double government spending on early childhood education, taking it from $1 billion to $2 billion over the next few years.

29   *Head Start program*: A longitudinal study by the U.S. Department of Health and Human Services show a slight academic bump for primary students enrolled in Head Start programs, but that those gains are no longer distinguishable after third grade.

30   *Difficult to catch them up*: A trio of longitudinal studies in the late 1990s showed "late bloomers," who start off behind and later "bloom," are extremely rare. Students who were poor readers in their first years of school tended to remain poor readers, the studies found.

30   *Incarceration rates*: There is a 2012 study from the Annie E. Casey Foundation that says students who are behind in reading at the third-grade level are several times more likely to drop out of high

school. And a 2009 study out of Northwestern University says students who drop out of high school are 63 percent more likely to get incarcerated than college graduates.

32   *In China*: From a 2019 survey by the China National Children's Center.

Chapter Two: High Standards for Teachers

39   *From the Philippines*: Goldstein, "Teacher Pay is so Low…"
39   *In South Korea*: OECD, "Policy Lessons for Korea."
40   *Starting teacher's salary*: Data compiled by the National Education Association.
46   *China regularly ranks*: Data from the Global Teacher Status Index.
52   *Nearly 2,000*: From the National Council on Teacher Quality.
55   *60 percent, 3 percent*: NCES data.
59   *Hours teachers spend*: OECD data from 2021 on the average number of hours teachers spend in their classroom teaching each year.

Chapter Three: Restructuring the School Experience

69   *Taiwanese students, Irish students*: NCES data.
69   *Students in Shanghai:* OECD data.
71   *Amount spent*: OECD data, bar chart by Brooke Staggs.
73   *Kids who aren't supervised*: FBI data shows teens are more likely to commit crimes in the hours immediately after school gets out, while the Office of Juvenile Justice and Delinquency Program shows they're more likely to get into trouble on weekdays.
74-75   *Length of school day, school year*: NCES data.

Chapter Four: Vocational Education Puts Student Choice First

92   *70 percent*: OECD data.
93   *Volumes of research*: In the 1970s, a large study by David N. Aspy and Flora N. Roebuck found giving students more choices was a key to boosting engagement. That concept has been reenforced by study after study over the years, including a 2010 study called "The effectiveness and relative importance of choice in the classroom" that specifically showed how giving students choice with their homework greatly improved the odds that kids would complete the assignment.

94   *In the 1800s*: Tucker, *Leading High-Performing*…

95   *Problems quickly emerged*: Oakes, *Keeping Track.*

96   *Massachusetts*: The 2018 study "The Effect of Career and Technical Education on Human Capital Accumulation: Causal Evidence from Massachusetts" showed strong vocational programs there boosted graduation rates by 7 to 10 percent even for higher-income students, and much more for poorer students.

98   *Suicide rates*: A longitudinal study completed by the U.S. Centers for Disease Control in 2015 found all veterinarians had higher rates of suicide than other professions, with females 3.5 times more likely to kill themselves than the general population.

100   *Required to attend school*: European Commission, "Compulsory Education in Europe."

102   *By the numbers*: Infographic by Brooke Staggs with data from City & Guilds Group, "Case Study…"

Chapter Five: High-Stakes Testing with Different Stakes

121   *100 standardized tests*: See page 125

121   *Growing acceptance*: Strauss, "It Looks Like…"

123   *Dozens of hours*: The Council of the Great City Schools study referenced on page 125 says students spend 20 to 25 hours each school year taking standardized tests, with many more hours spent on preparation.

123   *Grown more unhappy*: Results of the latest Metlife Survey of the American Teacher show educators have gotten less happy in their jobs over the past 20 years, while the 2022 Merrimack College Teacher's Survey showed job satisfaction at an all-time low.

124   *2012 study*: References the Brookings Institution report "Strength in Numbers: State Spending on K-12 Assessment Systems."

128   *Cheat*: In 2015, a jury in Atlanta convicted 11 teachers of a scheme to cheat on standardized tests, with an investigation that grew to include 109 teachers and administrators. There was also a scandal in 2010 at an elementary school outside Houston, with investigations also everywhere from Massachusetts to Nevada.

129   *Declared a flop*: A massive 2018 report by the RAND Corporation and the American Institutes for Research said the Bill and Melinda Gates' Foundation donation to evaluate teachers using test scores was not effective in meeting its intended goals.

132   *Research has found*: Data on testing vendors is also from the 2012 Brookings Institution report referenced above.

135 *Inequities in the tests*: Racial biases in SAT and ACT tests have been well documented, including a 2020 study from the Brookings Institution called "SAT Math Scores Mirror and Maintain Racial Inequity."

Chapter Six: Technology is Secondary

151 *Top of the charts*: OECD compiles data on student access to computers for schoolwork, with most recent data from the 2018 PISA exam.

152 *Ed tech* valuations: A 2019 study from firm Markets and Research projected the ed tech market would hit $350 billion by 2025.

161 *Research is showing*: While most people think of the digital divide as a lack of access to internet service and other technology for low-income people, the New York Times and other media outlets along with nonprofit groups and advocates, in recent years have been documenting how poor kids are being pushed to use technology in their classrooms much more than rich kids, with well-off schools and families opting out of too much screen time due to concerns over the negative implications.

Chapter Seven: The Arts and Culture are Essential

171 *Dropout rates*: The 2015 study "Arts Education and the High School Dropout Problem," which followed 175,000 students for five years, found a significantly lower risk of dropping out for students who'd had regular arts education.

171 *Reducing anxiety*: The 2010 study "Connection Between Art, Healing, and Public Health: A Review of Current Literature" found significant mental health benefits for those who engaged in the arts, with music particularly found to help reduce anxiety.

171 *Cortisol*: The 2016 study "Reduction of Cortisol Levels and Participants' Responses Following Art Making" found a noticeable reduction in cortisol levels for those who'd made art for 45 minutes.

172 *Academic achievement*: The 2019 Nation's Report Card showed a significant jump in both reading and math scores for students who had regular arts education, even after controlling for other factors.

172 *Pathways in the brain*: A five-year study by USC's Brain and Creativity Institute concluded in 2016 that music training accelerated brain development in young children.

173 *Historic events*: A history of arts budgets cuts was traced in the 2009 article "On the Chopping Block, Again" in Harvard Ed. Magazine.

Chapter Eight: The Equity Question

188 *Poorest 10 percent*: Andreas Schleicher, director of education and skills at the OECD, cited this fact in his analysis of the 2015 PISA results.

188-189 *Series of metrics*: All of the comparative data on equity in education on these pages comes from OECD, "Equity and Equality..."

193 *Teachers in Mississippi*: Data tracked by OECD

193 *New York spends*: State education expenses from 2021 U.S. Census Bureau data

195 *More racial divides*: A 2020 report from UCLA's *The Civil Rights Project* found the percentage of Black students who attended schools with a majority of White students has plummeted from a 1987 peak of 38 percent to a 2018 low of 19 percent.

201 *Homogenous population*: Foreign-born resident data tracked by OECD

210 *Told reporters*: Newberry, "More Parents..."

210 *10 percent:* NCES data

About the Authors

Keith Ballard has taught music, and much more, to thousands of public school students over the past 27 years.

To reach middle schoolers at his district in the southern tip of San Diego County, a couple miles from the Mexican border, he introduced mariachi and steel drum programs that drew national attention, sparking student performances on *The Today Show* and in front of former Presidents Bill Clinton and George W. Bush. Keith's efforts to infuse lessons about scales and chords with messages about self-esteem, cultural sensitivity and the importance of academics have helped him earn more than 25 teaching awards. That includes winning the 2003 *Milken National Educator Award*, which is widely known as "The Oscars of Teaching." That same year, Keith was inducted into the hall of fame at his alma mater, Arizona State University. And he received the Congressional Outstanding Educator Award in 2017. He's also been published in professional education journals, has written op-eds about teaching in local

newspapers and has been an invited speaker at more than a dozen education conferences. And Keith's quest to study the world's best schools has helped him land national TV appearances, a spot on the TEDx Talk stage and a YouTube channel that has millions of views.

Keith lives in a San Diego suburb with his wife, who's a nurse, and his teenage son. When he's not focused on education, he stays busy as a certified skydiver, snake wrangler and avid traveler. He's also training to be on the reality show *Naked and Afraid*, which accepted him as a cast member with a delay until he retires from teaching. *Stealing from the World's Best Schools* is his first book.

Brooke Staggs has masters degrees and has won industry recognition for her work in both journalism and education.

She got her start teaching high school English and journalism at a high school in the Inland Empire, where she was quickly put into leadership roles and named her school's "Best of the Best." But frustration with the system, combined with a new passion for journalism, drove Brooke to leave in 2006 to be a student again herself. She earned a master's degree in journalism from New York University while freelancing for various publications. At the *Daily Press* in Victorville, California, her work triggered grand jury and FBI investigations. During that time, she

also taught writing and journalism courses at a local community college. In January 2013, Brooke joined the *Orange County Register*, where she's covered topics including schools, politics and cannabis. In those roles, she's won some of the top journalism awards in the western United States and appeared on major TV and radio programs across the country, including *ABC*, *Fox News* and *NPR*. She has previously ghost written three nonfiction books.

Brooke lives in Southern California with her DJ-husband, Chris, their dear dog, Bruce Hornsby, and two much-loved cats. Her free time is filled with traveling, hiking, reading, volunteering and scheming about new ways to make the world a better place.

9 798218 013233

PRAISE FOR

Stealing from the World's Best Schools

"So, who said one man can't make a difference? This revealing masterpiece proves otherwise."

—Karen Sayward, Boston University

"[Ballard is] the first schoolteacher I have met in the United States who has taken it upon him or herself in a serious way to understand what these countries that are vastly outperforming us are doing and to accept the thought that they might actually have something to teach us. I have spent my life trying to help make teaching a profession, and what [he is] doing is what a real professional in education ought to be doing. So I see [Ballard] as a pioneer."

—Marc Tucker, founder of the National Center on Education and the Economy

"Keith Ballard attacks the myths surrounding 'American exceptionalism' and the myths of American education. ... He gives us workable ideas that improve teachers through emphasis on teacher collegiality, development of higher esteem among teachers, teacher mentorship programs, different work schedules for teachers and more significant involvement in curriculum building. Keith's book provides a genesis for a rebirth of American schools."

—William Frantz, EdD and retired Canadian educational administrator

"This is the medicine many of America's educators don't want to take. Don't blame the messenger for the realistic and honest diagnosis of our educational system."

—Marcus Butler, associate professor in Southern California

"Mr. Ballard's research, delineation and synthesis of education systems across the globe is presented in very real and very raw truth that should cause us ALL to take up a vigilant charge for change in the United States educational system."

—Lynn M Barker, EdD

"What [Ballard has] done is unprecedented as an educator. I agree ... that the U.S. education system is not giving students what they need and what employers need. I applaud [Ballard for his] mission to improve education in America."

—Mike Rose, late research professor at UCLA